ECCO COOK[...]

Books by Helen Hecht

Cold Cuisine

Cuisine for All Seasons

Gifts in Good Taste
(with Linda LaBate Mushlin)

Simple Pleasures

Cold Cuisine

HELEN HECHT

New and Expanded

THE ECCO PRESS
New York

I am grateful to Daniel Halpern and Lee Ann Chearneyi of The Ecco Press, who made this new edition of Cold Cuisine *possible.*

Copyright © 1981, 1990 by Helen Hecht
All rights reserved

First published in 1990 by The Ecco Press
26 West 17th Street, New York, NY 10011
Published simultaneously in Canada by
Penguin Books Canada Ltd., Ontario
Printed in the United States of America

Library of Congress Cataloging-in-Publication Data

Hecht, Helen.
  Cold cuisine / Helen Hecht.
    p. cm.
  1. Cookery (Cold dishes) I. Title.
TX830.H42   1990   89-71430   CIP
641.7'9—dc20

ISBN 0-88001-254-4

The text of this book is set in Garamond.

For Tony and Evan,
my most valued culinary critics

Contents

Introduction

SUMMER is the time of year when I most enjoy entertaining. Whether it be an informal patio lunch or a fancy dinner party, I can be as relaxed as the guests (at least until they go home and I have to confront the dishes). No, I do not have a cook, but I do have a system: I always serve chilled food. That is the subject of this book—a collection of chilled soups, entrées, and desserts, which can be prepared in advance, avoiding any last-minute fuss and anxiety. They can all be made a day or more ahead of serving and left in the refrigerator, where they will be busy cooling or setting while you are at leisure.

You will find recipes here suitable for the most elegant or informal occasion, and none requires that you even go near the oven after the guests arrive. No one, in any season of the year, wants to be steaming in the kitchen while guests are languidly sipping cold drinks, but in hot weather, it is a particularly cheerless activity. You should have little more to do than toss the salad and lift platters from refrigerator to table. Your menu might include Cream of Sorrel Soup, Chicken Breasts Stuffed with Pâté in Tarragon-Wine Aspic, Tomato and Avocado Salad, and Frozen Lime Soufflé—all served effortlessly and easily cleaned up and put away without greasy pots and pans to blight the kitchen. Cold food is also well suited to outdoor dining, since you may serve it in a leisurely fashion without any anxiety about keeping it hot.

During the summer months you may, of necessity, do more entertaining than usual, for it is a season when you are likely to have weekend guests. Try serving them fresh berries and scones for breakfast; a chilled soup and a salad or mousse for lunch or supper; a dish in aspic for fancy dinners. Your guests should be delighted (perhaps reluctant to leave), while you will be at liberty to entertain them and to lounge about sipping gin and tonics in an idle and carefree manner.

The dishes included here are also selected for their seasonal appeal. Summer food should be fresh, light, and often quite simple. It should also look colorful and appetizing, and use to advantage all the fruits, vegetables, and herbs plentiful during the spring and summer months. The appearance of a dish is especially important in the summer. While a steaming hot cassoulet may require no further embellishment than its own enticing aroma and an appetite stimulated by winter chill, summer food must rouse appetites languishing or dormant in stifling weather. You can transform an ordinary-looking dish into something attractive and appealing with a few simple touches and an eye for color, arrangement, and detail. A carefully set border of watercress, a glittering bed of chopped aspic, a sprinkling of herbs, or a garnish of ripe tomatoes can brighten a simple meal and charm a reluctant palate into submission.

While these recipes are intended for spring and summer, their use is not restricted to warm weather. They have been made and consumed by me and my family in every month of the year. I began work on this book in the summer. By late October, when the weather had turned noticeably chilly, my husband ventured, rather sheepishly, to inquire if he were to be served chilled mousses, salads, and aspics all winter long. "That all depends," I replied cagily. As it happens, he was, and in a climate not known for mild weather. (Rochester winters are a serious matter, not for amateurs. We live in what is called, with touching understatement, "the snow belt.") However, I cheered him up quite often by warming many of the chilled soups. Most of the soups are, in fact, very good served hot. And, although they would be cold comfort at the dinner table, salads are not bound by the season when served as lunch dishes. Chilled and frozen desserts are a different matter—appealing in any season of the year. So, while I am not suggesting that a salmon mousse, however attractively decorated, would do for Christmas dinner, a Cream of Fennel Soup or Frozen Grapefruit Soufflé would make quite a respectable addition to a meal on any occasion.

(1981)

NOTE FOR THE REVISED EDITION

Shortly after the original edition of *Cold Cuisine* was published, my family and I moved to Washington, D.C. Here it seems even more imperative to serve cooling meals during our wonderfully protracted and thoroughly hot summer season. I never stop experimenting with new ideas for summer entertaining. For this new edition, I have added several new soups, salads, and entrées, as well as a number of new desserts, the most notable being Tony's Fifth Birthday Cake, continuing a tradition that began years ago with my first cookbook.

(1990)

Notes on Ingredients

AMARETTI   A hard, Italian macaroon, flavored with bitter almonds and available at specialty food shops.

"BLUE" CHEESE   Do not substitute domestic blue cheese or even domestic Gorgonzola or Roquefort when an imported Gorgonzola, Roquefort, or Stilton is specified in a recipe. Domestic blue-veined cheeses are often sharper and bitter in flavor and will not give a satisfactory result.

CALAMATA OLIVES   These are not as bitter as most imported olives and are available at Greek grocery stores and some delicatessens.

CHIVES   When these are not available, the tender dark green tops of scallions may be substituted.

CREAM   It is important to use good-quality cream in soups, mousses, and desserts, since it is usually a central ingredient. If possible, buy it directly from a dairy; it will be better and fresher than what is available on a supermarket shelf.

EGGS   Recipes are based on USDA-graded large eggs.

FETA CHEESE   Bulgarian feta is creamier and less salty than Greek feta.

FLOUR   Unless otherwise specified, all-purpose flour is intended, preferably unbleached all-purpose flour.

LEMON OR LIME JUICE   Always use fresh.

LEMONS AND LIMES   These fruits vary in flavor with the season; at times they may be more acid or bitter. Always use them cautiously.

LETTUCE   In summer, various locally grown leaf lettuces become available. These are excellent and can be substituted for most other lettuces in a recipe.

MAYONNAISE   Use only homemade mayonnaise when it is served as a sauce. If it is one of many ingredients in a recipe, a good-quality bottled mayonnaise, such as Hellman's, is perfectly acceptable, but never use anything labeled "salad dressing."

MUSHROOMS   When fresh, mushrooms are firm and white and there is no separation between the stems and caps.

OLIVE OIL   Use only good-quality, imported olive oil. Those from Lucca, Italy, are excellent and there are also some good, and less expensive, Spanish oils.

POTATOES   The red, waxy "new" potatoes are best for potato salads. When boiled, they are less mealy and crumbly than Idaho potatoes.

VINEGAR   Use good-quality wine vinegars, which are less acid than white or cider vinegar. If possible, flavor your vinegar with fresh herbs.

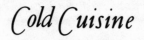

Cold Cuisine

1 : Cold Soups

CHILLING a soup will affect its flavor and texture in several ways that you should keep in mind when preparing the soups in this chapter. A soup thickened with egg yolks or potatoes will become still thicker after it has been chilled. Always check the consistency of the soup before serving; it may be necessary to thin it with a little extra broth or milk.

Proceed cautiously if you are tempted to add extra lemon or lime juice or more herbs. While their flavor may not be strong initially, they will intensify after standing for several hours.

Always season very carefully and adjust, if necessary, after chilling. If you are using a canned broth, it is unlikely that additional salt will be required.

Many of the soups in this chapter are thickened with an egg yolk or custard base. Instructions for making custards are included in the Introduction to Chapter 5, Desserts. When flour is used to thicken, it is usually added to melted butter to make a roux. Stock or other liquid is then added. It is important to blend this liquid into the flour slowly and gradually, beating with a wire whisk so that the mixture is smooth. To thicken, heat to simmering, stirring constantly to prevent lumps.

Almost any of the soups in this chapter can be served hot, if desired. Heat gradually, stirring frequently, and do not boil any soup with a custard or cream base.

The quality of your soup will be vastly affected by the stock you use. While a good-quality canned soup is usually acceptable, a soup with homemade stock will taste much better. There are many different ways of making a good stock. A very flavorful chicken stock can be made every time you poach chicken breasts for use in a salad or some other recipe simply by adding 1 or 2 chicken bouillon cubes to the water. Or, you can boil a collection of bones and carcasses with a few vegetables and herbs in a large kettle until the broth is well flavored. Or you can make stock from soup bones, a stewing chicken or chicken backs, or fish heads and bones, adding vegetables and herbs for flavor. Once you have learned to depend on homemade stock, you will not be careless about throwing away used bones, leftover gravies, and vegetable trimmings. Recycle your scraps: almost everything has potential for the stockpot. While most modern cooks do not have a stockpot constantly simmering at the back of the stove as a receptacle for such leftovers, most of us do have a freezer to store ingredients for future use in a stock.

Three recipes for homemade stocks follow. They are meant simply as guidelines and can be varied at will according to the ingredients you have on hand. Salt and other seasonings should be added sparingly because the liquid will be greatly reduced in cooking and because the soup in which you eventually use the stock may not need much seasoning. Since they all produce a fairly gelatinous stock, they work best in those chilled soups thinned with a greater proportion of cream or other liquid.

Stock will keep for 3 or 4 days under refrigeration. The surface layer of fat will help to preserve it and should not be removed until the stock is used.

CHICKEN STOCK

One 3-to-4 pound chicken,
    including neck and
    giblets; or 4 pounds
    chicken backs
2 large carrots, scraped and
    chopped
2 large celery stalks, chopped
Several celery leaves

2 medium yellow onions,
    peeled and quartered
Several sprigs of parsley
    and/or other fresh herbs
1 bay leaf
8 peppercorns
1 teaspoon salt
Approximately 4 quarts
    water

Wash the chicken and put it in a large pot with the vegetables, herbs, and seasoning and add water to cover. Bring to a boil and remove any scum. Simmer very gently, partially covered, for 3 to 4 hours, or until the broth has a good, strong flavor and the chicken meat falls from the bones. Strain, pressing down on the solids to extract their juices. Cool to room temperature and refrigerate. Use within 3 or 4 days, or freeze for longer storage. Remove the layer of fat just before using.

YIELD: APPROXIMATELY 2 QUARTS

BEEF STOCK

――――――――――

2 beef shank or soup bones (about 3 pounds)	1 cup mushrooms or stems, if available
3 large celery stalks, chopped	Several sprigs of parsley and/or other fresh herbs
Several celery leaves	8 peppercorns
2 large carrots, scraped and chopped	1 bay leaf
2 medium onions, peeled and chopped, or 1 onion and 1 leek	1 teaspoon salt
	Approximately 4 quarts water

Place all the ingredients in a large pot, cover with water, bring to a boil, and remove the scum. Simmer, partially covered, for 3 to 4 hours, or until the broth has a good, strong flavor. Strain, pressing down on the solids to extract all the juices, and cool to room temperature before refrigerating. Use within 3 or 4 days, or freeze for longer storage. The layer of fat should not be removed until the soup is used.

YIELD: APPROXIMATELY 2 QUARTS

FISH STOCK

――――――――――

4 pounds fish heads and bones, well washed	Several sprigs of fresh parsley
1 large yellow onion, peeled and quartered	Several fresh tarragon leaves or ½ teaspoon dried
1 large carrot, scraped and chopped	1 bay leaf
	6 peppercorns
1 large celery stalk, chopped	1 teaspoon salt
A few celery leaves	6 cups water
	1 cup dry white wine

Place all ingredients in a large pot. Bring to a boil and remove any scum. Simmer, partially covered, for 45 minutes to 1 hour. Strain, cool to room temperature, and refrigerate. Use within 3 days or freeze for longer storage.

YIELD: APPROXIMATELY 6 CUPS

ASPARAGUS SOUP

2 pounds fresh asparagus,
    washed, trimmed, and
    scraped
1⅓ cups chicken stock or
    broth
1 cup heavy cream

2 egg yolks, lightly beaten
¾ cup sour cream
1 tablespoon lemon juice
Salt
Fresh-ground pepper

Steam the asparagus or simmer in a little water for 5 to 7 minutes or just until tender. Cut into 2-inch lengths and purée in a food processor or blender, adding the broth in a thin stream.

Mix the cream with the egg yolks and cook, stirring, over medium heat for approximately 5 minutes or until thickened. Do not allow to boil. Stir this into the asparagus purée with the sour cream and lemon juice. Season to taste and chill.

YIELD: APPROXIMATELY 5 CUPS

AVOCADO SOUP

A smooth, creamy soup. Serve it with small wedges of sesame Toasted Syrian Bread (page 253).

2 *medium avocados*
2 *teaspoons lime juice*
1 1/4 *cups sour cream*
6 *tablespoons mayonnaise*

2 *tablespoons prepared white horseradish, drained*
1 1/2 *cups chicken stock or broth*
Salt

FOR THE GARNISH

4 *very thin slices of lime*

Cut the avocados in half, discard the pits, scoop out the flesh, and put it in the bowl of a food processor with the lime juice. Add the sour cream, mayonnaise, and horseradish, and purée. Empty into a mixing bowl, stir in the chicken stock or broth, and chill.

Garnish each serving with a thin slice of lime.

YIELD: 4 CUPS

CARROT AND PEACH SOUP

The peaches in this soup subtly complement the flavor of the carrots but are not readily identifiable. The soup can be served warm, but I think the flavor is best when chilled.

1 *pound carrots*
1 3/4 *cups chicken stock or*
 canned broth
2 *medium-size peaches (1/2*
 pound), peeled and
 sliced

1/2 *cup heavy cream*
A pinch of ground ginger

Scrape the carrots and cut them into 1-inch lengths. Put them in a saucepan with the chicken stock, cover tightly, and simmer until the carrots are tender. Drain the carrots and reserve the broth. Purée the carrots in a food processor with the peaches. Stir in the broth and cream, and season with ground ginger. Chill before serving.

YIELD: 3 TO 4 SERVINGS

CHILLED BEET SOUP

Grated fresh gingerroot gives this soup an extraordinary flavor. It blends beautifully with the beets, contributing a refreshing, slightly piquant taste.

1 1/2 *pounds trimmed fresh*
 beets
2 *cups beef stock or strong*
 broth
1 *large tomato, peeled,*
 cored, and seeded
1/3 *cup minced red onion*

1 *large garlic clove, peeled*
 and cut in half
1 *tablespoon plus 1/2 teaspoon*
 grated fresh gingerroot
3/4 *cup sour cream*
1 *tablespoon lime juice*

Peel the beets and slice 1/4 inch thick. Simmer, covered, with the beef stock, tomato, onion, garlic, and gingerroot for 30 to 40 minutes, or until the beets are tender. Remove from the heat and strain, reserving the broth. Purée in a food processor. Stir in the reserved broth, the sour cream, and lime juice. Chill before serving.

YIELD: APPROXIMATELY 4½ CUPS OR 4 TO 6 SERVINGS

CLEAR BORSCHT

A stunning claret-colored soup, which does not require clarifying.

1 pound fresh beets
5 cups beef stock or strong beef bouillon
2 tablespoons red wine vinegar

¼ cup dry white wine
2 teaspoons strained lemon juice

FOR THE GARNISH

Sour cream

Peel the beets and slice them lengthwise into very thin julienne strips no thicker than ⅛ inch. Put them in a saucepan with the beef stock or bouillon and simmer for about 10 minutes, or until the beets are tender but not soft. Remove from the heat and stir in the vinegar, wine, and lemon juice. Cool to room temperature and chill.

Serve the soup with a dollop of sour cream in each bowl.

YIELD: APPROXIMATELY 6 CUPS

CREAM OF ALMOND SOUP

The pear flavoring in this soup is too subtle to be identified, but the effect is mellow and interesting.

2 cups chicken stock or broth
3 egg yolks
1 cup heavy cream
1 cup blanched almonds
½ cup peeled and chopped
    Bartlett pear

Grated rind of half a small
    lemon
1 teaspoon lemon juice
A pinch of nutmeg

Heat the chicken broth to simmering. Combine the egg yolks and cream in a small bowl and stir in a little of the hot broth. Then, stirring vigorously, pour the yolk-cream mixture into the broth and cook over medium heat, stirring, for 15 minutes or until slightly thickened. Do not allow the mixture to boil.

Grind the almonds to a fine powder in a food processor or blender. Add the chopped pear and purée with the almonds. With the motor running, add the cream and broth mixture in a thin, steady stream. Pour the soup into a saucepan and stir over medium heat, without boiling, for 10 minutes. Remove from the heat and stir in the lemon rind and juice and nutmeg to taste. Cool to room temperature and chill.

If the soup becomes too thick after chilling, stir in a little milk, cream, or broth to thin to desired consistency.

YIELD: APPROXIMATELY 1 QUART

CREAM OF BROCCOLI SOUP

———

*1 pound fresh broccoli,
    washed and scraped*
*1¼ cups chicken stock or
    broth*
½ cup heavy cream
1 egg yolk, lightly beaten
½ cup sour cream

*1 tablespoon plus 1 teaspoon
    lemon juice*
*1 tablespoon minced fresh
    tarragon or 1 teaspoon
    dried*
Salt
Fresh-ground pepper

Steam the broccoli until just tender and chop it coarse. Purée in a food processor or, in batches, in a blender, adding the chicken stock in a steady stream.

Mix the heavy cream and egg yolk and cook, stirring, over medium heat for about 5 minutes or until thickened, but do not allow to boil. Stir this into the broccoli purée. Add the sour cream, lemon juice, tarragon, and seasoning to taste. Chill. Before serving, thin with a little extra chicken stock, if necessary.

YIELD: APPROXIMATELY 4 CUPS

CREAM OF CARROT SOUP

———

A fine, thick soup, delicately flavored with Madeira and nutmeg.

*1½ pounds carrots, scraped
    and cut into 1-inch
    lengths*
*2½ cups chicken stock or
    broth*

1 egg yolk
1½ cups heavy cream
2 tablespoons Madeira
⅛ teaspoon nutmeg
Salt

FOR THE GARNISH

Carrot curls

Cook the carrots, covered, in the stock until tender. Drain, reserving the stock; you should have approximately 2⅓ cups. Purée the carrots, in batches, in a food processor or blender, adding a little of the reserved stock, until you have a smooth purée.

Stir the egg yolk into ½ cup of the cream and cook over low heat, stirring constantly, until thickened. Do not boil. Stir this into the carrot purée with the remaining reserved stock, the remaining cup of cream, the Madeira, and nutmeg. Taste, and add a little salt, if necessary.

Chill. Taste before serving, and add a little more Madeira and nutmeg, if desired. For the garnish, scrape strips from a carrot with a vegetable parer. Roll up each strip, secure with a toothpick, and place in a bowl of ice water to set. Before serving, remove the toothpicks and place a few carrot curls in each bowl.

YIELD: APPROXIMATELY 5½ CUPS

CREAM OF CELERY SOUP

This is a delicate-flavored soup, accented with tarragon or dill weed, which are acceptable in dried form. But since it is a soup that adapts well to almost any fresh herb flavoring, experiment with different combinations if you have an herb garden.

1 *large head celery, washed,*
   trimmed, and cut into
   1-inch lengths
1 *medium potato, peeled and*
   sliced (½ pound)
1 *small onion, peeled and*
   quartered
3 *garlic cloves, peeled and*
   halved
A *few sprigs of parsley*

4 *cups chicken stock or broth*
2 *egg yolks*
1 *tablespoon lemon juice*
1 *teaspoon fresh tarragon or*
   dill weed or ¼ tea-
   spoon dried
1 *cup heavy cream*
½ *teaspoon soy sauce*
Salt

FOR THE GARNISH

A *few teaspoons of fresh tarragon leaves or dill weed, if available*

Simmer the celery in a covered saucepan with the potato, onion, garlic, parsley, and chicken broth until tender. Purée the mixture a little at a time, in a food processor or blender.

Mix the egg yolks and lemon juice. Heat the soup and stir a little into the yolks. Then pour the egg mixture into the soup and cook over medium heat, stirring, for 5 or 6 minutes. Do not let the soup boil. Remove from the heat and stir in the tarragon or dill, cream, soy sauce, and salt to taste. Cool to room temperature and chill.

To serve, ladle into soup bowls and sprinkle with fresh herbs.

YIELD: APPROXIMATELY 6 CUPS

CREAM OF FENNEL SOUP

Bulb fennel, available in the spring and fall, has a crisp and refreshing anise flavor that lends itself to many preparations. This soup is delicious hot or cold, and I recommend you make it whenever you see fresh fennel in the market.

4 medium-large fennel bulbs
    (4 pounds untrimmed)
1 large potato, peeled and
    sliced
1 medium yellow onion,
    peeled and quartered
3 garlic cloves, peeled and
    halved
Several sprigs of parsley

4½ cups chicken stock or
    broth
3 egg yolks, lightly beaten
1 cup heavy cream
1 tablespoon lemon juice
2 tablespoons Pernod
2 teaspoons minced fresh
    tarragon or ½ teaspoon
    dried
Salt

OR THE GARNISH

Minced fennel ferns

'rim off and discard the green fennel stalks, reserving a few of the
erns for garnish. Wash the fennel bulbs and slice them into 1-inch
ieces. In a covered saucepan, simmer the fennel, potato, onion,
arlic, and parsley in the chicken stock until tender. Strain and then
urée the vegetables in batches in a food processor or blender, with
 little of the broth. Turn into a mixing bowl and stir in the
emaining broth.

Mix the egg yolks and cream and cook over medium heat, stir-
ng, for 5 or 6 minutes, or until thickened. Do not boil. Remove
om the heat and stir into the soup with the lemon juice, Pernod,
nd tarragon. Taste and season with a little salt, if necessary. Cool
 room temperature and chill. Thin with extra broth if too thick.

Garnish each serving with minced reserved fennel ferns.

IELD: APPROXIMATELY 8 CUPS

CREAM OF MUSHROOM SOUP

——————

An appetizer to make for special dinner parties or just for yoursel
when you're feeling special. It is thick and creamy, with a fine an
delicate flavor.

1 pound firm white
  mushrooms
3 tablespoons unsalted butter
¼ cup chopped shallots or
  scallions
2 teaspoons lemon juice
2 tablespoons dry white wine

1 tablespoon flour
2 cups chicken stock or broth
1 bay leaf
2 egg yolks, lightly beaten
1 cup heavy cream
Fresh-ground pepper

FOR THE GARNISH

Reserved mushrooms

Clean the mushrooms by wiping with a damp towel, or rinse briefl
under cold water and dry. Reserve 2 or 3 for garnish. Slice th
remainder, trimming the ends from the stems.

Melt the butter in a large skillet. Add the chopped shallots o
scallions and the mushrooms and sauté until the vegetables begin t
soften. Add the lemon juice and wine and continue cooking ove
medium heat for about 10 minutes, until the mushrooms are quit
soft and liquid has collected in the pan. Remove from the heat an
purée the mushrooms and shallots in a food processor or blender
adding their cooking juices in a thin stream.

Dissolve the flour in a little cold water and stir into the chicke
broth. Add the bay leaf and heat to simmering. Combine the eg
yolks and cream in a small bowl; stir a little of the hot broth int
this mixture and then pour it all into the rest of the broth, stirrin
vigorously. Continue cooking over moderate heat for 10 to 15 mir

utes, stirring constantly until thickened. Do not boil. Remove from the heat and discard the bay leaf. Combine the broth with the mushroom purée, cool to room temperature, and chill.

Before serving, taste for seasoning and add pepper and a little salt, if necessary. If the soup is too thick, stir in a little milk or cream. Slice the reserved mushrooms very thin and use to garnish each bowl of soup.

YIELD: APPROXIMATELY 4½ CUPS

CREAM OF SORREL SOUP

A lovely, tart soup with which to herald early spring.

1½ pounds sorrel (12 cups, packed)
3½ cups chicken stock or broth

4 egg yolks, lightly beaten
2 cups heavy cream
Salt
Fresh-ground white pepper

Wash the sorrel and discard the stems and any wilted leaves. Cook in a covered pot, in the water clinging to the leaves, until wilted. Drain and purée in a food processor or blender.

In a large saucepan, heat the chicken stock to simmering. Stir together the egg yolks and cream and add a little of the hot stock. Pour this mixture into the rest of the stock and cook, stirring, over medium-high heat for 10 to 15 minutes, or until slightly thickened, but do not boil. Remove from the heat, cool, and whisk in the sorrel purée. Season to taste and chill. Thin with a little extra stock, if necessary.

YIELD: 5½ TO 6 CUPS

CREAM OF WATERCRESS SOUP

━━━━◆━━━━

*1 large potato (10 ounces),
   peeled and sliced thin*
*2 cups watercress leaves,
   loosely packed*
2 cups chicken stock or broth

2 egg yolks, lightly beaten
1 cup heavy cream
Fresh-ground white pepper
Salt

FOR THE GARNISH

Several sprigs of watercress

In a covered saucepan, simmer the sliced potato and watercress in the chicken stock for 5 to 10 minutes, or just until the potato is tender. Purée in a food processor or blender, adding the broth in a thin stream.

Combine the egg yolks and cream and cook over medium heat, stirring constantly, for about 5 minutes, or until slightly thickened. Do not allow it to boil. Stir into the puréed mixture, season to taste, and chill.

Garnish each serving with a sprig of watercress.

YIELD: APPROXIMATELY 4 CUPS

CUCUMBER AND HONEYDEW SOUP

━━━━◆━━━━

I've always felt that cucumbers and honeydew have an affinity for each other, and I wasn't surprised to learn that they are related botanically. The addition of honeydew to a cucumber soup creates a particularly cooling potion for a humid summer day.

2 tablespoons unsalted butter
3 tablespoons flour
1 1/2 cups chicken stock or
    canned broth
3 large cucumbers (2 1/4 to
    2 1/2 pounds)

2/3 cup fresh mint leaves,
    loosely packed
1 small honeydew melon
Salt

FOR THE GARNISH

Sprigs of mint

Melt the butter in a small saucepan and stir in the flour. Gradually add the chicken stock, and cook, stirring, until the mixture comes to a boil and thickens. Remove from the heat.

Peel the cucumbers, cut off and discard the ends, and quarter them lengthwise. Discard the seeds. Chop the cucumber coarse and purée with the mint leaves in a food processor. Add the thickened stock and blend. Turn into a container, cover airtight, and refrigerate. About 2 hours before serving, scoop out the honeydew from its rind. Cut enough of the melon into small cubes to measure 2 1/2 cups. Add to the soup and season to taste. Refrigerate until serving. Garnish each serving with a sprig of mint.

YIELD: APPROXIMATELY 5 CUPS

CUCUMBER-MINT SOUP

A refreshing start to a meal. For a lighter version, omit the sour cream.

3 tablespoons unsalted butter
3 tablespoons flour
1 ½ cups chicken stock or
    broth
3 large cucumbers, peeled,
    seeded, and cut into
    2-inch lengths

⅓ cup fresh mint leaves,
    packed
½ cup sour cream (optional)
Salt

FOR THE GARNISH

Several sprigs of fresh mint

Melt the butter and gradually stir in the flour. Add the chicken stock slowly, blending with a whisk. Heat, stirring, until the broth simmers and is thickened. Remove from the heat.

Purée the cucumber with the mint leaves in a food processor or blender and stir into the chicken broth. Fold in the sour cream, if desired, and chill.

Before serving, taste for seasoning and add salt, if necessary. Garnish each bowl of soup with a sprig of fresh mint.

YIELD: APPROXIMATELY 5 ½ CUPS

CURRIED COCONUT-CRABMEAT SOUP

An interesting combination of flavors, with accents of mint, lime juice, and chutney.

3 tablespoons unsalted butter
1/4 cup flour
2 cups half-and-half
1 cup flaked, unsweetened coconut*
2 cups fish stock or bottled clam juice
1 tablespoon chopped fresh mint leaves or 1 teaspoon dried

1 teaspoon curry powder
A pinch of ginger
1 tablespoon mango chutney juice or sieved chutney
3/4 cup sour cream
5 teaspoons lime juice
6 ounces cooked crabmeat, fresh or frozen and defrosted

* If you use sweetened, packaged coconut, soak it in 3 cups of cold water for about 15 minutes and drain well.

FOR THE GARNISH

Several sprigs of fresh mint or 2 tablespoons of sliced almonds

Melt the butter in a saucepan and stir in the flour. Add the half-and-half, a little at a time, beating with a wire whisk until smooth. Cook, stirring, until the mixture comes to a boil and thickens. Add the coconut, fish stock or clam juice, mint leaves, curry powder, ginger, and chutney, and cook over medium heat, stirring occasionally, for about 15 minutes. Remove from the heat and strain, pressing out as much liquid as possible. Whisk in the sour cream, add the lime juice and crabmeat, cool to room temperature, and chill.

To serve, garnish each bowl with a sprig of fresh mint or with a few sliced almonds.

YIELD: APPROXIMATELY 5 CUPS

FRESH PARSLEY SOUP

Quantities of fresh, uncooked parsley are used in this soup for a crisp and defined flavor.

3 tablespoons unsalted butter
¼ cup flour
2 cups chicken stock or broth
4 cups washed and stemmed
    parsley sprigs, loosely
    packed

2 tablespoons chopped fresh
    mint leaves
1 tablespoon chopped chives
2 anchovy fillets
1 cup heavy cream
¾ cup sour cream

FOR THE GARNISH

Parsley sprigs

Melt the butter in a saucepan, stir in the flour, and gradually add the chicken broth, whisking until smooth. Heat gently, stirring constantly, until the mixture comes to a boil and thickens. Remove from the heat.

Mince the parsley, mint leaves, chives, and anchovies in a food processor. With the motor running, add the thickened broth in a thin stream. Turn into a mixing bowl and stir in the heavy cream and sour cream. Chill.

Garnish each serving with a sprig of parsley.

YIELD: APPROXIMATELY 4 CUPS

GAZPACHO

There are many ways of making this Spanish soup. The following recipe is one I particularly like.

1 garlic clove, peeled

2 tablespoons parsley sprigs

2 large ripe tomatoes, peeled, cored, and chopped coarse (1 to 1 1/4 pounds)

1 medium sweet green pepper, cored, seeded, and chopped coarse

2 or 3 scallions, chopped or 1/2 medium Bermuda onion, chopped

1 medium cucumber, peeled and chopped coarse

2 tablespoons chopped fresh basil or 1/2 teaspoon dried

2 1/2 cups tomato juice

2 1/2 tablespoons olive oil

3 tablespoons red wine vinegar

Salt

Fresh-ground pepper

Tabasco sauce

FOR THE GARNISH

1 cup garlic-flavored Croutons (page 243)

Mince the garlic and parsley in a food processor or blender. Add the chopped tomatoes, green pepper, scallions, cucumber, and basil to the work bowl. With the motor running, add the tomato juice in a stream, processing only until the vegetables are chopped fine but not puréed. The consistency of the soup should be quite thick and coarse. Turn into a mixing bowl and stir in any remaining tomato juice, the oil, vinegar, and seasoning to taste. Chill. Before serving, thin with a little extra tomato juice, if desired, and garnish each portion with croutons.

YIELD: APPROXIMATELY 6 CUPS

GAZPACHO BLANCO

This is a light soup, quickly made from fresh, raw vegetables. It is an interesting alternative to the popular tomato gazpacho.

2 medium cucumbers, peeled and chopped coarse

2 white celery stalks, chopped coarse

1 medium-size sweet green pepper, seeded and chopped coarse

6 scallions with tender green ends, chopped coarse

1/4 cup parsley sprigs, packed

3 tablespoons chopped fresh mint leaves

2 large garlic cloves, peeled

2 tablespoons prepared white horseradish, drained

1 cup plain yogurt

1 cup sour cream

1 1/2 tablespoons lime juice

Salt

6 drops Tabasco sauce, or to taste

FOR THE GARNISH

4 or 5 scallions, celery stalks, or cucumber sticks

In two batches, chop all the vegetables and herbs in a food processor but do not purée them. The soup should be coarse in texture. Turn into a mixing bowl and stir in the horseradish, yogurt, sour cream, and lime juice. Season to taste with salt and Tabasco. Chill.

Serve in individual mugs, garnishing each with a scallion, celery stalk, or cucumber stick.

YIELD: APPROXIMATELY 1 QUART

ICED HONEYDEW-PEAR SOUP

This lovely sea-green soup provides a cooling start to a hot-weather meal.

1 large honeydew melon	*½ cup dry white wine*
2 Bartlett or Anjou pears	*A large pinch of cinnamon*
1½ tablespoons lemon juice	

FOR THE GARNISH

Several sprigs of fresh mint

Cut the melon in half, discard the seeds, and scoop out the flesh. Purée, in batches, in a food processor or blender and empty into a mixing bowl.

Peel and core the pears and chop into small pieces. Put them in a small, heavy saucepan with the lemon juice and slowly bring to a simmer. Cook gently, stirring occasionally, for 10 to 12 minutes or until soft. (This prevents the pears from darkening.) Purée the pears in a food processor or blender and stir into the honeydew purée. Add the wine and cinnamon and chill.

Serve ice-cold and garnish each cup with a sprig of mint.

YIELD: APPROXIMATELY 5 CUPS

ICED PEAR-CELERY SOUP

An unusual and light hot-weather soup.

6 cups chopped celery	*⅓ cup dry white wine*
3 cups chicken stock or broth	*A dash of cinnamon*
1 cup peeled and chopped	
Anjou or Bartlett pear	

Simmer the celery in the chicken stock, uncovered, for about 15 minutes or until soft. Drain and purée the celery and pear in a food processor or blender, a little at a time, adding the hot broth in a thin stream. Empty into a mixing bowl and stir in the wine and cinnamon. Cool to room temperature and chill.

YIELD: 5 TO 6 CUPS

ICED TOMATO SOUP

This is a wonderfully cooling soup for a sweltering day. Because it is both elegant and simple to make, it should be in every host's repertoire. The recipe comes from our friend James Merrill.

FOR EACH SERVING

3/4 pound ripe tomatoes
1 teaspoon grated onion
1/2 teaspoon minced fresh
  herbs, such as tarra-
  gon, basil, or dill

Salt
Fresh-ground pepper

FOR THE GARNISH

A dollop of sour cream or mayonnaise flavored with a pinch
  of curry powder

Slice the tomatoes in half crosswise and scoop out the seeds. Grate the tomato halves by hand on the coarse teeth of the grater. (The skin will remain on the top side and can be easily discarded.) Add the onion and herbs and season to taste with salt and pepper. Freeze the mixture until it is mushy and slightly crystallized. This will take 1 to 2 hours, depending on the quantity and the temperature of your freezer. Scoop into individual serving bowls and put a dollop of curry-flavored sour cream or mayonnaise on top of each serving. Serve immediately.

LEMON-MINT SOUP

A smooth and cooling concoction based on the Greek egg and lemon soup, with the addition of mint and a little basil.

2 scallions with tender green ends, minced
1 tablespoon unsalted butter
1 tablespoon flour
2¼ cups chicken stock or broth
3 tablespoons chopped fresh mint leaves or ¾ teaspoon dried

1 tablespoon chopped fresh basil leaves or ½ teaspoon dried
6 egg yolks, lightly beaten
½ cup heavy cream
⅓ cup sour cream
¼ cup lemon juice
Salt

FOR THE GARNISH

4 very thin slices of lemon
4 sprigs of fresh mint

In a saucepan, sauté the scallions in the butter until soft, but do not brown. Stir in the flour and gradually add the chicken stock, stirring until smooth. Add the mint and basil and heat until almost simmering. Stir a little of the hot stock into the egg yolks and then add the yolk mixture to the saucepan, stirring vigorously. Continue to cook and stir over medium heat until slightly thickened, but do not boil. Cool to room temperature and mix in the heavy cream, sour cream, lemon juice, and salt to taste. Chill.

Garnish each serving with a slice of lemon and a sprig of mint.
YIELD: APPROXIMATELY 3 CUPS

LOBSTER BISQUE

This thick, rich soup is almost a meal in itself. Serve it for supper with Melba Toast (page 249), one of the green entrée salads, and a fruit ice for dessert.

One 1½-pound live lobster
1 tablespoon unsalted butter
2 tablespoons flour
1 large garlic clove, peeled and minced
1 small yellow onion, peeled and sliced
1 tablespoon minced fresh tarragon or 1 teaspoon dried
A few sprigs of fresh parsley

1 bay leaf
1 pound ripe tomatoes, cored and chopped
½ cup dry white wine
1½ tablespoons Madeira, Pernod, or brandy
½ cup reserved lobster broth
1 cup heavy cream
Salt
Fresh-ground white pepper

Bring a very large pot of salted water to a boil, put in the lobster, cover the pot, return to a boil, and cook for 15 minutes. Place the lobster on a large platter with a well or in a shallow baking dish, to catch all the broth from the shells as the lobster is cut up. Cut down the center of the chest and remove the meat from the chest, tail, claws, and legs, placing it in a small bowl. Drain the cooking juices into a measuring cup and reserve. (You should have about ½ cup.)

Melt the butter in a large skillet; add the flour and stir to blend. Add the garlic, onion, tarragon, parsley, bay leaf, and tomatoes. Stir and sauté gently until the tomatoes start to liquefy. Pour in the wine and Madeira, Pernod, or brandy, according to your own preference, and cover the pan. Simmer for 20 minutes and then strain through a food mill into a mixing bowl.

While the broth is simmering, cut up the meat from the chest and tail of the lobster and put it in a food processor or blender with any scraps from the legs, but reserve the claw meat. Purée, adding the reserved cooking juices in a thin stream. Stir into the strained tomato mixture. Slice the reserved claw meat and add it to the soup with the heavy cream and seasoning to taste. Chill.

YIELD: APPROXIMATELY 4 CUPS

MADRILÈNE WITH AVOCADO AND CAVIAR

This is an elegant and light appetizer. Homemade beef stock is flavored with tomato, Madeira, and lemon juice; jellied; and set over sliced avocado. It is garnished with a dollop of sour cream and a bit of red caviar.

4 cups good, strong-flavored, homemade beef stock
1 cup tomato purée
1/2 cup Madeira
1/4 cup fresh lemon juice
10 peppercorns, slightly crushed
6 cloves
3 egg whites
Crushed shells of 3 eggs
1 envelope plus 2 teaspoons unflavored gelatin
1/3 cup cold water
1 large avocado
2 tablespoons lemon juice mixed with 1 tablespoon water

FOR THE GARNISH

Approximately 1/3 cup sour cream
Approximately 2 teaspoons red caviar (lumpfish or salmon roe)

In a large saucepan, stir together, off the heat, the beef stock, tomato purée, Madeira, lemon juice, peppercorns, and cloves. Beat the egg whites lightly to break them up and add them to the pan, along with the crushed eggshells. Place over medium heat and bring the mixture slowly to a boil, whisking constantly back and forth across the bottom of the pan. When the mixture reaches a full boil, the egg whites will coagulate and rise to the surface. Remove from the heat and let stand undisturbed for a few minutes.

Wring out a cotton dish towel in cold water and secure it as a lining inside a large sieve. Place the sieve over a deep bowl and slowly pour the stock into it, a bit at a time, if necessary. Allow it to drip through without disturbing the crust of egg whites. Allow plenty of time for this and do not remove and discard the egg whites until the dripping has stopped completely. At that point, remove the sieve and measure the clarified broth. You should have approximately 3⅔ cups.

Soften the gelatin in the cold water and dissolve over low heat, stirring constantly. Stir the dissolved gelatin into the clarified broth.

Cut the avocado in half lengthwise, peel it, and discard the pit. Slice each half into ¼-inch-thick crosswise sections, dipping them into the diluted lemon juice as you do so. Arrange them on the bottoms of 6 small glass bowls (1-to-1½-cup capacity). Carefully pour a shallow layer of madrilène over each. Refrigerate until set. (This will prevent the avocado slices from floating to the top.) Then ladle equal portions of the remaining madrilène into the bowls. (Each serving will have approximately ⅔ cup.) Refrigerate until set.

Just before serving, spoon a dollop of sour cream onto the center of each bowl of madrilène and place a bit of red caviar on top of the sour cream.

YIELD: 6 SERVINGS

PEA AND FENNEL SOUP

Puréed fresh peas and fennel are a fine complement of flavors in this creamy, jade-green soup.

3 medium-large fennel bulbs	*2½ pounds unshelled peas*
(3 pounds untrimmed)	*(12 ounces shelled)*
Approximately 4 cups	*1 cup heavy cream*
chicken stock or broth	*Salt*

FOR THE GARNISH

Chopped fennel ferns

Trim the fennel bulbs, discarding the green stalks, but reserve a handful of the ferns for garnish. Chop the white bulbs coarse and simmer in a covered saucepan in 3 cups of the chicken stock for 10 to 15 minutes or until tender. Drain and purée the fennel in batches in a food processor or blender, reserving the stock. Measure the stock and add enough additional to equal 3 cups.

Shell the peas and cook them in a vegetable steamer or colander until tender. Purée through a food mill in order to strain out the skins. Combine the puréed fennel, peas, stock, and cream and season to taste. Chill. Garnish each serving with a few chopped fennel ferns.

YIELD: 7½ TO 8 CUPS

RUSSIAN GAZPACHO

When I first made this soup, I was attempting a chilled borscht. The result was a slightly tangy purée of beets and raw vegetables that seemed more like a Russian gazpacho. So here is a cross-ethnic summer soup, to be served ice-cold.

Two 1-pound cans whole
    beets drained and juice
    reserved
1 medium Bermuda onion,
    peeled (3 ounces)
1 medium-size sweet red
    pepper, cored and seeded
1 medium-large cucumber,
    peeled

8 red radishes
2 garlic cloves, peeled
3/4 cup chicken stock or broth
1/3 cup lemon juice
2 tablespoons white wine
    vinegar
2 teaspoons sugar
Salt to taste

FOR THE GARNISH

Very thin lemon slices
1 cup sour cream

Chop each of the vegetables coarse, mix together and purée them in batches in a food processor or blender, adding the beet juice in a thin stream. Turn into a mixing bowl and stir in the remaining ingredients. Chill.

    Serve ice-cold, garnishing each bowl with a wafer-thin slice of lemon. Serve the sour cream on the side.

YIELD: APPROXIMATELY 6½ CUPS

SENEGALESE SOUP

This is a splendid, mildly curried chicken soup, suitable for a special dinner party, or substantial enough to serve as the main course for lunch or supper.

3 tablespoons unsalted butter
1 large celery stalk, scraped and chopped
1 large garlic clove, peeled and minced
3 tablespoons flour
1 1/2 teaspoons curry powder
1 tablespoon Major Grey's chutney
1 tablespoon lime juice
1 large carrot, scraped and chopped
3 scallions, chopped
2 tablespoons tomato purée
4 cups chicken stock or broth
1/2 cup heavy cream
1/3 cup sour cream
3/4 cup shredded cooked chicken breast (1/2 breast)

FOR THE GARNISH

Several sprigs of fresh mint

Melt the butter in a heavy saucepan or Dutch oven and add the celery, carrot, scallions, and garlic. Cook gently for a few minutes and then gradually sprinkle in the flour, stirring with a whisk or wooden spoon to blend. Stir in the curry powder, chutney, lime juice, and tomato purée and slowly add the chicken stock, whisking to incorporate with the butter and flour mixture. Cover and simmer gently for 30 to 40 minutes, or until the vegetables are tender.

Purée the vegetables, adding a little of the soup, in a food processor or blender. Empty into a mixing bowl, add the rest of the soup, and cool to room temperature. Stir in the heavy cream, sour cream, and the shredded chicken. Chill.

Garnish each serving with a sprig of fresh mint.

YIELD: 5 TO 5 1/2 CUPS

SHRIMP BISQUE

I first made this soup for our friend, the Caribbean poet Derek Walcott. Although he comes from a part of the world abundant in seafood, he generously approved this Rochester version.

3 cups water	2 cups reserved stock
1 celery stalk	2 egg yolks
½ small onion, peeled	1¼ to 1½ cups heavy cream
1 small bay leaf	2 to 3 tablespoons Madeira
1 garlic clove, peeled	1 tablespoon minced fresh
1 teaspoon salt	parsley
1 pound unshelled large	1 teaspoon fresh tarragon or
shrimp	¼ teaspoon dried

Boil the water with the celery, onion, bay leaf, garlic, and salt, covered, for about 10 minutes. Add the unshelled shrimp to the boiling water, return to a boil, and simmer uncovered for 2 to 3 minutes, or just until the shrimp are opaque. Drain, reserving the stock; you should have approximately 2 cups. Lightly beat the egg yolks and stir them into the stock. Cook over low heat, stirring constantly for 5 to 10 minutes or until slightly thickened. Do not boil. Remove from the heat.

Shell and devein the shrimp. Purée them in a food processor, or in batches in a blender, adding 1 cup of the stock mixture in a thin stream. Turn into a mixing bowl and stir in the remaining stock, the cream, Madeira, parsley, and tarragon. Refrigerate until serving.

YIELD: APPROXIMATELY 4 CUPS

SORREL AND MINT SOUP

Sorrel and mint are among the first herbs to appear in spring. I've seen them side by side in my neighbor's garden, and this suggested to me a natural affinity, which I thought might be used to culinary advantage. My experiments produced a delicately flavored chilled soup. Because the sorrel is puréed without being cooked, it retains its fresh green color.

2 tablespoons unsalted butter
3 tablespoons flour
3½ cups chicken stock or
    broth
3 egg yolks, lightly beaten
¾ pound sorrel leaves with-
    out stems (6 cups
    packed)

½ cup sour cream
1 cup plus 2 tablespoons
    heavy cream
¼ cup plus 1 tablespoon
    minced fresh mint leaves

FOR THE GARNISH

Sprigs of mint

Melt the butter in a saucepan and blend in the flour. Add the chicken broth gradually, whisking to blend. Bring to a simmer and cook for 1 or 2 minutes. Stir a little of the hot broth into the beaten egg yolks. Return the yolks to the pan and cook over medium-low heat for about 15 minutes, stirring constantly, until thickened. Do not allow to boil. Remove from the heat and cool to room temperature.

After the broth has cooled, purée the sorrel, in batches, in a food processor, adding a little of the broth mixture. Turn into a bowl and add the remaining broth. Whisk in the sour cream; then add the heavy cream and mint. Taste and add a little salt if necessary. Chill, tightly covered, until serving. Garnish each serving with a sprig of fresh mint.

YIELD: 6 CUPS

SOUR CREAM-CHIVE SOUP

This familiar combination of flavors makes a fine creamed soup.

>   3 tablespoons unsalted butter   3 egg yolks
>   ¼ cup flour   ½ cup heavy cream
>   4 cups chicken stock or broth   1 cup sour cream
>   ½ cup minced chives

Melt the butter in a large saucepan, stir in the flour, and gradually whisk in the chicken stock. Add the chives and cook, stirring, until the mixture comes to a boil and thickens. Remove from the heat.

Beat the egg yolks lightly with the heavy cream. Stir in a little of the hot broth and then return the mixture to the saucepan. Cook over medium heat, stirring constantly, for about 10 minutes to thicken, but do not let the soup boil. Remove from the heat and cool to room temperature. Whisk in the sour cream and chill.

YIELD: 4½ TO 5 CUPS

SPICED PEACH SOUP

This is a cooling appetizer for a mid-summer luncheon. Follow with a green salad such as Caesar Salad (page 54) or Spinach Salad (page 87).

>   1½ pounds peaches   ½ teaspoon Chinese 5-spice
>   ¼ cup orange juice   powder
>   2 tablespoons white port   A pinch of allspice
>   ⅔ cup buttermilk   A pinch of ginger

Peel the peaches after immersing them in boiling water for about 20 seconds. Chop them coarse and purée in batches in a food processor or blender. Stir in the remaining ingredients and refrigerate. Serve ice-cold.

YIELD: APPROXIMATELY 3½ CUPS

SPINACH AND MINT SOUP

The flavor of mint combines well with spinach to create a cooling and delicious summer soup. I use peppermint (the variety that flourishes in—invades—most backyards), as it has no trace of bitterness.

Three 10-ounce packages
    fresh spinach
2½ tablespoons unsalted
    butter
3½ tablespoons flour
4 cups chicken stock or
    canned broth

2 egg yolks
1⅓ cups sour cream
⅔ cup heavy cream
2 scant tablespoons lemon
    juice
⅓ cup minced fresh mint
    leaves

FOR THE GARNISH

Sprigs of fresh mint or very thin lemon slices

Wash the spinach well and discard any stems or wilted leaves. Cook, covered, in a large enameled pot in the water clinging to the leaves. Drain well in a colander, pressing out as much water as possible with the back of a wooden spoon. Purée in a food processor and reserve.

Melt the butter in a large saucepan and stir in the flour. Gradually add the chicken stock or broth, whisking until the mixture comes to a boil and thickens. Lower the heat and cook below a simmer for a few minutes. Stir a little hot broth into the egg yolks; then add the yolk mixture to the pan, whisking vigorously. Cook for 5 to 10 minutes to thicken slightly, stirring often. Do not let the soup boil or the eggs will curdle. Remove from the heat and let cool to room temperature. When cool, stir in the spinach. Add the sour cream, stirring with a wire whisk, and then the cream, lemon juice, and mint. Cover and refrigerate until ready to serve. Garnish each serving with a mint sprig or lemon slice.

YIELD: 7 CUPS

SUMMER GARDEN SOUP

---

1 head Boston lettuce, washed, with tough outer leaves discarded
1 1/2 cups chicken stock or broth
1/4 cup watercress leaves

2 tablespoons minced parsley
1 tablespoon chopped chives
1 tablespoon chopped fresh basil leaves
1/2 cup sour cream
Salt

Blanch the lettuce leaves in the chicken broth for 2 minutes, or until wilted. Strain, reserving the broth, and purée in a food processor, adding the watercress leaves, parsley, basil, and chives. Stir in the sour cream, reserved broth, and salt to taste. Chill.

YIELD: APPROXIMATELY 2 1/2 CUPS

TOMATO AND ORANGE SOUP

This is a recipe developed by our friend Jill Stallworthy. The combination of flavors is marvelous—and it is a very agreeable way to cool off on a hot day.

2 pounds ripe tomatoes
1 large garlic clove, peeled and minced
1 tablespoon unsalted butter
1 bay leaf
Several whole peppercorns

1 cup chicken stock or broth
¾ cup orange juice, preferably fresh
1 tablespoon minced mint leaves or basil leaves
Salt

FOR THE GARNISH

Paper-thin orange slices

Wash, core, and chop the tomatoes coarse. Sauté them gently with the garlic, butter, bay leaf, and peppercorns for a few minutes. Add the chicken stock, cover the pan, and simmer for 20 minutes. Strain through a food mill, pressing through as much pulp as possible. Stir in the orange juice and mint or basil and add salt to taste. Chill thoroughly. Garnish each serving with an orange slice.

YIELD: APPROXIMATELY 4½ CUPS

TOMATO AND PEACH SOUP

The flavor of the peaches is too subtle to be identified readily, bu
it creates an interesting effect.

3 pounds ripe tomatoes, cored
and chopped coarse
1 large garlic clove, peeled
and cut in half
1 1/2 tablespoons unsalted
butter

2 teaspoons grated fresh
gingerroot
2 cups (scant) chicken stock
or broth
3 large peaches
Salt

Sauté the tomatoes gently with the garlic and butter for a few
minutes. Add the grated gingerroot and chicken stock, cover the
pan, and simmer for 20 minutes. Strain through a food mill, press
ing through as much pulp as possible.

Peel the peaches after immersing in boiling water for about 2
seconds. Discard the pits, chop coarse, and purée in a food proces
sor. Stir into the tomato mixture. Add salt to taste and chill before
serving.

YIELD: APPROXIMATELY 8 CUPS

TOMATO-FENNEL SOUP

This is a very pleasing, if unexpected, combination of flavors.

1 large fennel bulb, washed and chopped (about 1¼ cups), with green tops reserved

2 tablespoons unsalted butter

1 medium yellow onion, sliced

3 medium-size ripe tomatoes, peeled, seeded, and chopped coarse (1½ cups)

3 tablespoons flour

½ cup dry white wine

One 24-ounce can tomato juice (3 cups)

1 tablespoon lime juice

Grated rind of 1 lime

2 cups beef stock or broth

2 tablespoons Pernod or anise-flavored liqueur

FOR THE GARNISH

Minced fennel ferns

Sauté the fennel in the butter for 5 minutes. Add the onion and sauté until the vegetables are soft but do not brown. Add the tomatoes, cook for a few minutes, and blend in the flour. Add the wine, simmer briefly, stirring, and remove from the heat. Purée the cooked vegetables, with any liquid in the pan, in a food processor or blender. Empty into a large bowl and stir in all the remaining ingredients except the garnish. Chill, and garnish each bowl of soup with a few fennel ferns.

YIELD: APPROXIMATELY 7 CUPS

TOMATO-GINGER SOUP

A simple tomato soup recipe that is given character by the addition of fresh ginger. Do not substitute dried, ground ginger. This soup is good served hot or cold.

3½ pounds ripe tomatoes,
    cored and chopped coarse
2 garlic cloves, peeled and
    halved
2 tablespoons unsalted butter

1 tablespoon grated fresh
    gingerroot
2 cups chicken stock or broth
Salt

Sauté the tomatoes gently with the garlic and butter for a few minutes. Add the grated ginger and chicken stock, cover the pan, and simmer for 20 minutes. Strain through a food mill, pressing through as much pulp as possible. Taste, and add a little salt, if necessary. Serve chilled or hot.

YIELD: APPROXIMATELY 7 CUPS OR 8 SERVINGS

TOMATO-MINT SOUP

A chilled, light soup to make when vine-ripened tomatoes are at their peak.

4½ pounds tomatoes,
    washed, cored, and
    chopped coarse
2 teaspoons minced garlic
1½ tablespoons unsalted
    butter

1 bay leaf
4 whole peppercorns
2⅔ cups chicken stock or
    broth
6 tablespoons fine-minced
    fresh mint leaves

In a large skillet, gently sauté the tomatoes and garlic in the butter for a few minutes. Add the bay leaf, peppercorns, and chicken stock. Cover tightly and simmer for about 30 minutes. Strain through a food mill, pressing through as much pulp as possible. Cool to room temperature. Stir in the mint leaves and chill until serving.

YIELD: 9 CUPS

VICHYSSOISE

Here is a slightly muted version of this classic and popular chilled soup. Six variations on the basic recipe follow.

> *3 large leeks (10 to 12*
> *ounces trimmed or 2½*
> *cups chopped)*
> *2 tablespoons butter*
> *1 pound potatoes (approxi-*
> *mately 2 large)*

> *3 cups chicken stock or broth*
> *1 cup heavy cream*
> *Salt*
> *Fresh-ground white pepper*

FOR THE GARNISH

> *¼ cup chopped chives*

Wash the leeks well. Trim off and discard the dark green ends and slice the white part and some of the tender light green portion into ½-inch lengths. Cook in the butter, covered, until soft; do not let them brown.

Peel and slice the potatoes into ½-inch pieces and simmer them, covered, in the chicken stock until tender. Drain and reserve the broth.

Purée the leeks and potatoes in batches, in a food processor or blender, adding the chicken stock in a thin, steady stream. Cool to room temperature. Stir in the cream, season to taste, and chill.

To serve, garnish each bowl of soup with a sprinkling of chopped chives.
YIELD: APPROXIMATELY 5½ CUPS

Artichoke Vichyssoise

Follow the basic recipe above, but purée 8 to 9 ounces canned artichoke hearts with the leeks and potatoes.
YIELD: APPROXIMATELY 6 CUPS

Celery Root Vichyssoise

Peel and slice 1 large or 2 small celery roots (10 ounces). Proceed as in the basic recipe above, but cook the celery root with the potatoes and increase the chicken stock to 4½ cups. Purée the celery root with the potatoes and leeks, adding the stock in a thin stream. Increase the cream to 1½ cups. Chill. If necessary, thin the soup to desired consistency with a little extra chicken stock.
YIELD: 7½ TO 8 CUPS

Cucumber Vichyssoise

Prepare the basic recipe on pages 43–44, reducing the cream to ⅓ cup. Purée enough peeled, seeded, and chopped cucumber to equal 4 cups. Stir this into the soup with 1 teaspoon minced fresh dill weed or ¼ teaspoon dried.
YIELD: APPROXIMATELY 6½ CUPS

Gorgonzola Vichyssoise

Follow the basic recipe on pages 43–44 with these changes: purée 2½ to 3 ounces mild, imported Gorgonzola cheese with the leeks

nd potatoes. Thin the soup with an additional ½ cup chicken stock
r broth.

YIELD: APPROXIMATELY 6 CUPS

Rosemary Vichyssoise

ollow the basic recipe on pages 43–44, but increase the chicken
tock to 3½ cups and simmer it with 1 tablespoon dried rosemary
or 10 minutes. Strain the stock and discard the rosemary before
ooking the potatoes.

YIELD: APPROXIMATELY 5½ CUPS

Snow Pea Vichyssoise

auté until tender ½ pound snow peas or Chinese pea pods. Proceed
s in the basic recipe on pages 43–44, puréeing the snow peas with
he leeks and potatoes. Thin with a little extra broth, if necessary.

YIELD: APPROXIMATELY 6 CUPS

ZUCCHINI-BASIL SOUP

refreshing, summery combination. If you don't grow fresh basil,
y to find someone who does.

2 pounds small, firm zucchini	1 cup half-and-half
¼ cup chopped scallions	1 cup sour cream
1 tablespoon olive oil	1 tablespoon lemon juice
½ cup minced fresh basil leaves	1 cup chicken stock or broth
	Salt
	Fresh-ground white pepper

OR THE GARNISH

Several sprigs of fresh basil, if available

Wash and dry the zucchini, slice crosswise, and sauté with the scallions in the olive oil over low heat for a few minutes. Do not allow it to brown. Cook very gently, partially covered, until tender. Purée the zucchini and scallions with the basil in a food processor or blender, in batches, adding the half-and-half in a thin stream. Empty into a mixing bowl and stir in the sour cream, lemon juice, and chicken stock. Season to taste with salt and pepper and chill.

Thin with a little extra chicken stock or milk, if necessary, before serving. Garnish each bowl with a sprig of fresh basil.

YIELD: 5 TO 6 CUPS

2: Entrée Salads

T H E salads included in this chapter are all substantial enough to serve as the main course for lunch or supper. Many of them can, as well, be used as side dishes to accompany the entrées in Chapters 3 and 4.

Salads should be made from the freshest possible ingredients, and it is important to store them properly. Different greens should be stored under different conditions, and I have found the following methods work best:

Lettuce: Wash, dry, roll up in one layer in paper towels, put in a plastic bag, and place in the vegetable drawer of your refrigerator. Or, put washed and dried lettuce in a colander, wrap the underside of the colander in waxed paper to catch any water, and refrigerate.

Watercress: Rinse and completely immerse in a bowl of water and refrigerate.

Parsley: Place the stem ends in a glass of water, cover the leaves with a plastic bag, and refrigerate.

Other fresh herbs: Wash and dry thoroughly. Store in the refrigerator in airtight plastic bags or containers.

Use fresh herbs whenever possible and be cautious when purchasing dried. Dried herbs vary in quality from one brand and variety to another; some, such as dill and oregano, can be very bitter. Also, dried herbs do not have an indefinite shelf life. Those you've had for years are not likely to have any identifiable flavor left in them; when their aroma is nondescript and dusty, it is time to replace them.

I have to confess to making vinaigrette dressing for years on a ratio of 2 parts oil to 1 part vinegar. It was not until reading Elizabeth David's recommendations that I realized how barbaric this was and began to take a more critical view of salad dressings. The overpowering acidity of vinegar masks other flavors; in her view, even a ratio of 4 to 1 is a bit excessive, and she advocates a ratio of 6 parts oil to 1 part vinegar. My own current preference for most salad dressings is a 4 to 1 ratio. This is, of course, largely a matter of personal taste and you must determine your own level of tolerance. Ideal proportions are also greatly affected by the kind of vinegar you use. Vinegars vary in sharpness according to both variety and quality. White vinegar is the most acid and should be used for pickling, but not for salad dressings. Cider vinegar is more acid than red or white wine vinegar. And a cheap wine vinegar is more acid than one of good quality. Wine vinegars flavored with herbs are ideal for use in salads. If you have fresh herbs, it is easy enough—and more economical—to make your own. Simply add about 1 cup of fresh herbs, such as tarragon, sage, basil, burnet, or a combination of herbs, to 2 quarts of red or white wine vinegar in a large covered crock or nonmetallic container. Let stand in a cool, dark place for 2 or 3 weeks, shaking or stirring occasionally. Strain into clean bottles, adding a few sprigs of fresh herbs to each bottle, if desired.

It is also important to use a very good quality, fresh olive oil in any salad dressing. Those made and packed in Lucca, Italy, are excellent, although some good and less expensive Spanish oils are also available. I would avoid domestic olive oil.

BASIC VINAIGRETTE

---

1 garlic clove, peeled and cut
      in half
¾ cup olive oil

3 tablespoons wine vinegar

Combine the ingredients and let stand for several hours. Remove the garlic before using.

YIELD: APPROXIMATELY 1 CUP

AEGEAN SALAD

This splendid salad made with a tangy lime vinaigrette is more hearty and filling than the Greek Salad on page 66. It can be assembled and dressed well in advance of serving. Accompany it with the sesame Toasted Syrian Bread (page 253).

FOR THE LIME VINAIGRETTE

1 large garlic clove, crushed
½ cup olive oil

¼ cup lime juice
¼ teaspoon dill weed

FOR THE SALAD

1 cup raw rice
1 pound cooked, shelled, and
      deveined medium-large
      shrimp
½ cup Calamata olives,
      pitted
⅓ cup chopped scallions

1 medium cucumber, peeled
      and sliced thin
⅓ cup fresh parsley sprigs,
      packed
1 cup crumbled feta cheese
Fresh-ground pepper to taste

FOR THE GARNISH

5 or 6 cup-shaped Boston or romaine lettuce leaves

Mix all the ingredients for the vinaigrette and reserve.

Cook the rice in a very large pot of rapidly boiling salted water for 15 to 20 minutes, or until tender but slightly firm. Drain and rinse. Combine the rice, shrimp, and half the lime vinaigrette and let stand until the mixture reaches room temperature. Mix in the remaining ingredients and the rest of the vinaigrette and chill.

Before serving, arrange the lettuce leaves on a platter and fill each with a portion of the salad, or serve the salad from a glass bowl.

YIELD: 6 SERVINGS

AL FRESCO SALAD

A colorful and highly flavored green salad, which is nice for a picnic or patio lunch. Serve with Corn Muffins (page 243).

8 thin slices bacon
2 ripe avocados
1 tablespoon lemon juice
3 medium-size ripe tomatoes
1 cup pitted black olives, halved
1 small Bermuda onion, peeled and sliced thin
2 ounces blue cheese, crumbled (½ cup)

½ pound fresh spinach, washed, stemmed, and dried
Salt
Fresh-ground pepper
1 recipe Basic Vinaigrette (page 49)

Sauté the bacon until crisp. Drain on paper towels and then crumble.

Peel the avocados, slice into a bowl, and toss with the lemon juice. Core the tomatoes and chop into bite-size pieces. Combine the bacon, avocados, tomatoes, olives, onion, blue cheese, and spinach in a salad bowl. Season to taste and toss with the vinaigrette before serving.

YIELD: 6 SERVINGS

AVOCADOS WITH CHICKEN SALAD

Serve with the lemon-pepper Toasted Syrian Bread (page 253).

FOR THE DRESSING

1 egg yolk
1/2 cup olive oil
2 teaspoons Dijon mustard
2 teaspoons lemon juice
3 tablespoons sour cream
1 tablespoon minced fresh
parsley

1 teaspoon minced fresh tarragon or 1/4 teaspoon dried
1 tablespoon minced chives
Salt
Fresh-ground white pepper

FOR THE SALAD

1 very large whole chicken
breast, split
2 cups chicken broth or water
5 slices bacon, fried until
crisp, drained, and
crumbled

1 large tomato, peeled, seeded, and cut into strips
1/2 cup watercress sprigs
2 large ripe avocados
3 tablespoons chopped pecans
(optional)

To make the dressing, place the egg yolk in a small mixing bowl. Beat with an electric mixer or wire whisk while adding the olive oil drop by drop and, as the mixture thickens, in a very thin stream. Stir in the mustard, lemon juice, sour cream, minced herbs, and salt and pepper to taste.

Poach the chicken in the stock or broth for about 20 minutes, or until just cooked. Do not overcook. When cool enough to handle, strip off the skin and bones and cut chicken into julienne strips about ¼ inch wide and 2 inches long.

In a mixing bowl, combine the chicken, bacon, tomato, watercress, and dressing. Cut the avocados in half lengthwise and rub the cut sides with a little lemon juice to prevent discoloring. Fill each half with a portion of the chicken salad and, if desired, sprinkle with chopped pecans.

YIELD: 4 SERVINGS

BYZANTINE ARTICHOKES

Whole artichokes are steamed in a sweet-and-sour marinade, then chilled and filled with either shrimp or mussels vinaigrette.

6 *large artichokes*
2 *medium yellow onions,*
   sliced
1 *tablespoon sugar*
Juice of 2 lemons
⅔ *cup olive oil (or half*
   olive oil and half vege-
   table oil)

1 *cup water*
1 *teaspoon salt*
A large pinch crushed red
   pepper

FOR THE FILLING

2 cups cooked shrimp or mus-
    sel meat
¼ cup chopped scallions
2 tablespoons minced fresh
    parsley, packed

⅓ cup olive oil
2 tablespoons white wine
    vinegar
1 garlic clove, peeled and cut
    in half

FOR THE GARNISH

Fresh parsley

1 lemon, cut into 6 wedges

TO PREPARE THE ARTICHOKES

Wash them well under cold running water. Cut off the top third of each and then snip the thorny tips off all the remaining leaves with a pair of shears. Cut off the stems so that the artichokes are flat on the bottom. Stand them up in a large enameled or stainless steel pot (other metals cause discoloration). Add the sliced onions, sugar, lemon juice, oil, water, salt, and crushed red pepper. Cover tightly and cook over medium heat for approximately 45 minutes. Artichokes are done when the bottom can be pierced easily with a fork. Let stand until they reach room temperature.

TO MAKE THE FILLING

Combine the shrimp or mussels with the scallions and parsley. Mix the olive oil and vinegar separately, add the cut garlic clove, and let stand for a few hours, until the garlic flavor has permeated the vinaigrette. Discard the garlic and toss the shrimp or mussel mixture in the vinaigrette. Cover and refrigerate until serving.

TO SERVE

Remove the central cone of purplish leaves from each artichoke and scrape out the fuzzy choke that lies beneath. Fill each cavity with the shrimp or mussels. Arrange on a platter with fresh parsley and lemon wedges.

YIELD: 6 SERVINGS

CAESAR SALAD

This salad may seem Mediterranean in flavor, but it was the inspiration of a California restaurateur. Serve it with a crusty loaf of Cuban Bread (page 245) or Gougère (page 248).

F O R   T H E   S A L A D

2 medium-size heads romaine
   lettuce (10 to 12 ounces
   each), or 1 large head
1 small can anchovy fillets,
   drained
3 hard-boiled eggs, peeled
   and cut into quarters

3 tablespoons fresh-grated
   Parmesan cheese
Fresh-ground pepper
3/4 cup garlic-flavored
   Croutons (page 243)

F O R   T H E   D R E S S I N G

1 egg, *lightly beaten*
1 garlic clove, *peeled and
   crushed*

2/3 cup olive oil
3 tablespoons lemon juice

Wash the lettuce well, discarding the tough outer leaves, and dry. Tear into bite-size pieces and put in a large salad bowl with the anchovies, the quartered hard-boiled eggs, the Parmesan, and pepper to taste. Combine the ingredients for the salad dressing.

Just before serving, add the croutons to the salad and toss with the dressing.

YIELD: 4 GENEROUS SERVINGS

CALAMARI SALAD

A delicious combination of shrimp, squid, and artichoke hearts marinated in a light vinaigrette.

FOR THE MARINADE

1 cup olive oil
2 tablespoons white wine vinegar
2 tablespoons lemon or lime juice

1 small garlic clove, peeled and minced
1 tablespoon fresh dill weed, or ½ teaspoon dried

FOR THE SALAD

1 pound squid, cleaned*
1 pound unshelled shrimp (or ¾ pound shelled)
⅓ cup chopped scallions
8 or 9 ounces canned artichoke hearts, well drained and quartered

2 tablespoons capers
¼ cup minced fresh parsley
Salt
Fresh-ground pepper

* The spiny, transparent rod, the skin covering the head and tentacles, the ink sac at the base of the head, and the intestines should be removed, preferably by a fishmonger. Or use frozen, cleaned squid. Wash the squid well.

FOR THE GARNISH

4 large Boston lettuce leaves

In a large mixing bowl, combine the ingredients for the marinade.

Bring a large pot of salted water to a boil. Add the squid and cook for 15 to 20 minutes. Drain well, cut into ½-inch pieces, and add to the marinade.

Refill the pot with water, add salt, and again bring to a boil. Peel, devein, and wash the shrimp and cook in the boiling water for about 2 minutes, or until pink and firm. Drain thoroughly and toss in the marinade while the shrimp are still warm. Mix in the scallions, artichoke hearts, capers, parsley, and salt and pepper to taste. Allow to marinate several hours or overnight in the refrigerator. Remove from the refrigerator about ½ hour before serving. Place each portion on a large lettuce leaf.

YIELD: 4 SERVINGS

CELERY RÉMOULADE SALAD

Roast beef, mushrooms, and capers have been added to the traditional celery rémoulade.

4 cups celery root, peeled and cut into julienne strips	¼ pound rare roast beef, cut into julienne strips
1 tablespoon white wine vinegar	3 tablespoons capers
6 ounces mushrooms, cleaned and sliced ¼ inch thick	2 tablespoons minced fresh parsley

FOR THE MUSTARD-CREAM DRESSING

2 cups sour cream	1 tablespoon lemon juice
2½ tablespoons Dijon mustard	

FOR THE GARNISH

    2 tablespoons chopped chives

Parboil the celery root in a large pot of boiling water for 2 to 3 minutes, until it is slightly softened but not limp. Drain, rinse under cold water, and dry with paper towels. Toss in a bowl with the vinegar and then add the sliced mushrooms, roast beef, capers, and parsley.

    Mix the ingredients for the mustard-cream dressing and combine with the salad. Turn into a serving bowl and sprinkle with chopped chives.

YIELD: 4 SERVINGS

CHICKEN SALAD ELIZABETH

Strips of chicken sautéed in lemon and butter are combined in a lemon-mustard vinaigrette with bacon, avocado, basil, tomatoes, and pine nuts. It is named for our good friend, Elizabeth Sullam.

FOR THE DRESSING

    ⅓ cup olive oil
    2 tablespoons lemon juice
    2 teaspoons Dijon mustard

    1 tablespoon mayonnaise
    1 garlic clove, peeled and cut
        in half

FOR THE SALAD

2 large whole chicken breasts
   (1 ¼ pounds), skinned,
   boned, and split in
   half
2 tablespoons butter
2 tablespoons lemon juice
7 lean slices of bacon
1 cup cherry tomatoes, cut in
   half

1 ¼ cups fresh basil, torn
   into small pieces and
   lightly packed
¼ cup pine nuts
1 avocado
1 bunch of watercress
Fresh-ground pepper

At least 1 hour before serving the salad, whisk together all the ingredients for the dressing.

Cut the chicken into strips about ⅜ inch wide and 2½ inches long. Heat the butter in a very large skillet, add the chicken, and sprinkle with the lemon juice. Cook, turning, over moderately high heat for 2 or 3 minutes, or just until lightly browned and cooked through. Remove from the heat and cool to room temperature.

Cook the bacon until crisp in a skillet or microwave, or on a shelf placed at least 6 inches below the broiler. Drain on paper towels and break into bite-size pieces.

Shortly before serving, combine the chicken, bacon, cherry tomatoes, basil, and pine nuts in a large serving bowl. Peel the avocado, cut in half lengthwise, and slice crosswise into ¼-inch-thick pieces. Add to the salad bowl with the watercress. Remove the garlic clove from the dressing and toss the salad with the dressing. Season to taste with ground pepper.

YIELD: 4 SERVINGS

CHICKEN SALAD MADRAS

This chicken salad is dressed in a mild curried sauce that combines walnuts, currants, and seedless green grapes for a variety of textures as well as an Eastern flavor. Serve with sesame Toasted Syrian Bread (page 253).

*2 large whole chicken
    breasts, split*

*2 cups chicken broth or water
Juice of ½ lime*

FOR THE DRESSING

1 cup sour cream
¼ cup mayonnaise
¾ teaspoon curry powder
*2½ teaspoons Chut-Nut
    Colonial chutney*
*1 tablespoon chopped fresh
    chives*

*½ cup coarse-chopped wal-
    nuts*
3 tablespoons currants
*½ cup seedless green grapes
    (or chopped fresh pine-
    apple)*

FOR THE GARNISH

Lettuce leaves
Several small bunches of seedless green grapes (optional)

Poach the chicken, partially covered, in simmering stock or water for 20 minutes, or just until cooked through. Be careful not to overcook or it will be dry. Drain, and when cool enough to handle, strip the skin and bones from the chicken and cut it into julienne strips, about 2 inches long and ½ inch wide, following the grain of the meat. Combine thoroughly with the lime juice and allow to marinate for several hours or until ready to serve.

Combine all the ingredients for the dressing. Just before serving, toss the chicken with the dressing and mound on a bed of lettuce leaves. Surround with a few small bunches of green grapes, if desired.

YIELD: 4 SERVINGS

CHICKEN SALAD OTHELLO

Both simple and elegant, this chicken salad is composed almost entirely of julienne strips of chicken breast, with a little shredded lettuce added for texture, and tossed in a dressing that is light, creamy, and piquant. Serve it with Melba Toast (page 249) or Oatmeal Crackers (page 251).

3 whole chicken breasts, split
3 cups chicken broth or water
2 cups packed Boston or ice-
 berg lettuce, cut into
 julienne strips

1 1/3 cups thin-sliced celery

FOR THE DRESSING

1 small garlic clove, peeled
3 scallions
1/4 cup fresh parsley sprigs,
 packed
1 teaspoon Worcestershire
 sauce

2 tablespoons white wine
 vinegar
3/4 cup mayonnaise
2/3 to 1 cup sour cream

FOR THE GARNISH

2 bunches of watercress, washed and dried

Place the chicken in a large skillet with the chicken broth or water. Poach, partially covered, over medium heat until just done. This should take about 20 minutes; do not overcook or the chicken will be dry. Remove the chicken from the broth. When it is cool enough to handle, strip the skin and bones from the chicken and cut it into long, narrow strips about ⅜ inch wide, following the grain of the meat.

To make the dressing, mince the garlic, scallions, and parsley in a food processor or blender. Add the Worcestershire sauce, vinegar, and mayonnaise and blend. Turn into a small bowl and fold in ⅔ to 1 cup sour cream, according to taste.

Just before serving, combine the chicken strips, shredded lettuce, celery, and dressing. Mound onto a platter and surround with the watercress.

YIELD: 6 SERVINGS

CHICKEN SALAD WITH CREAMY HERB DRESSING

The dressing for this salad is a lovely smooth combination of sour cream and mayonnaise, sparked with a little lemon juice and a great deal of fresh mint. Watercress adds a crisp flavor and texture to the salad.

FOR THE DRESSING

¼ cup fresh parsley sprigs
¾ cup chopped fresh mint leaves
1 to 1½ tablespoons lemon juice

1 cup sour cream
¾ cup mayonnaise

FOR THE SALAD

3 *small whole chicken breasts, split in half (not boneless)*	2 *tablespoons chopped fresh chives or tender scallion ends*
3 *cups chicken broth*	1 *bunch of watercress, washed and trimmed*
1 *cup small pitted black olives*	

It is best to make the dressing several hours or even a day ahead, to allow time for the mint flavor to develop. Mince the parsley and mint in a food processor. Add the lemon juice, sour cream, and mayonnaise and blend. (If you make the dressing by hand, beat it vigorously with a wire whisk or it will be too thick.) Turn into a bowl, cover, and refrigerate.

To poach the chicken breasts: Put them in a large skillet in a single layer with the broth. Partially cover and simmer gently for 17 minutes, or just until cooked through. Remove from the skillet and let cool on a platter. Remove the skin and bones and cut the chicken into strips about 3 inches long by ⅜ inch wide. Cover and refrigerate until serving.

Just before serving, put the chicken, olives, chives or scallion ends, and watercress in a salad bowl and toss with the dressing.

Note: If you add the dressing to the salad too long before serving, the chicken will absorb too much of the dressing and the mixture will be dry.

YIELD: 6 SERVINGS

COLD CURRIED SHRIMP

Shrimp, avocado, cucumber, and herbs are combined in a mildly curried vinaigrette dressing. This is a light, refreshing hot-weather dish.

F O R   T H E   D R E S S I N G

6 *tablespoons olive oil*
3 *tablespoons lime juice*
1 *tablespoon juice from a jar of Major Grey's chutney, preferably Sun Brand*

$\frac{1}{3}$ *teaspoon curry powder*
A pinch of ground coriander
1 *garlic clove, peeled and cut in half*

F O R   T H E   S A L A D

1½ *pounds raw, unshelled large shrimp*
Salt
3 *tablespoons lime juice*
1 *medium-small cucumber*

¼ *cup minced fresh chives*
¾ *cup chopped fresh mint leaves*
1 *large or 2 small avocados*

Combine the ingredients for the dressing at least 1 hour before needed, to allow time for the garlic flavor to develop.

Shell and devein the shrimp. Bring a large pot of water to a boil. Add salt and the shrimp and cook 2 minutes or just until the shrimp are pink and firm. Drain and toss the shrimp immediately with the lime juice. Cool to room temperature.

Peel the cucumber, quarter lengthwise, and discard the seeds. Slice into julienne strips, about ¼ inch wide and thick and 2½ to 3 inches long. Drain off any lime juice not absorbed by the shrimp. Combine the shrimp, cucumber, chives, and mint leaves in a salad bowl, and refrigerate, covered, until serving.

To serve, peel and halve the avocado. Remove the pit and slice crosswise about ¼ inch thick. Add to the salad. Remove the garlic clove from the dressing and toss the salad with the dressing.

YIELD: 4 SERVINGS

CUCUMBER BOATS

Cucumber halves are filled with a seafood and cottage cheese mixture combined with a tangy dressing. Serve with Melba Toast (page 249).

2 medium-small cucumbers, peeled, halved, and seeded
Salt
1 cup large-curd creamed cottage cheese
1½ cups medium-size shrimp, cooked and cleaned (½ pound)

¼ pound smoked salmon, cut into bite-size pieces (optional)
¼ cup chopped chives
Fresh-ground pepper

FOR THE DRESSING

½ cup plain yogurt
1 tablespoon lime juice
2 teaspoons Major Grey's chutney, minced or sieved

½ teaspoon fennel seeds

FOR THE GARNISH

1 lime, quartered

1 bunch of watercress

Sprinkle the cucumbers with salt, invert, and drain on paper towels for about ½ hour. Rinse and pat dry.

Place the cottage cheese, shrimp, salmon, chives, and pepper to taste in a mixing bowl. Combine the ingredients for the dressing and toss with the salad.

To serve, fill each cucumber half with the salad mixture. Garnish with watercress and lime wedges.

YIELD: 4 SERVINGS

DUCK SALAD

Sliced radishes add a slightly sharp and crisp accent to this salad. The dressing is a lime hollandaise with sour cream.

One 5-to-6-pound duck, quartered and roasted (page 140)

2 cups shredded Bibb lettuce

1 cup seedless green grapes, cut in half

1 cup radishes, washed, trimmed, and sliced thin

FOR THE DRESSING

6 egg yolks

6 tablespoons lime juice

10 tablespoons unsalted butter

1 tablespoon minced fresh parsley

⅔ cup sour cream

Fresh-ground white pepper

A pinch of salt

Strip the skin and bones from the duck and cut into bite-size pieces. Combine with the shredded lettuce, green grapes, and sliced radishes.

Using a wire whisk, beat the egg yolks and lime juice in the top of a double boiler over hot, not boiling, water until they begin to thicken. Gradually add the butter, a few tablespoons at a time, beating constantly until the sauce is thick and fluffy. Do not let the sauce get too hot or it will separate. (Should this happen, rehomogenize it by beating in a tablespoon of boiling water.) Remove from the heat and let cool to room temperature. Fold in the parsley, sour cream, and a little salt and pepper.

Combine the duck salad with the dressing just before serving.
YIELD: 4 SERVINGS

GREEK SALAD

1 medium head of romaine
    or leaf lettuce
1 medium cucumber, peeled
    and sliced
1 large or 2 small tomatoes,
    peeled and cut into
    bite-size pieces
24 pitted Calamata olives
    (²/₃ cup)

½ pound feta cheese,
    crumbled
½ medium Bermuda onion,
    sliced thin
1 small can anchovy fillets,
    rinsed and patted dry
Fresh-ground pepper to taste

FOR THE VINAIGRETTE

1 garlic clove, peeled and
    halved
½ cup olive oil

2 tablespoons red wine
    vinegar
¼ teaspoon oregano or basil

Wash and dry the lettuce; tear into bite-size pieces and combine with the remaining ingredients for the salad.

Combine the ingredients for the vinaigrette, allowing the garlic to marinate in the dressing for a while. Before serving, remove the garlic clove and toss the salad with the dressing.

YIELD: 3 SERVINGS

INSALATA ROMANA

This is a hearty salad, ideal for buffets, since it can be completely assembled and dressed well in advance of serving. It is one of those recipes people always request.

Three 7-ounce cans solid
    white tuna fish in oil,
    drained
7 to 10 ounces canned arti-
    choke hearts, quartered
1 large can medium-size
    pitted black olives,
    drained
One 7-ounce jar Progresso
    roasted sweet peppers,
    cut into small pieces

1 small jar capers, drained
1 small can anchovy fillets,
    drained
6 ounces hard salami, sliced
    and cut into julienne
    strips
1 cup small cherry tomatoes
1/2 cup chopped scallions
2 tablespoons minced fresh
    parsley, packed

FOR THE DRESSING

2/3 cup olive oil
1/4 cup red wine vinegar

1 garlic clove, peeled and
    crushed

Place all the salad ingredients in a large mixing bowl. Combine the olive oil, vinegar, and garlic for the dressing; pour it over the salad and mix thoroughly. Cover and refrigerate until serving.

YIELD: 6 SERVINGS

ITALIAN CHEF SALAD

If you've grown tired of the traditional American chef salad, try this translation of it.

½ pound thin-sliced prosciutto
½ pound Jarlsberg, Emmenthal, or Gruyère cheese
1 cup medium-size pitted black olives, halved

3 cups cleaned and trimmed thin-sliced mushrooms
4 large bunches of arugola or watercress, washed and dried

FOR THE DRESSING

1 cup olive oil
⅓ cup red wine vinegar
2 teaspoons lemon juice

1 small garlic clove, pressed
Fresh-ground pepper

Cut the prosciutto and cheese into long julienne strips. Combine with the olives, mushrooms, and arugola or watercress. Combine the ingredients for the dressing in a separate bowl and toss with the salad just before serving.

YIELD: 4 SERVINGS

JERUSALEM ARTICHOKE SALAD

Jerusalem artichokes, or "sunchokes," have become widely available in recent years. They have an interesting, nutty flavor, not unlike that of celery root. In this salad they are combined with ham and Swiss cheese in a mustard vinaigrette.

FOR THE SALAD

*1 pound Jerusalem arti-
  chokes, peeled*
*One 6-ounce slice of baked
  ham, cut in
  ¼-inch-thick strips*
*¼ pound sliced Swiss cheese,
  cut in ¼-inch-wide
  strips*
*2 cups shredded Bibb or
  iceberg lettuce*

*3 tablespoons minced fresh
  parsley*
*2 tablespoons chopped chives
  or scallions*
*2 tablespoons fresh dill or ¾
  teaspoon dried*
Fresh-ground pepper

FOR THE DRESSING

1 tablespoon Dijon mustard
¾ cup olive oil

*3 tablespoons white wine
  vinegar*

Cut any large artichokes in half. Place in a saucepan in water to cover, and simmer for 10 to 20 minutes (depending on their size) or until tender but not soft. Drain, refresh under cold water, and dry with paper towels. Cool to room temperature. Cut into julienne strips about ¼ inch thick. Place in a bowl with the remaining salad ingredients.

Stir together the dressing ingredients, and toss the salad with the dressing just before serving.

YIELD: 4 SERVINGS

LOBSTER SALAD

A luxurious salad in a creamy rémoulade dressing. Serve it with Biscuits (page 241).

One 1½-pound lobster,
    boiled according to di-
    rections on page 28

1 cup shredded Boston or
    leaf lettuce
1 cup halved cherry tomatoes

FOR THE DRESSING

½ cup sour cream
2 tablespoons mayonnaise
2 teaspoons lemon juice
1 teaspoon Dijon mustard
1 generous tablespoon minced
    chives or scallions
1 tablespoon minced fresh
    tarragon or ½ teaspoon
    dried

1 tablespoon capers, well
    drained
Reserved lobster tomalley
Reserved lobster coral, if
    available

FOR THE GARNISH

2 large Boston lettuce leaves

2 hard-boiled eggs, quar-
    tered

Remove the lobster meat from the chest, tail, legs, and claws and reserve the green tomalley and coral, if any, for the dressing. Cut the lobster into bite-size chunks and place in a mixing bowl with the shredded lettuce and tomatoes. Cover and refrigerate.

Combine all the ingredients for the dressing, cover, and refrigerate. Just before serving, mix the dressing with the salad. Serve each portion on a lettuce leaf and surround with hard-boiled egg quarters.

YIELD: 2 SERVINGS

MANGO CHICKEN SALAD

This may be my favorite chicken salad. Mango, avocado, preserved ginger, and fresh mint are combined with chicken and tossed in a lime and ginger vinaigrette. While it is evocative of palm trees and tropical beaches, it would probably make a big hit in Cleveland on a hot August day.

FOR THE DRESSING

7 *tablespoons olive oil*
3 *tablespoons lime juice*
2 *tablespoons white wine vinegar*

1 *tablespoon syrup from a jar of preserved ginger stem*
1 *garlic clove, peeled and cut in half*

FOR THE SALAD

3 *whole chicken breasts, cut in half*
3 *cups chicken broth*
1 1/2 *cups peeled, sliced mango*
1 *large avocado, peeled and sliced*

1/4 *cup thin-sliced preserved ginger stem*
1/4 *cup minced fresh mint leaves*

FOR THE GARNISH

Spinach or lettuce leaves

Combine the ingredients for the dressing and reserve.

Poach the chicken, partially covered, in simmering broth in a large skillet for 20 minutes, or just until cooked through. Be careful not to overcook or it will be dry. Drain, and when the chicken is cool enough to handle, strip the skin and bones and cut the chicken

into julienne strips about 2½ inches long and ½ inch wide, following the "grain" of the meat.

In a mixing bowl, combine the chicken with the mango, avocado, ginger stem, and mint. Just before serving, remove the garlic
clove from the dressing and gently toss the salad and dressing. Serve
on a bed of spinach or lettuce leaves.

YIELD: 6 SERVINGS

MEDITERRANEAN PEPPER SALAD

Roasted peppers and marinated potatoes are combined with a medley of other ingredients to make a flavorful and hearty salad.

FOR THE VINAIGRETTE

½ cup olive oil
¼ cup red wine vinegar

1 garlic clove, peeled and
crushed

FOR THE SALAD

1½ pounds red new potatoes,
scrubbed
3 pounds large sweet red and
green peppers
⅔ cup pitted black olives

½ to ⅔ cup minced red
onion
¼ pound salami, cut into
¼-inch-wide strips
Fresh-ground pepper
¾ cup crumbled feta cheese

Combine the ingredients for the vinaigrette.

Boil the potatoes in salted water to cover for 20 to 25 minutes
or just until tender. Peel, slice, and marinate in the vinaigrette
dressing while they are still warm. Let stand until they reach room
temperature.

Roast the peppers under the broiler, about 2 inches from the heat, turning frequently, until the skin is blistered on all sides. Peel them under cold running water, remove the seeds, and cut into ½- to ¾-inch-wide strips. Let stand in a colander for about ½ hour, or until well drained.

After they have drained, put the peppers in the bowl with the potatoes and vinaigrette dressing. Add the olives, onion, salami, and pepper to taste. Toss the salad and sprinkle the feta cheese over the top. Chill until serving.

YIELD: 6 SERVINGS

MOZZARELLA AND TOMATO SALAD

This very simple dish is commonly served in Italy—a cool and light lunch for a hot day.

FOR EACH SERVING

3 thick slices from a large, peeled tomato
1 large lettuce leaf
Salt
Fresh-ground black pepper
Several fresh basil leaves, chopped, or ⅛ teaspoon dried

Two ¼-inch-thick slices from a 1-pound mozzarella
2 anchovies, rinsed and patted dry
1 tablespoon Basic Vinaigrette (page 49)
1 teaspoon capers

FOR THE GARNISH

3 slices hard salami

6 Calamata olives

Arrange the tomato slices over the lettuce leaf and sprinkle with salt, pepper, and the basil leaves. Lay the mozzarella on top of the tomatoes, crisscross with the anchovies, and drizzle the vinaigrette over everything. Scatter the capers over the salad and add more fresh-ground pepper.

Roll up each slice of salami and secure with a toothpick. Arrange the olives and salami on the plate around the salad.

MUSSEL AND POTATO SALAD

In this recipe, mussels are cooked as for *moules marinière* and combined with potato salad in a vinaigrette. Serve with a dry white wine.

FOR THE MUSSELS

4 pounds mussels (3 quarts)
1½ cups dry white wine
3 garlic cloves, peeled and minced

⅓ cup chopped shallots or scallions
1 bay leaf

FOR THE VINAIGRETTE

½ cup olive oil
¼ cup white wine vinegar

¾ cup reserved, strained mussel broth

FOR THE POTATO SALAD

2½ pounds red new potatoes
⅔ cup chopped scallions (including green tops)

Salt
Fresh-ground pepper
¼ cup minced parsley, packed

FOR THE GARNISH

6 large Boston lettuce leaves

2 bunches of watercress

Scrub the mussels well under cold running water until free of all sand and seaweed. Put them into a large, heavy, lidded kettle with the wine, garlic, shallots or scallions, and bay leaf. Cover tightly, bring to a simmer, and cook for about 5 minutes, or until the mussels have opened. Discard any mussels that fail to open and remove the rest from their shells. Strain and reserve the broth.

Combine the ingredients for the vinaigrette in a small saucepan.

Boil the potatoes in a large pot of boiling water until just tender. Drain, peel, and slice ⅛ inch thick while they are still warm. Heat the vinaigrette to simmering and pour over the potatoes. Add the scallions, mussels, and seasoning to taste and stir to combine. Cool and mix in the parsley.

To serve, arrange the 6 lettuce leaves on a large platter, and spoon individual servings into each leaf. Arrange the watercress in a border around the edge of the platter. Serve at room temperature.

YIELD: 6 SERVINGS

MUSSEL, RICE, AND ROAST PEPPER SALAD

I particularly like this version of mussel and rice salad. The roasted sweet red pepper adds a bright flavor as well as color to the combination.

FOR THE VINAIGRETTE

½ *cup olive oil*
¼ *cup lemon juice*

1 small garlic clove, peeled

FOR THE SALAD

> 4 pounds mussels
> 3 garlic cloves, peeled and
>   cut in half
> 2/3 cup dry white wine
> 2 large sweet red peppers
> 1 1/3 cups rice
> 1/4 cup minced fresh parsley
>
> 1/3 cup chopped fresh basil, if
>   available
> 3 tablespoons minced scal-
>   lions with tender green
>   ends
> Salt
> Fresh-ground pepper

Combine the oil and lemon juice for the vinaigrette. Grate a little of the garlic into the mixture, then drop in the rest of the clove.

Scrub the mussels well under running water and remove the beards. Put the mussels into a large, heavy pot with the garlic and wine. Cover, bring to a boil, and cook for 5 minutes, or just until the shells open wide. (Discard any that fail to open.) Remove the mussels and shell them. Strain the mussel broth through a sieve lined with a damp towel and reserve 1/4 cup plus 2 tablespoons.

Preheat the broiler. Put the peppers in a pan about 4 inches below the heat source and broil until the skin blisters and blackens, and turn to char all sides. When cool enough to handle, peel off the skin under cold running water, and discard the core and seeds. Pat dry and cut into strips 1 to 1 1/2 inches wide.

Bring a very large pot of water to a rolling boil. Add a little salt and the rice and cook for 17 minutes, or until the rice is tender but firm. Drain well in a colander, rinse under hot tap water, and turn into a salad bowl. Toss with the vinaigrette (remove the garlic clove) while the rice is still warm. Let cool to room temperature, then mix in the mussels, peppers, the reserved mussel broth, the parsley, basil, and scallions. Season with a little salt, if necessary, and plenty of pepper. Serve either slightly chilled or at room temperature.

YIELD: 6 SERVINGS

PALM COURT SALAD

This is a variation on a chef salad, with strips of cucumber to add an agreeably crisp taste as well as texture. It is my own fantasy of a salad served in New York's Plaza Hotel in the old days.

FOR THE SALAD

¼ pound rare roast beef, sliced ¼ inch thick

2 ounces aged Swiss or Jarlsberg cheese, sliced

½ large cucumber, peeled and seeded

1 cup shredded spinach, packed

2 tablespoons chopped scallions or chives

1 hard-boiled egg, chopped fine

Fresh-ground pepper

Salt

FOR THE DRESSING

1 tablespoon mayonnaise

½ teaspoon Dijon mustard

A dash of Worcestershire sauce

1 tablespoon white wine vinegar

¼ cup olive oil

FOR THE GARNISH

1 large ripe tomato, cut into wedges

Cut the roast beef, cheese, and cucumber into uniform julienne strips, about ¼ inch thick. Combine in a salad bowl with the spinach, scallions or chives, and salt and pepper to taste.

To make the dressing, stir the mayonnaise, mustard, and Worcestershire sauce in a small cup with the wine vinegar; add the oil and stir well to combine.

Before serving, toss the salad with the dressing. Sprinkle the chopped egg over the top and surround the salad with tomato wedges.

YIELD: 2 SERVINGS

PASTA SALAD PRIMAVERA

———————

This is a refreshing and light summer meal. It should be served with chilled white wine, warm Cuban Bread (page 245), and cheese and fruit for dessert.

12 ounces green fettucine	*¾ to 1 cup fresh basil leaves*
2 tablespoons vegetable oil	*1 recipe Basic Vinaigrette*
2 tablespoons salt	*(page 49)*
½ cup olive oil	*Salt*
4 large ripe tomatoes, peeled	*Fresh-ground pepper*
and chopped coarse	
1 cup medium-size pitted	
black olives	

Cook the pasta in a very large pot of rapidly boiling water, to which 2 tablespoons vegetable oil and 2 tablespoons salt have been added for about 8 minutes, or until tender but not soft. Drain and toss immediately with the olive oil to prevent the noodles from sticking together. Let the pasta stand until it reaches room temperature.

Before serving, toss the pasta with the tomatoes, olives, basil leaves, and vinaigrette dressing. Add salt and fresh-ground black pepper to taste.

YIELD: 6 TO 8 SERVINGS

PASTA SALAD WITH MUSHROOMS
AND FRESH HERBS

This is a very simple but elegant Northern Italian dish. Serve it with a dry white wine and Whole Wheat Cuban Bread (page 246). You might begin the meal with Iced Tomato Soup (page 26) or Gazpacho (page 23) and end with strawberries or sliced peaches.

FOR THE DRESSING

½ cup heavy cream

3 tablespoons sour cream

1 tablespoon lemon juice

FOR THE SALAD

4 ounces small ruffle-edged egg noodles

3 tablespoons olive oil

4 ounces firm white mushrooms, cleaned, trimmed, and sliced

2 tablespoons minced chives

1 tablespoon minced fresh basil

1 tablespoon minced fresh parsley

2 teaspoons minced fresh tarragon

Salt

Fresh-ground pepper

1 bunch of arugola or watercress, large stems removed (1 cup, packed)

Combine the ingredients for the dressing and reserve.

Cook the noodles according to the package directions, adding a little vegetable oil to the boiling water to prevent the noodles from sticking together. Drain and toss with the olive oil. Cool to room temperature and add the mushrooms, chives, basil, parsley, tarragon, salt to taste, and plenty of fresh-ground pepper.

Before serving, combine with the arugola or watercress and toss with the dressing. Serve at room temperature.

YIELD: 2 SERVINGS

PASTA SALAD TONNATO

A colorful salad that looks particularly attractive served in a glass bowl.

FOR THE DRESSING

1 large garlic clove, peeled   *¾ cup olive oil*
and crushed   *3 tablespoons lemon juice*

FOR THE SALAD

4 ounces small ruffle-edged   *¼ cup capers*
egg noodles   *⅓ cup minced fresh parsley,*
Two 7-ounce cans solid   *packed*
white tuna fish in oil,   *Salt*
drained and flaked   *Fresh-ground pepper*
1 cup pitted black olives,
halved
1 large sweet red pepper,
seeded and cut into
slivers

Combine the ingredients for the dressing and reserve.

Cook the noodles according to the package directions, adding a little vegetable oil to the boiling water to prevent the noodles from sticking together. Drain and toss with the dressing. Add the tuna, olives, pepper, capers, and parsley. Season with a little salt, if necessary, and add plenty of fresh-ground black pepper. Toss to combine and serve at room temperature or slightly chilled.

YIELD: 4 SERVINGS

PROVENÇAL SALAD

This is a hearty composed salad similar to salade Niçoise. It is full of pungent flavors—roasted red peppers, basil, capers, and anchovies.

FOR THE VINAIGRETTE

½ cup olive oil
2 tablespoons wine vinegar
1 small garlic clove, peeled and pressed

1 teaspoon Dijon or Düsseldorf mustard

FOR THE SALAD

1 ½ pounds small red-skinned new potatoes
½ cup thin-sliced red onion
½ pound green beans, trimmed
2 large sweet red peppers (1 pound)
One 2-ounce tin of anchovy fillets

12 Calamata olives, halved and pitted
2 tablespoons well-drained capers
*¾ cup chopped fresh basil**
Fresh-ground pepper

* If fresh basil is not available, substitute about ⅓ cup minced fresh parsley.

Whisk together the ingredients for the vinaigrette.

Boil the potatoes until tender. While they are still warm, peel and slice them ¼ inch thick, and then toss them with the vinaigrette in a large, shallow bowl. Mix in the sliced onion.

Cook the beans in about an inch of salted water in a saucepan with a tight-fitting lid until tender but not soft. (Check after 7 minutes.) Drain in a colander, refresh under cold running water, and turn onto paper towels to absorb excess moisture. Toss with the potato mixture.

Preheat the broiler. Place the peppers on a baking sheet about 4 inches from the heat source and cook until the skin blackens, and turn to char all sides. Let peppers cool slightly, then peel under cold running water, and discard the stems and seeds. Cut into ½-inch strips and pat dry. Rinse the anchovies and dry on paper towels. Add the peppers, anchovies, olives, capers, and basil to the salad, and season to taste with pepper. Serve at room temperature.

YIELD: 4 SERVINGS

RATATOUILLE VINAIGRETTE

Ratatouille is commonly served as a hot vegetable dish, but it is very satisfying for a summer lunch or supper when chilled and tossed in a light vinaigrette. I recommend baking the eggplant and zucchini in the oven, rather than sautéing them as you would for a regular ratatouille, to avoid an excessive amount of oil being absorbed by the eggplant.

1½ pounds eggplant
Salt
1 pound zucchini
¾ pound sweet red peppers
2 tablespoons olive oil
½ pound yellow onions,
    peeled and sliced thin
    (2 cups)
2 garlic cloves, peeled and
    minced

1 pound ripe tomatoes,
    peeled, seeded, and
    chopped coarse
¾ cup pitted Calamata
    olives
3 tablespoons chopped fresh
    basil leaves or ½ tea-
    spoon dried
2 tablespoons capers
Fresh-ground pepper

FOR THE VINAIGRETTE

1 *tablespoon olive oil*   1 *tablespoon white wine*
3 *tablespoons lemon juice*   *vinegar*

FOR THE GARNISH

2 *tablespoons minced chives*

Trim the ends off the eggplant and slice crosswise into ¼-inch-thick rounds. Sprinkle heavily with salt, tossing to distribute it evenly. Place the slices in a colander with a heavy weight directly on top of them. Allow the eggplant to stand for 30 minutes or until it has been drained of its acrid juices. Slice, salt, and drain the zucchini in the same manner. Rinse the vegetables well to remove salt and pat dry.

Preheat the oven to 400°. Lightly oil a large baking sheet and place the eggplant slices on the sheet in a slightly overlapping layer. Bake for 20 to 30 minutes, turning over once during the cooking, or until tender. Cook the zucchini in the same way for approximately 15 minutes.

Core, seed, and slice the red peppers into ¼-inch-wide strips and sauté gently in the olive oil for about 10 minutes. Add the onions and garlic and continue cooking until the vegetables are tender, but do not let them brown. Add the tomatoes to the pan and cook, stirring occasionally, for 4 or 5 minutes.

Cut the eggplant slices into quarters and combine, in a large mixing bowl, with the zucchini, the sautéed vegetables, the olives, basil leaves, capers, and fresh-ground pepper to taste. Mix the ingredients for the vinaigrette and toss with the ratatouille. Turn into a glass serving bowl, sprinkle with the chives, and chill.

YIELD: 4 SERVINGS

SHRIMP IN ZUCCHINI BOATS

A refreshing shrimp salad, accented with mint and hearts of palm, is used to stuff marinated zucchini halves.

>   3 medium zucchini (½ to ¾ pound each and 6 to 7 inches
>   long)

FOR THE MARINADE

>   ¼ cup olive oil
>   2 tablespoons white wine
>   vinegar
>   1 small garlic clove, peeled
>   and crushed

>   ¼ teaspoon chervil
>   ¼ teaspoon tarragon
>   Salt
>   Fresh-ground pepper

FOR THE SHRIMP SALAD

>   ½ cup raw rice
>   ½ pound cooked medium-size
>   shrimp
>   6 hearts of palm, cut into
>   ¼-inch-thick slices

>   ⅓ cup chopped scallions
>   ¼ cup minced fresh parsley
>   2 tablespoons chopped fresh
>   mint leaves, packed

FOR THE SALAD DRESSING

>   2 egg yolks
>   ¾ cup olive oil
>   1½ tablespoons lemon juice
>   1½ teaspoons Düsseldorf or
>   Dijon mustard

>   3 tablespoons sour cream
>   Salt

FOR THE GARNISH

>   6 large lettuce leaves
>   Several sprigs of fresh mint or parsley

Cut the zucchini in half lengthwise. Place them, skin side down, in a large saucepan or skillet in about 1 inch of water. Partially cover and simmer gently for 10 to 15 minutes, or until cooked but still firm and slightly crisp. Take care not to overcook them; they should not be limp. While the zucchini are cooking, combine all the ingredients for the marinade. When the zucchini are done, drain them and scrape the seeds from the center, leaving a cavity for stuffing. Place them in a shallow pan and spoon the marinade over them and into the cavities. Let stand for several hours.

Cook the rice in a large pot of rapidly boiling water for 15 to 20 minutes, or until cooked through but slightly firm. Drain and rinse thoroughly under cool running water. Combine with the remaining ingredients for the salad.

For the salad dressing, make a mayonnaise by beating the egg yolks and adding the olive oil, drop by drop, until the mixture begins to thicken. Then, beating constantly, add the remaining oil in a thin stream. Stir in the lemon juice and mustard, fold in the sour cream, and add salt to taste.

Before serving, drain the zucchini boats. Mix the salad with the dressing and fill the cavities of the 6 zucchini halves. Serve on lettuce leaves and surround with sprigs of mint or parsley.

YIELD: 6 SERVINGS

SHRIMP SALAD BAHIA

¾ pound fresh shrimp, large
   or medium
1 tablespoon butter
1 tablespoon lemon juice
4 ounces feta cheese, preferably Bulgarian
One 7¾-ounce can hearts of
   palm
¾ cup diced cucumber
1 cup cherry tomatoes, cut in
   half

3 tablespoons minced fresh
   parsley
2½ tablespoons chopped scallions, with greens
⅓ cup chopped fresh mint
   leaves
Grated zest of 1 lemon
1 small bunch of watercress
Fresh-ground pepper

FOR THE VINAIGRETTE

¼ cup olive oil
1½ tablespoons lemon juice

1 garlic clove, peeled and cut
   in half

Combine the ingredients for the vinaigrette at least one hour before serving the salad.

Shell and devein the shrimp. Heat the butter in a skillet. Add the shrimp, sprinkle with the lemon juice, and cook, turning, just until the shrimp turn pink. Remove from the heat, drain if necessary, and reserve.

Cut the feta cheese into ¾-inch cubes, place in a strainer, and rinse well under cold running water. Dry with paper towels. Rinse and dry the hearts of palm and slice crosswise ¼ inch thick. Place the shrimp, cheese, hearts of palm, and the remaining ingredients in a salad bowl. Remove the garlic clove from the vinaigrette and toss the salad with the vinaigrette just before serving.

YIELD: 3 SERVINGS

SPINACH SALAD

There are many ways of preparing a spinach salad but this one, with avocado, mushrooms, bacon, and feta cheese, is my favorite. Serve it with Oatmeal Bread (page 250).

8 to 10 ounces fresh spinach, washed, stemmed, and dried
1 large ripe avocado
2 teaspoons lemon juice
½ pound firm white mushrooms, cleaned, trimmed, and sliced

8 slices bacon, fried, drained, and crumbled
Fresh-ground pepper
1 cup crumbled feta cheese (about ⅓ pound)

FOR THE DRESSING

1½ teaspoons Dijon mustard
⅓ cup herbed white wine vinegar

¾ cup olive oil
1 garlic clove, peeled and halved

Tear the spinach into manageable pieces and place in a salad bowl. Peel the avocado, cut in half lengthwise, and discard the pit. Slice into long strips and toss very gently with the lemon juice. Combine the avocado, mushrooms, bacon, and plenty of fresh-ground black pepper with the spinach. Sprinkle the feta cheese over the top.

To make the dressing, put the mustard in a small bowl and gradually add the vinegar, stirring to homogenize. Add the olive oil and garlic clove and let the garlic marinate for a while. Before serving, remove the garlic and toss the salad with the dressing.

YIELD: 4 SERVINGS

STEAK SALAD I

This salad is very quick and easy to put together and it makes an elegant summer meal. Serve it with Deviled Eggs (page 256).

1 1/2 pounds trimmed boneless top sirloin, 1 1/4 inches thick*

1 cup medium-size pitted black olives

8 scallions, chopped or 1/2 medium Bermuda onion, sliced thin

1 bunch of watercress, washed and dried

Salt

Fresh-ground pepper

* Leftover rare steak or roast beef may be substituted.

FOR THE DRESSING

1 large garlic clove

1/4 teaspoon sugar

1/4 teaspoon sea salt

2 teaspoons Dijon mustard

1 1/2 tablespoons minced fresh tarragon or 1/2 teaspoon dried

2 tablespoons red wine vinegar

1/2 cup olive oil

FOR THE GARNISH

1 lemon, quartered

1 large ripe tomato, cut into wedges

Several cornichons

Broil the steak close to the flame for 3 to 5 minutes on each side, or sauté quickly in a skillet. Watch it carefully to keep it quite rare. Slice into strips about 1/8 inch thick and 3 to 4 inches long. Stack the strips together and cover tightly with plastic wrap. Refrigerate until serving time.

To make the dressing, slice the garlic thin and crush it with the back of a spoon with the sugar and salt. Add the mustard, tarragon, and wine vinegar, stirring to dissolve the mustard. Add the olive oil and pour into a screw-top jar.

Just before serving, combine the steak in a mixing bowl with the olives, scallions, and watercress. Shake the jar of dressing and pour it over the salad. Toss, and season to taste with salt and fresh-ground black pepper. Serve on a platter and surround with lemon wedges, tomato wedges, and cornichons.

YIELD: 3 TO 4 SERVINGS

STEAK SALAD II

FOR THE VINAIGRETTE

¾ cup olive oil

3 tablespoons red wine
vinegar

1 small garlic clove, peeled
and pressed or grated

1 tablespoon Dijon mustard

FOR THE SALAD

3½ pounds sirloin steak
with bone in or 3
pounds boneless (1½
inches thick)

15 slices bacon

3 medium-large tomatoes
(1½ pounds), peeled,
cored, and sliced

½ cup thin-sliced red onion

3 tablespoons well-drained
capers

1½ cups chopped fresh basil

Salt

Fresh-ground pepper

Combine the ingredients for the vinaigrette and reserve.

Broil the steak for about 8 minutes on each side for rare meat. Let cool to room temperature and reserve.

Broil or fry the bacon until crisp, drain on paper towels, and crumble coarse. Slice the steak into thin strips and toss in a salad bowl with the vinaigrette to prevent the meat from darkening. Add the bacon, tomatoes, onion, capers, basil, and seasonings to the salad just before serving.

YIELD: 6 SERVINGS

SUMMERHOUSE SALAD

Serve this salad with Cuban Bread (page 245) and chilled white wine.

2 large whole chicken
   breasts, split
2 cups chicken broth or water
12 slices bacon, fried,
   drained, and crumbled
1/4 pound Roquefort cheese,
   crumbled

1/2 cup pitted black olives,
   cut in half
3 ounces fresh spinach, preferably small, tender
   leaves, washed and
   dried
3 scallions, chopped
Fresh-ground pepper

FOR THE MUSTARD-CREAM DRESSING

1 1/3 cups heavy cream
3 tablespoons Dijon mustard
1 1/2 tablespoons white wine
   vinegar

1 tablespoon cognac
1/4 teaspoon dried tarragon

FOR THE GARNISH

1 large ripe tomato, cut into
   wedges

8 Deviled Egg halves (page
   256)

Poach the chicken breasts in 2 cups of chicken broth or water, partially covered, for 20 minutes or just until cooked through. Do not overcook or the chicken will be dry. Remove from the broth and, when cool enough to handle, strip the skin and bones from the chicken. Cut the chicken meat into long, narrow strips, about ⅜ inch wide, following the grain of the meat. Cover tightly and refrigerate until serving.

Combine all the ingredients for the mustard-cream dressing, stirring with a whisk to dissolve the mustard, and refrigerate.

Before serving, combine the chicken, bacon, Roquefort cheese, olives, spinach, and scallions. Toss with the dressing and add fresh-ground pepper to taste. Serve on a platter and surround with tomato wedges and deviled eggs.

YIELD: 4 SERVINGS

TABOULI

This Middle Eastern salad makes a pleasantly tart and refreshing hot-weather lunch. It is composed of fresh raw vegetables, mint, and parsley with a light binding of bulgur in a lemony vinaigrette. I have included feta cheese in the recipe to contrast with the vegetables and make the salad more filling. While most of the salad can be prepared in advance, the tomatoes and cucumbers should not be added until just before serving, or they will drain and make the salad watery. Serve with sesame Toasted Syrian Bread (page 253).

1 cup cracked wheat
   (bulgur)
1 large sweet red pepper,
   seeded and chopped (²/₃
   cup)
1 sweet green bell pepper,
   seeded and chopped (¹/₃
   cup)
¹/₂ cup chopped scallions
¹/₃ cup coarse-chopped mint
   leaves

¹/₃ cup minced parsley
1 cup crumbled feta cheese
1 large cucumber
3 medium tomatoes
   (1 pound)
¹/₄ cup olive oil
¹/₄ cup lemon juice
1 tablespoon white wine
   vinegar
Salt
Fresh-ground pepper

Put the cracked wheat in a small bowl, cover with cold water, and
let soak for 20 minutes. Drain well, pressing out as much water a
possible, and dry on paper towels.

Put the wheat in a salad bowl with the chopped red and green
peppers, scallions, mint, parsley, and feta cheese. Cover and refrig
erate. Put the cucumber and tomatoes in the refrigerator as well

Before serving, peel, seed, and chop the cucumber, chop the
tomatoes, and add both to the salad. Add the olive oil, lemon juice
vinegar, salt to taste, and plenty of fresh-ground pepper and toss
well, using a fork to separate the grains of wheat.

YIELD: 3 OR 4 SERVINGS

TOMATOES WITH SHRIMP RÉMOULADE

The shrimp are marinated in a sweet-and-sour version of a rémou
lade sauce. You may vary the recipe by serving them on avocad
halves or lettuce leaves rather than in tomato cases.

FOR THE DRESSING

3 tablespoons lemon juice
2 tablespoons sugar
1 cup sour cream
½ cup mayonnaise

2½ tablespoons capers, well drained
1 small Bermuda onion, sliced thin

FOR THE SALAD

1½ pounds cooked medium shrimp

6 extra-large ripe tomatoes
Fresh-ground white pepper

FOR THE GARNISH

1 bunch of watercress or parsley

Combine the ingredients for the dressing, toss with the shrimp, and allow to marinate in the refrigerator for several hours or overnight.

Slice about ½ inch off the stem end of each tomato. Scoop out the seeds and pulp, invert, and drain on paper towels for about 15 minutes.

Just before serving, fill each tomato case with equal portions of the shrimp, season with pepper, and garnish with watercress or parsley.

YIELD: 6 SERVINGS

TOMATOES WITH TUNA

———————

This is not the usual tuna-with-mayonnaise salad. Serve it with cold asparagus or green beans and the herb-Parmesan Toasted Syrian Bread (page 253).

4 extra-large ripe tomatoes
Two 7-ounce cans solid
    white tuna, drained
24 pitted green olives,
    halved
6 tablespoons minced Ber-
    muda onion
1/4 cup minced sweet red pep-
    per
3 tablespoons capers

6 ounces crumbled feta cheese
    (1 generous cup)
2 to 3 tablespoons minced
    fresh herbs (such as
    basil, oregano, parsley,
    thyme, mint)
Fresh-ground pepper
1 recipe Basic Vinaigrette
    (page 49)

Cut 1/2 inch off the stem end of each tomato, scoop out the seeds and pulp, invert, and drain on paper towels for about 15 minutes.

Combine the remaining ingredients and fill each tomato with the salad, mounding it above the shell.

YIELD: 4 SERVINGS

WALNUT AND KIWI CHICKEN SALAD

———————

A light and cooling chicken salad tossed in a lime vinaigrette.

FOR THE SALAD

3 large chicken breasts, split
in half
6 kiwi
1 large avocado
⅓ cup chopped scallions with
tender green ends

3 cups chicken broth
1 large cucumber
¾ cup broken walnuts,
toasted*
1 bunch of watercress

FOR THE VINAIGRETTE

½ cup walnut or olive oil
2 tablespoons lime juice

2 tablespoons white wine
vinegar

Put the chicken breasts and the broth in a large skillet. Partially cover and bring to a simmer. Cook gently for 20 minutes, or just until the chicken is cooked through; do not overcook or it will be dry. Drain, and when cool enough to handle, strip off the skin and bones. Cut the meat into strips, about 2½ inches long and ½ inch wide, following the grain. Peel and seed the cucumber and slice lengthwise into strips about 2½ inches long and ¼ inch thick. Peel the kiwi and slice crosswise. Cut the avocado in half, peel it, remove the pit, and slice lengthwise. Wrap the avocado slices tightly in plastic wrap to prevent discoloring.

To serve, combine the chicken, cucumber, kiwi, avocado, scallions, walnuts, and watercress in a bowl. Mix the ingredients for the vinaigrette and toss with the salad just before serving.

YIELD: 6 TO 8 SERVINGS

* Spread in a baking pan and toast for 5 to 7 minutes in a 350° oven.

WHITE BEAN AND TUNA SALAD

This is an easy salad to put together for a casual summer lunch. For dried beans, use Great Northerns and boil according to package directions. Canned beans can be almost as good; use the large white kidney beans (cannellini) packed in water without any pork rind or flavoring.

4 cups cooked white beans or two 20-ounce cans large white kidney beans (cannellini)

Two 6½-ounce cans solid white tuna in water

⅓ cup minced fresh parsley

½ cup chopped fresh mint, packed

½ cup diced celery

½ cup diced sweet red pepper

⅓ cup minced mild white or red onion

Fresh-ground pepper

1 recipe Basic Vinaigrette (page 49)

If you are using canned beans, place them in a colander and rinse well under cold running water. Drain. In a salad bowl, mix the beans, tuna, parsley, mint, celery, red pepper, onion, and ground pepper to taste. After removing it from the vinaigrette, grate a little of the garlic clove into the vinaigrette, and toss the salad with the dressing.

YIELD: 4 SERVINGS

WHITE SALAD WITH PROSCIUTTO

A few years ago in a Venetian restaurant, I had a fine appetizer composed of thin-sliced Parmesan, mushrooms, and celery. This is a more substantial version, to be served as a lunch or supper entrée, enriched with fresh mozzarella and prosciutto. Do not use packaged mozzarella, which has a rubbery texture. If you cannot find fresh mozzarella, Armenian string cheese, soaked overnight in milk to cover, is a good substitute.

FOR THE VINAIGRETTE

½ cup olive oil
2 tablespoons lemon juice

*1 garlic clove, peeled and cut
    in half*

FOR THE SALAD

*6 ounces fresh, firm white
    mushrooms, sliced thin*
*1 ½ cups thin-sliced white
    celery*
*4 ounces imported Parmesan
    cheese (not grated)*

*6 ounces prosciutto, sliced
    very thin*
6 ounces fresh mozzarella
Fresh-ground pepper

FOR THE GARNISH

1 bunch of arugola or watercress

Combine the ingredients for the vinaigrette at least one hour before serving the salad.

Put the mushrooms and celery in a salad bowl. With a sharp carving knife, shave the Parmesan into wafer-thin slices. Cut the prosciutto and mozzarella into narrow strips, and add them to the salad bowl with the sliced Parmesan. Season with pepper. Just before serving, remove the garlic clove from the vinaigrette and toss the salad with the vinaigrette. Place a bed of arugola or watercress on each of 4 individual plates or on a serving platter and put the salad on top.

YIELD: 4 SERVINGS

3: Entrée Mousses

E N T R É E mousses are composed of puréed meat, fish, vege-tables, or cheese, with added liquid and flavorings. Uncooked mousses are held together by a gelatin or liquid aspic base; others are set with eggs and steamed in a water bath in the oven. While many mousses are served hot, those in this chapter are intended to be chilled and unmolded before serving. They are generally light in texture but substantial enough to serve as the main course for lunch or supper.

When preparing any recipe requiring gelatin, do not alter the proportion of liquid or puréed ingredients to the amount of gelatin specified. Although the general rule is that 1 envelope of gelatin will set about 2 cups of liquid, this ratio varies with the type of "liquid" being set. For example, sour cream, whipped cream, or puréed foods, which are already thick, require less gelatin. You may double or halve a recipe but the proportions must remain constant or you may end up with a mousse that either fails to set or bounces back at you with a self-willed spring and elasticity.

Premeasured envelopes of gelatin indicate that the amount con-tained in each packet has the gelling power of 1 tablespoon. The packet actually contains 2⅓ teaspoons, so if you are making half a recipe which calls for 1 envelope, take this into account—a half-packet would be 1⅙ teaspoons. A teaspoon or fraction thereof should be measured level with standard measuring spoons.

To dissolve gelatin: Gelatin must, of course, be dissolved before it can be used. There are many ways of doing this, but I find the following method most reliable. First fill a small metal cup (I use a stainless steel measuring cup) with the amount of cold water specified in the recipe. Sprinkle the gelatin granules over the water and stir to combine. Do not let it "stand 10 minutes to soften," as some recipes direct. It will dissolve more readily, with less chance of burning, if it is heated right away. Put the cup directly over very low heat and stir the liquid constantly to prevent burning. Never allow it to boil. After a few minutes, when the liquid looks clear, with no trace of granules, the gelatin will be melted. Remove it from the heat and stir to cool before adding it to the other ingredients. If hot gelatin is added to a cold mixture, or if the gelatin has stood too long and begun to set, it will not blend. The mousse will not set properly and will be riddled with rubbery little lumps. Ideally, all ingredients should be at room temperature before blending. If the gelatin *has* begun to set before you add it to the mousse, stir it over low heat or hot water until smooth and liquid. In some recipes, dissolved gelatin is combined with a large amount of liquid before folding into whipped cream or beaten egg whites. The gelatin mixture is then stirred over ice cubes or refrigerated until it becomes syrupy. It can then be combined with the whipped cream or beaten egg whites without separating and without deflating them, as would too much thin liquid.

Always fold whipped cream or beaten egg whites carefully into other ingredients with a flexible rubber or plastic spatula. Use broad strokes, scraping from the bottom of the bowl to the top. If you are working with large quantities, it is easiest to use a wide, flat-bottomed bowl.

To mold a mousse: Lightly oil the inside of the mold before filling, unless you are setting a clear aspic, which should not be clouded with a film of oil. In that case, rinse the mold thoroughly in cold water and leave it wet. As soon as the mold is filled, put it in the refrigerator to set. The length of time required to set a mousse or aspic will vary according to the ingredients in the recipe, the temperature of your refrigerator, the size of the mold, and the material it is made of. Few recipes, however, require more than 4 hours to set.

To unmold a mousse: Loosen the sides of the mousse by pulling away the sides of the mold or running a knife around the edges, taking care not to disturb any decorative pattern on the sides. Invert a chilled and slightly dampened platter over the mold and, holding both together, reverse so that the plate is right side up. Rap lightly on the counter, and the mousse should dislodge. If it is stubborn, find a bowl that is larger than your mold and fill it with hot tap water. Lower the bottom of the mold into it; don't go too deep or the water will push its way over the edge. Hold for a few seconds only (or the mousse will start to melt), and then repeat the procedure for unmolding onto the platter.

Two of the mousses in this chapter are coated with a layer of clear aspic. For full instructions on clarifying stock for an aspic, refer to the introduction to Chapter 4.

ARTICHOKE MOUSSE

A rich, creamy, and flavorful mousse. Serve it for lunch or supper with a green salad vinaigrette, Toasted Syrian Bread (page 253), and chilled dry white wine.

1 *pound canned artichoke hearts**

1 *cup milk*

6 *ounces mushrooms, cleaned, trimmed, and sliced*

4 *scallions, chopped*

1 ½ *tablespoons butter*

Salt

Fresh-ground white pepper

2 *tablespoons dry white wine*

1 *cup part-skim-milk ricotta cheese*

½ *cup sour cream*

2 *tablespoons minced parsley*

1 ½ *teaspoons fresh dill weed or* ½ *teaspoon dried*

2 *envelopes unflavored gelatin*

½ *cup cold water*

* If using frozen or fresh artichoke hearts rather than canned, add 1 ½ tablespoons lemon juice and reduce the water to ⅓ cup.

FOR THE GARNISH

1 *bunch of watercress*

Purée the artichoke hearts in a food processor or in batches in a blender, adding the milk in a thin stream.

Sauté the mushrooms and scallions in the butter for a few minutes. Turn up the heat, add the wine, and cook, stirring, until the moisture has evaporated. Remove from the heat, and stir into the artichoke purée. Add the ricotta, sour cream, parsley, dill, and salt and pepper to taste.

Soften the gelatin in the cold water. Place over low heat and stir until dissolved. Combine thoroughly with the mousse mixture. Lightly oil a 4- or 5-cup decorative mold. Spoon in the mousse and chill until set.

To serve, unmold onto a platter and garnish with the watercress.

YIELD: 6 SERVINGS

ASPARAGUS MOUSSE

A creamy mousse with a hollandaise flavoring. Serve it with a green salad.

1 1/4 pounds asparagus
3 ounces cream cheese
2 egg yolks, lightly beaten
1 tablespoon lemon juice
5 tablespoons unsalted butter, cut into several pieces
1 teaspoon minced fresh tarragon or 1/4 teaspoon dried
2 teaspoons white wine vinegar
Salt
Fresh-ground white pepper
1 1/2 teaspoons gelatin
3 tablespoons cold water
1/2 cup heavy cream

FOR THE GARNISH

1 bunch of parsley

Trim the tough ends and thorny scales off the asparagus, wash well, and steam or cook it in a little water until tender but not soft. Trim off the tips and reserve. Cut the stalks into 2-inch pieces and purée in a food processor with the cream cheese.

To make the hollandaise sauce, combine the egg yolks and lemon juice in the top of a double boiler and stir over simmering water until lukewarm. Add the butter, bit by bit, beating with a wire whisk until the sauce thickens. Do not let the water boil. Should the sauce separate, beat in a tablespoon of boiling water to re-emulsify. Fold the hollandaise into the asparagus purée with the reserved asparagus tips, the tarragon, wine vinegar, and salt and pepper to taste.

Soften the gelatin in the cold water and dissolve over low heat, tirring constantly. Stir the dissolved gelatin into the asparagus mixture, combining well. Whip the cream until it holds soft peaks and fold it into the mousse. Turn into a lightly oiled 3- or 4-cup mold and chill until firm.

To serve, unmold the mousse and garnish with the parsley.

YIELD: 4 SERVINGS

AVOCADO-SHRIMP MOUSSE

2 large ripe avocados
2 tablespoons lime juice
1/2 cup sour cream
3 tablespoons mayonnaise
1/2 teaspoon Worcestershire
   sauce
1 tablespoon fresh minced
   mint leaves, packed
1 medium-size ripe tomato,
   peeled, seeded, and
   chopped coarse

6 ounces cooked, shelled, and
   deveined shrimp, small
   to medium size
1/4 teaspoon salt or to taste
1 envelope plus 1/4 teaspoon
   unflavored gelatin
1/4 cup cold water

OR THE GARNISH

Watercress or parsley
1 large ripe tomato, cut into
   wedges

2 limes, cut into wedges

ut the avocados in half. Leave half of one in its shell, cover with lastic wrap, and reserve. Scoop the pulp from the remaining 3 alves and purée in a food processor or blender or mash well with a rk. You should have 1 1/2 cups purée. Blend in the lime juice, sour eam, mayonnaise, and Worcestershire sauce. Empty into a large mixing bowl and combine with the chopped mint leaves, chopped tomato, and shrimp. Add salt to taste. Peel the reserved half avocado, chop it coarse, and add to the mixture. Soften the gelatin in the cold water and dissolve over medium heat, stirring constantly. Combine it thoroughly with the avocado mixture. Turn into a lightly oiled 4- or 5-cup mold and chill until firm. Before serving, unmold and garnish with watercress or parsley, tomato, and lime wedges.

YIELD: 4 SERVINGS

CHICKEN MOUSSE

This is a light-textured mousse combining seedless green grapes, almonds, herbs, and strips of chicken. It is topped with a decorative layer of aspic. Serve with Biscuits or Scones (pages 241 and 252).

    2 whole chicken breasts, split
    3 cups chicken stock or broth

FOR THE ASPIC LAYER

    1 egg white, lightly beaten   *2 tablespoons cold water*
    Crushed shell of 1 egg   *6 thin slices of lime*
    Reserved stock   *Watercress leaves*
    1 1/4 teaspoons unflavored
      gelatin

FOR THE MOUSSE

Reserved chicken
Reserved stock
3 tablespoons dry white wine
1 envelope unflavored gelatin
¼ cup cold water
1 tablespoon minced fresh
　　parsley, packed
1 tablespoon fresh tarragon
　　or a scant ½ teaspoon
　　dried

½ cup seedless green grapes,
　　cut in half
⅓ cup sliced almonds
1 cup heavy cream, lightly
　　whipped
⅓ cup mayonnaise
Salt
Fresh-ground white pepper

FOR THE GARNISH

1 bunch of watercress

Poach the chicken breasts in the stock or broth, partially covered for 20 minutes or just until tender. Do not overcook. Remove the chicken to a platter and reserve. Pour the stock into a jar and chill it in the refrigerator until the fat rises to the surface and congeals. Skim off the fat and then boil the stock over high heat until it is reduced to 2 cups. Reserve ¾ cup for the mousse mixture.

TO MAKE THE ASPIC LAYER

Add the egg white and crushed shell to the stock remaining in the saucepan. Heat the mixture slowly, stirring, until it boils and the egg white rises to the top of the saucepan. Remove from the heat and strain through a sieve lined with a dampened cotton dish towel. You should have 1 cup clarified stock. Soften 1¼ teaspoons gelatin in 2 tablespoons cold water and dissolve it over medium heat, stirring constantly. Stir it into the clarified stock. Pour half the stock into a 6-cup ring or decorative mold. Refrigerate until set. Place the lime slices over the set aspic, press a few watercress leaves in between, and carefully pour the remaining clarified stock on top. Return the mold to the refrigerator and chill until the second layer of aspic is almost set, but slightly tacky.

TO MAKE THE MOUSSE MIXTURE

Strip the skin and bones from the chicken breasts. Cut a half-breast into julienne strips and reserve. Chop the remainder coarse, and purée in a food processor, or a little at a time in a blender. Add the reserved ¾ cup reduced chicken stock and the wine and blend. Soften the 1 envelope of gelatin in the ¼ cup cold water and dissolve over medium heat, stirring constantly. With the motor on, pour the dissolved gelatin into the mousse mixture in a thin stream. Turn the mousse into a large mixing bowl. Stir in the parsley, tarragon, grapes, almonds, and the reserved julienne chicken. Fold in the lightly whipped cream and the mayonnaise, combining everything thoroughly. Season to taste with salt and fresh-ground white pepper.

Remove the ring mold containing the set aspic from the refrigerator. Spoon the chicken mousse evenly over the aspic and refrigerate until firm. To serve, unmold and surround with sprigs of watercress.

YIELD: 6 SERVINGS

CRABMEAT MOUSSE

This makes an elegant supper or lunch, when served with asparagus vinaigrette and a dry white wine. The mousse itself is surrounded with tomatoes and watercress and accompanied by Avocado Sauce or Green Mayonnaise.

2 envelopes *unflavored gelatin*
½ *cup cold water*
¼ *cup dry white wine*
2½ *cups sour cream*
¾ *pound (2 cups) cooked crabmeat, fresh or frozen and defrosted*
¼ *cup chopped chives*
⅓ *cup fine-chopped cucumber*

¼ *cup lime or lemon juice*
i cup mayonnaise
¼ *cup watercress leaves*
Fresh-ground white pepper
i cup Avocado Sauce (page 258) or Green Mayonnaise (page 261)

FOR THE GARNISH

i bunch of watercress
2 *medium tomatoes, cut into wedges*

Soften the gelatin in the cold water and dissolve over low heat, stirring constantly. Whisk together the lime juice, mayonnaise, white wine, and sour cream and stir in the dissolved gelatin.

Flake the crabmeat and stir it into the mousse mixture with the chives, cucumber and watercress, and fresh-ground white pepper to taste. Turn into a lightly oiled 6-cup decorative mold and chill until firm.

To serve, unmold onto a platter and surround with the watercress and tomato wedges. Serve the Avocado Sauce or Green Mayonnaise on the side.

YIELD: 4 TO 6 SERVINGS

CUCUMBER-GRAPE ASPIC WITH CHICKEN SALAD

A translucent ring of sea-green aspic with green grapes piled in the center is served with chicken salad in a creamy, slightly piquant dressing.

i recipe Chicken Salad Othello (page 60)

FOR THE ASPIC

2 to 3 large cucumbers (or
    enough to make 2½
    cups purée)
¾ cup apple juice
2 tablespoons plus 2 tea-
    spoons lime juice
2 tablespoons light honey
1 envelope plus 1 teaspoon
    unflavored gelatin

¼ cup cold water
¾ cup halved seedless green
    grapes
2 tablespoons minced fresh
    mint leaves
Salt

FOR THE GARNISH

2 bunches of seedless green
    grapes

Several sprigs of fresh mint

Peel the cucumbers, cut off and discard the ends, and cut each in half lengthwise. With the tip of a spoon, scrape out the seeds, retaining as much pulp as possible. Chop the cucumbers coarse and, in a food processor or blender, purée enough to yield 2½ cups.

In a mixing bowl, combine the cucumber purée, apple juice, lime juice, and honey. Soften the gelatin in the cold water and dissolve over low heat, stirring constantly. Stir to cool slightly and add the gelatin to the cucumber mixture, combining thoroughly. Mix in the grapes and mint leaves and add salt to taste. Turn into a lightly oiled 4- or 5-cup ring mold and chill until firm.

To serve, unmold the aspic onto a platter. Fill the center of the ring with bunches of green grapes and arrange the mint around the outside of the mousse. Serve the Chicken Salad Othello in a separate bowl.

YIELD: 6 TO 8 SERVINGS

HAM MOUSSE

This very creamy mousse is delicately flavored with wine, herbs, and chives. It can be served with Mousseline Sauce (page 265) and Biscuits (page 241) or Cuban Bread (page 245).

3/4 pound lean ham, all fat and gristle removed
6 ounces cream cheese, at room temperature
1 cup sour cream
1 cup heavy cream
2 1/2 tablespoons minced fresh parsley
1 1/2 tablespoons minced fresh tarragon, or 1 1/2 teaspoons dried

1 1/2 teaspoons minced fresh thyme, or 1/4 teaspoon dried
2 tablespoons chopped fresh chives
1 small garlic clove, minced or crushed
1/4 cup dry white wine
Fresh-ground pepper
1 envelope unflavored gelatin
1/4 cup cold water

FOR THE GARNISH

1 bunch of watercress
2 medium ripe tomatoes, cut into wedges

If the ham is too salty, place it in a large pot of cold water, bring it to a boil, and drain. Grind the ham in a food processor and reserve.

Beat the cream cheese until it is light and fluffy. Fold in the sour cream, heavy cream, herbs, chives, garlic, and ground ham, combining thoroughly. Stir in the wine and season to taste with pepper. It is unlikely that any salt will be needed.

Soften the gelatin in the cold water and dissolve over medium heat, stirring constantly. Stir off the heat for a few minutes to cool slightly and then stir it into the mousse, combining well.

Pour the mousse into a lightly oiled 5-cup ring mold and chill until set. To serve, unmold, surround with watercress and tomato wedges and, if desired, serve with Mousseline Sauce on the side. YIELD: 6 SERVINGS

ROQUEFORT MOUSSE

A cooling and attractive dish for a summer luncheon, this mousse is molded in a ring and served surrounded by watercress with chopped ripe tomatoes piled into the center. It is important to use a good imported Roquefort (or imported Gorgonzola); a domestic "blue" cheese is likely to have a bitter flavor and to tint the mousse a peculiar blue-green.

5 ounces Roquefort cheese, softened
4 ounces cream cheese, softened
1½ cups sour cream
1½ cups small-curd creamed cottage cheese
1 cup light cream or half-and-half
¼ cup minced chives
½ cup watercress leaves
2 cups peeled, seeded, and chopped cucumber
2 envelopes unflavored gelatin
½ cup cold water

FOR THE GARNISH

2 bunches of watercress
3 large or 4 medium-size ripe tomatoes, peeled and chopped coarse
½ recipe Basic Vinaigrette (page 49)

Cream the Roquefort cheese with the cream cheese until smooth. Beat in all the remaining ingredients except the gelatin and water, combining thoroughly.

Soften the gelatin in the cold water. Heat gently, stirring, until dissolved. Cool slightly and add to the mousse mixture, stirring to mix well.

Oil a 6-cup ring mold and spoon in the mousse. Cover with plastic wrap and chill until set.

To serve, unmold the mousse onto a platter. Surround with the watercress. Mix the tomatoes with the Basic Vinaigrette and pile them in the center of the ring.

YIELD: 6 SERVINGS

SALMON MOUSSE

Chopped cucumber, tomato, green pepper, scallions, and capers are folded into this mousse, contributing different textures as well as flavors. It is served with a Sour Cream–Horseradish Sauce.

*1 pound cooked salmon,
    skinned and boned
    (fresh or canned)*
½ cup mayonnaise
1 cup sour cream
*4 teaspoons white horserad-
    ish, drained*
2 tablespoons lemon juice
2 tablespoons dry white wine
*1 medium-size ripe tomato,
    chopped and seeded (⅔
    cup)*
*½ cup peeled, diced cucumber
    (half of one medium-
    size)*

3 scallions, chopped
*1 small green bell pepper,
    seeded and chopped*
3 tablespoons capers, drained
*2 tablespoons minced fresh
    parsley, packed*
*1½ tablespoons fresh dill
    weed or ¼ teaspoon
    dried*
Salt
A few drops Tabasco sauce
1 envelope unflavored gelatin
¼ cup cold water

FOR THE GARNISH

*1 lemon, cut into 6 wedges
Parsley
Tomato wedges or cherry
    tomatoes*

*Double recipe Sour Cream–
    Horseradish Sauce
    (page 267).*

Purée the salmon in a food processor or blender. Add the mayonnaise, sour cream, horseradish, lemon juice, and white wine and
blend. Turn the mixture into a large bowl and stir in the chopped
vegetables, capers, and herbs. Season to taste with salt and Tabasco
sauce. Soften the gelatin in the cold water and dissolve over medium
heat, stirring constantly. Stir it into the mousse mixture, combining thoroughly. Turn into a lightly oiled 5-to-6-cup mold and chill
for several hours or overnight until set.

Before serving, unmold the mousse onto a platter and surround
with parsley, lemon wedges, and tomatoes. Serve the Sour Cream–
Horseradish Sauce separately.

YIELD: 6 SERVINGS

SMOKED SALMON MOUSSE IN LIME ASPIC

This makes a good appetizer, as well as an elegant luncheon dish. The aspic is not simply decorative: its texture and tart flavor are a foil for the richness of the mousse. Use a good-quality smoked salmon, which is not salty.

FOR THE MOUSSE

½ pound smoked Nova Scotia salmon

¾ cup plus 2 tablespoons Fish Stock (page 6)

2 teaspoons white wine vinegar

½ cup sour cream

2 teaspoons minced chives

Fresh-ground pepper

1 ¼ teaspoons unflavored gelatin

1 tablespoon lemon juice

1 tablespoon dry white wine

1 egg white

FOR THE ASPIC

2 cups Fish Stock (page 6)

⅓ cup fresh lime juice

2 egg whites, lightly beaten

Crushed shells of 2 eggs

2 teaspoons unflavored gelatin

3 tablespoons dry white wine

FOR THE GARNISH

Thin slices of lime

Long strips of chives

Chopped aspic

TO MAKE THE MOUSSE

Cut the salmon into small pieces and purée in a food processor or blender, adding ¾ cup of the fish stock in a thin stream. Add the vinegar and sour cream and blend. Turn into a mixing bowl and stir in the chives and pepper to taste.

Soften the gelatin in the 2 remaining tablespoons of fish stock, the lemon juice, and the white wine. Dissolve over low heat, stirring constantly, and blend thoroughly into the salmon purée. Beat the egg white until stiff and fold in.

TO MAKE THE LIME ASPIC

Combine the fish stock, lime juice, beaten egg whites, and crushed shells in a deep saucepan. Slowly bring the mixture to a boil while whisking back and forth. When it boils up, the egg whites will congeal on the surface. Remove from the heat and let stand for a few minutes. Wring out a clean cotton dish towel in cold water and secure it as a lining inside a sieve. Set the sieve over a deep bowl and pour the aspic mixture into it. Allow plenty of time for the liquid to drip through, and do not disturb the egg whites. After clarifying, you should have approximately 1½ cups of stock. Soften 2 teaspoons gelatin in 3 tablespoons white wine and dissolve over low heat, stirring constantly. Stir into the clarified stock.

Thoroughly rinse a 4-to-5-cup decorative mold, preferably a metal one, in cold water and leave it wet. Pour a thin layer of aspic into the bottom of the mold. Arrange the lime and chive garnish in the aspic and place in the refrigerator to set. Add another thin layer of aspic and refrigerate again. To coat the sides of the mold with aspic, stir the aspic over ice until it is very cold and syrupy. Then place the mold, on its side, over the ice and spoon in a little aspic. Hold until it sets and then rotate the mold, adding more aspic until all the sides are coated. Turn the mousse mixture into the aspic-lined mold, cover, and refrigerate until firm. Pour the remaining aspic into a small pan to make a shallow layer, refrigerate until set, and chop into dice.

To serve, unmold the mousse onto a serving platter and surround with the chopped aspic.

YIELD: 4 SERVINGS

SOLE AND TOMATO MOUSSE

This looks like a salmon mousse because the tomato purée gives it a pinkish tint. The sole, however, has a more delicate flavor and smoother texture than salmon. For a more elaborate meal, omit the Sour Cream–Horseradish Sauce and serve it with Shrimp Rémoulade (page 92).

1 carrot, scraped and cut up
1 celery stalk, cut up
¾ pound sole or flounder
   fillets
1 cup reserved fish stock
2 tablespoons parsley sprigs,
   packed
6 tablespoons tomato purée
⅔ cup mayonnaise
6 tablespoons sour cream
2 tablespoons dry white wine
5 teaspoons lemon juice or to
   taste

2 teaspoons prepared white
   horseradish, drained
1 envelope plus 1 teaspoon
   unflavored gelatin
¼ cup cold water
4 teaspoons red lumpfish
   caviar
Salt
1 recipe Sour Cream-
   Horseradish Sauce
   (page 267)

FOR THE GARNISH

1 lemon, cut into 6 wedges
2 large tomatoes, cut into
   wedges

1 bunch of watercress

Cook the carrot and celery in 1½ cups water, covered, for 10 minutes. Add the sole fillets and poach gently for 5 minutes or just until cooked. Drain, reserving 1 cup of the cooking liquid.

Mince the parsley in a food processor. Add the fish, and purée, pouring in the reserved fish stock in a steady stream. Blend in the tomato purée, mayonnaise, sour cream, wine, lemon juice, and horseradish.

Soften the gelatin in the cold water and dissolve over low heat, stirring constantly. Add to the fish purée, mixing thoroughly. Stir in the caviar, taste, and add salt if necessary. Turn into a lightly oiled 4-to-5-cup fish or ring mold and refrigerate until firm.

To serve, unmold and surround with the tomato and lemon wedges and the watercress. Serve the sauce separately.

YIELD: 4 TO 6 SERVINGS

TOMATO ASPIC

Made from fresh tomatoes, this aspic is very subtly flavored with orange juice and Madeira. It is set in a ring mold and the center can be filled with Chicken Salad (pages 57–63), Lobster Salad (page 70), or Shrimp Rémoulade (page 92). Or, serve it as a side dish with Sour Cream–Horseradish Sauce (page 267).

2 pounds fresh ripe tomatoes
1 tablespoon butter
1 large garlic clove, peeled
    and minced
1 bay leaf
6 peppercorns
2/3 cup tomato juice
1/4 cup tomato purée

2 envelopes unflavored gelatin
1/2 cup orange juice, prefera-
    bly fresh
2 tablespoons Madeira
Salt
Fresh-ground pepper
1/4 cup fine-chopped sweet
    green pepper

FOR THE GARNISH

1 bunch of watercress

Wash, core, and chop the tomatoes coarse. Sauté with the butter, garlic, bay leaf, and peppercorns for a few minutes. Add the tomato juice and tomato purée, cover the pan, and simmer for 25 to 30 minutes, stirring occasionally and crushing the tomatoes with a wooden spoon. Remove from the heat and strain through a food mill. You should have about 3⅔ cups liquid.

Soften the gelatin in the orange juice and dissolve over low heat, stirring constantly. Cool slightly and stir into the tomato mixture. Add the Madeira and seasoning to taste. Chill until slightly thickened and then stir in the chopped green pepper. Turn into a lightly oiled 5-cup ring mold and chill until firm.

To serve, unmold onto a serving platter and surround with the watercress. Fill the center of the ring with Chicken Salad, Lobster Salad, or Shrimp Rémoulade. Or, serve with Sour Cream–Horseradish Sauce as a side dish.

YIELD: 6 SERVINGS

4: Dishes in Aspic and Other Cold Entrées

WHILE this chapter contains some light entrées for picnics and patio suppers, such as the Tomato Tart, most are suitable for fancy dinners. (And all of them can, of course, be prepared ahead of time.) Entrées set under a crystalline aspic glaze are the most glamorous and appetizing. While they are not difficult to prepare, they do require a little extra time and attention. Directions for clarifying stock and setting in aspic are given with each recipe, but a fuller explanation may be helpful here.

To clarify stock: The stock should be cool or at room temperature and free of all grease. For every pint of liquid, add 1 lightly beaten egg white and the crushed shell of 1 egg. Use a large, heavy saucepan, set it over moderate heat, and constantly whisk back and forth until the mixture reaches a full boil. The egg whites will congeal and froth up at the surface. Immediately remove the pan from the heat and let it stand for 10 minutes. Meanwhile, wring out a clean, lightweight cotton dish towel in cold water and use it to line the inside of a large strainer or sieve. Do not use cheesecloth; even in several layers, it is too porous. Do not let the ends of the towel hang. Fasten them securely by wrapping around the handle and prongs of the sieve with a rubber band. Place the lined sieve over a deep bowl and pour in as much clarified stock as the sieve will hold without overflowing. Add the remaining stock after some has dripped through. This will take a long time, but you should not try to encourage it by stirring or disturbing the filter of egg whites. The stock that drips into the pan will be crystal clear. After all the stock has been clarified, you should measure it before adding the gelatin, since about ⅓ of the original quantity is lost in the clarification process. (Much of the flavor, as well, disappears in the discarded particles or sediment, and it is therefore necessary to use a particularly flavorful stock when making aspics.) Dissolve and add 1 envelope of gelatin for every pint of liquid. (Some recipes do not require additional gelatin, as the stock becomes sufficiently gelatinous from long cooking of the meat or fowl; others derive their gelatin from cooking knuckle bones or a calf's foot with the meat.)

The final step, after clarifying the stock and adding gelatin, is to cover the food with the aspic, either by coating or setting in a mold.

To coat with aspic: Pour a shallow layer of liquid aspic into the serving platter and refrigerate until set. Arrange the food and any garnish or decoration over the aspic layer. Place the rest of the liquid aspic over a large bowl filled with ice cubes and stir until it begins to thicken and feel syrupy. Then quickly spoon the aspic over the food, taking care to coat it thoroughly. Any leftover aspic should be melted and poured in a shallow layer into a pan and refrigerated. When it has set, it can be scored into small cubes and used as a decorative border around the edges of the serving platter.

The second method of setting in aspic is simpler: Rinse out a decorative mold in cold water and do not dry. (This facilitates unmolding; coating the mold with oil is not satisfactory as it leaves an oily film on the surface of the aspic.) Pour a thin layer of liquid aspic into the mold and set in any garnish, such as herbs, chives, and egg-white cutouts. Refrigerate until set. Arrange the food in the mold and pour in the remaining aspic to cover. If the food is to be molded in layers, it will be necessary to do this in several stages, setting each layer of food in aspic before adding another. Place the filled mold in the refrigerator until set and unmold when firm. (Note that some refrigerator shelves are not level, but tilt down toward the back. It may therefore be necessary to place a paperback book or tiles at the rear of the shelf under your platter or mold.) Directions for unmolding can be found in the introduction to Chapter 3.

Vegetables or side dishes served with the cold entrées in this chapter should be kept simple, and, with the exception of hot rolls or bread, should also be chilled or at room temperature. Sliced tomatoes with basil or watercress; asparagus, green beans, or whole artichokes vinaigrette; or a green salad are good choices. Menu suggestions can be found in the Appendix.

CHICKEN AND FENNEL PÂTÉ

This is a light pâté, suitable for a spring luncheon. Serve it with a green salad and Cuban Bread (page 245).

1 small whole chicken
    breast, split, skinned,
    and boned
1/3 cup dry white wine
1 tablespoon olive oil
2 medium whole chicken
    breasts, split, skinned,
    and boned (14 ounces
    meat)
2 eggs
12 ounces ground pork
    shoulder
4 ounces ground pork fat
1/2 cup heavy cream
1 1/3 cups fine-chopped fennel

1/4 cup minced green fennel
    ferns
1/4 cup chopped fresh parsley
1/3 cup pine nuts or
    blanched, slivered al-
    monds
2 tablespoons minced shallot
2 tablespoons minced fresh
    tarragon or 1 1/2 tea-
    spoons dried
1/2 teaspoon salt
Fresh-ground pepper
3/4 pound thin-sliced pork fat
    for larding

FOR THE GARNISH

> *1 recipe Mayonnaise Collée*   *1 bunch of watercress*
> *(page 262), optional*

Cut the meat from the small chicken breast lengthwise into ½-inch-wide strips and marinate in the white wine and olive oil for several hours. Drain and reserve the marinade.

With a large, sharp knife, mince the meat from the 2 larger chicken breasts into small dice or put it through a meat grinder. (Do not use a food processor, which would purée the meat.) Lightly beat the eggs in a large mixing bowl. Add the minced chicken, ground pork, ground pork fat, cream, fennel, fennel ferns, parsley, nuts, shallot, tarragon, salt, pepper, and the reserved marinade. Mix well. Sauté a spoonful and taste for seasoning.

Preheat the oven to 350°. Line a 1½-quart terrine or loaf pan with the pork fat, reserving some for the top. Spoon in ⅓ of the pâté mixture. Cover with half of the strips of chicken breast, laid lengthwise. Add another third of the pâté; cover with the remaining strips of chicken breast and spoon the rest of the pâté on top, packing it down firmly. Cover with the remaining pork fat, a double thickness of aluminum foil, and the terrine lid, if available. Set in a large pan half filled with hot water and bake for about 1 hour, 45 minutes, to 2 hours, or until the juices are a clear yellow and the pâté has shrunk slightly from the sides of the pan. Pour the water out of the large pan, place the terrine in it again, and weight the pâté by placing large, heavy cans or filled jars directly on top of the aluminum foil. Let stand until cool and unmold. If desired, slice approximately ½ inch thick, remove the surrounding fat, and spread one side of each slice with a coating of Mayonnaise Collée. Chill until the mayonnaise is set. Serve chilled or at room temperature, surrounded by sprigs of watercress.

YIELD: 8 OR MORE SERVINGS

CHICKEN BREASTS STUFFED WITH PÂTÉ IN TARRAGON-WINE ASPIC

This is a glamorous dish for special dinner parties. The chicken breasts are stuffed with a mild and creamy pâté and the whole covered with a flavorful aspic.

5 whole chicken breasts, split   *4 cups chicken stock or broth*

FOR THE PÂTÉ STUFFING

½ pound chicken livers
1 small yellow onion, peeled and quartered
1 cup chicken broth or water
6 tablespoons unsalted butter, softened

1 teaspoon cognac
1 teaspoon lemon juice
Salt
Fresh-ground pepper
¼ cup heavy cream, whipped

FOR THE ASPIC

Reserved chicken stock
Approximately 8 cups chicken broth
⅔ cup dry white wine
Juice and grated rind of 1 lime

1 teaspoon dried tarragon
3 or 4 tablespoons cognac
5 egg whites, slightly beaten
Crushed shells of 5 eggs
5 envelopes unflavored gelatin

FOR THE GARNISH

5 thin slices of lime with edges scalloped
5 thin slices of lemon with edges scalloped
10 capers

10 fresh sage or basil leaves
2 hard-boiled egg whites
3 or 4 black olives
Diced aspic
Several sprigs of fresh parsley

Poach the chicken breasts, partially covered, in 4 cups chicken stock or broth for 20 minutes, or just until done. Take care not to overcook them. Remove to a platter and, when cool enough to handle, strip off the skin and bones. Reserve the stock.

TO MAKE THE PÂTÉ STUFFING

Simmer the chicken livers with the onion in 1 cup chicken broth or water for 10 to 15 minutes, or until the livers are cooked but slightly pink in the center. Drain and allow to cool to room temperature. Purée the livers and onion in a food processor or blender, adding the butter a few tablespoons at a time. Turn into a bowl, stir in the cognac and lemon juice, and season to taste with salt and fresh-ground pepper. Fold in the whipped cream and refrigerate until firm.

TO MAKE THE ASPIC

Skim off any fat from the reserved stock used to cook the chicken breasts. Measure it and add enough chicken broth to make 12 cups. Add all the remaining aspic ingredients except the gelatin. Pour into a very large saucepan and heat slowly, stirring constantly, until the mixture boils and the egg whites froth up to the surface. Remove from the heat. Dampen a clean cotton dish towel and secure it around the inside surface of a large strainer or sieve. Slowly strain the stock through the lined sieve, allowing plenty of time for the liquid to drip through. Do not let the egg whites come in contact with the clarified stock. Remove 1 cup of the clarified stock to a clean saucepan and allow it to cool. Sprinkle with the gelatin and stir over medium heat until the gelatin is dissolved. Stir this into the rest of the clarified stock.

Pour approximately 2 cups of clarified stock into a shallow, flat-bottomed 9-by-13-inch pan for the diced aspic, refrigerate, and score into dice when set.

Select a large serving platter and pour ¼ inch of liquid aspic over the bottom. Refrigerate until set.

Slice each half chicken breast laterally in half, but leave one end intact, to form a pocket. Fill each pocket with 2 to 3 tablespoons of pâté, or as much as will fit without leaking out around the edges.

Arrange the stuffed chicken breasts over the set aspic on the serving platter. On top of each breast, place a lemon or lime slice with a caper in the center and a sage or basil leaf tucked under the edge of each slice. Cut 6 to 8 flower shapes out of slices of hard-boiled egg white and place a bit of black olive in the center of each. Set these on top of the bottom layer of aspic at the corners and sides of the platter. Stir the liquid aspic over a large bowl filled with ice cubes until it appears viscous and slightly thickened and is on the verge of setting. Quickly spoon the aspic over the chicken breasts and egg-white flowers, covering all exposed surfaces. Decorate the edges of the platter with the diced aspic and a few sprigs of parsley. Refrigerate until serving.

YIELD: 10 SERVINGS

CHICKEN CARCIOFI

It occurred to me that an interesting sauce could be made by substituting artichoke hearts for the tuna fish in a *tonnato* recipe. The artichoke, or *carciofi,* sauce is smoother, without the graininess of the tuna, and the flavor is delicate and distinctive. It has, too, the virtue of originality, since the *tonnato* version, although excellent, is well known. Both sauces are versatile and can be used for fish and vegetables as well as veal and chicken.

*4 large whole chicken
    breasts, split*

4 cups chicken stock or broth

FOR THE CARCIOFI SAUCE

2 egg yolks
2 teaspoons lemon juice or to
   taste
¾ cup olive oil
7 or 8 ounces canned artichoke hearts

3 anchovy fillets
⅓ cup reserved chicken stock
3 tablespoons capers
Fresh-ground white pepper

FOR THE GARNISH

1 bunch of parsley

2 lemons, cut into 8 wedges

Poach the chicken breasts gently, partially covered, in the stock until just done (about 20 minutes). Be careful not to overcook. Drain, reserving the stock, and when cool enough to handle, remove the skin and bones from the chicken. Lay each half breast flat on a cutting board and, holding the knife blade parallel to the board, cut each in half horizontally to make two thin pieces. Cover and reserve.

TO MAKE THE SAUCE

Blend the egg yolks and lemon juice in a food processor or blender. With the motor running, make a mayonnaise by adding the oil slowly, drop by drop, and as it thickens, in a thin stream. Drain the artichokes well, squeezing any excess moisture from each one. Add them to the mayonnaise with the anchovies and blend until smooth. Empty into a mixing bowl and thin with ⅓ cup reserved stock. Fold in the capers. Taste, add more lemon juice, if necessary, and season with pepper.

Spoon a little of the sauce over the bottom of a serving platter. Arrange the chicken pieces on top, slightly overlapping, and cover each piece of chicken with the sauce, spooning any additional sauce over the top. Cover completely with plastic wrap (it should be airtight) and refrigerate for at least 24 hours.

Remove the platter from the refrigerator about 30 minutes before serving to bring the chicken to room temperature, but leave it covered with plastic wrap until the last minute. Serve surrounded with parsley sprigs and lemon wedges.

YIELD: 8 SERVINGS

Vitello Carciofi

Cook 3½ to 4 pounds boneless veal as in the recipe for Sliced Veal with Funghi Trifolati in Aspic (page 155), reducing the cooking time to 1½ to 2 hours. Make the Carciofi Sauce above, substituting ⅓ cup degreased veal pan juices for the chicken stock. After the veal has cooled to room temperature, slice it thin and arrange on a platter with the carciofi sauce, as in the recipe for Chicken Carciofi (page 124).

YIELD: 8 SERVINGS

Chicken or Vitello Tonnato

Prepare 4 whole chicken breasts or 3½ to 4 pounds boneless veal as in the recipes above for Chicken Carciofi or Vitello Carciofi. Cover the sliced meat with the following Tonnato Sauce in place of the Carciofi Sauce.

FOR THE TONNATO SAUCE

2 egg yolks	2½ tablespoons lemon juice
¾ cup olive oil	¼ cup chicken or veal stock
3 anchovy fillets	3 tablespoons capers
One 7-ounce can white tuna fish in oil, drained	Fresh-ground white pepper

Put the egg yolks in the container of a food processor or blender and with the motor running add the oil drop by drop, as for a mayonnaise. As the sauce thickens, the oil can be added in a thin stream. Add the anchovies and tuna and blend until smooth. Add the lemon juice and stock and blend. Turn into a mixing bowl, fold in the capers, and season with fresh-ground pepper.

YIELD: 8 SERVINGS

CHICKEN IN LEEK AND GORGONZOLA ASPIC

For this unusual and cooling supper dish, poached chicken breasts are set on a bed of cucumbers and covered with an aspic of Gorgonzola Vichyssoise. Before you begin, find the right serving dish: it should be a fairly shallow bowl, approximately 10 inches in diameter—just large enough to hold the 6 chicken breast halves with 4 cups of aspic. Serve it with Biscuits (page 241) and a green salad vinaigrette.

3 small cucumbers
Salt
Fresh-ground white pepper
3 whole chicken breasts, split
4 cups chicken broth or water

2 envelopes unflavored gelatin
⅓ cup cold water
3⅔ cups Gorgonzola
Vichyssoise (page 44)

FOR THE GARNISH

6 reserved slices of cucumber
2 to 3 tablespoons minced parsley

Peel the cucumbers and cut them crosswise into paper-thin slices. Put them in a colander, sprinkle heavily with salt, and toss to distribute the salt evenly. Place a heavy weight on top of the cucumbers and allow them to drain for at least 30 minutes. Rinse, pat dry, and sprinkle with pepper.

Gently poach the chicken breasts in the broth or water, partially covered, for 15 to 20 minutes or until just cooked. Do not overcook. Remove from the hot broth and, when cool enough to handle, strip off the skin and bones.

To make the aspic, soften the gelatin in the cold water and dissolve over low heat, stirring constantly. Stir the dissolved gelatin into the Gorgonzola Vichyssoise.

Arrange 6 equal mounds of cucumber slices on the bottom of the serving dish, reserving 6 slices for garnish. Place half a chicken breast over each mound. Pour the Gorgonzola aspic over and around the chicken. It should just cover the chicken breasts. If it does not, place the serving dish over a pan of ice and spoon the aspic over the chicken until it is viscous enough to set. Garnish each piece of chicken with a cucumber slice and refrigerate until firm. Before serving, sprinkle with minced parsley.

YIELD: 6 SERVINGS

COLD BEEF FILLET WITH CAPER-MUSTARD SAUCE

Because it is served cold, the beef can be cooked a day ahead, but do not slice it until shortly before serving or it will lose its pink color.

One 4-pound beef tenderloin	*Ground allspice or ground*
Salt	*ginger*
Fresh-ground pepper	

FOR THE SAUCE

1 egg yolk	*4 tablespoons minced fresh*
1½ tablespoons Dijon	*parsley*
mustard	*3 tablespoons chopped capers*
1 cup fine, light olive oil	*½ cup sour cream (optional)*
4 teaspoons lemon juice	

FOR THE GARNISH

Watercress

TO COOK THE BEEF

Preheat the oven to 500°. Put the beef in a roasting pan and sprinkle with salt, pepper, and a little allspice or ginger. As soon as you put the meat in the oven, turn down the temperature to 225°. For rare meat, cook until a meat thermometer registers 145°. The cooking time will vary according to the thickness of the meat. A very thin tenderloin may take only 35 minutes, but the average size will require 1 to 1¼ hours cooking time. When the meat is done, let cool to room temperature, then cover with plastic wrap and refrigerate.

TO MAKE THE SAUCE

Combine the egg yolk and mustard in a small bowl. While beating continuously with a wire whisk, add the olive oil, at first drop by drop and then in a very thin stream as the mixture thickens, to make a mayonnaise. After the oil is absorbed, stir in the lemon juice, parsley, and capers, and sour cream, if desired. Cover and refrigerate until serving.

TO SERVE

Slice the meat ¼ inch thick and arrange pieces overlapping in a row in the middle of a platter. Spoon a thin strip of sauce down the center of the slices. Garnish the platter with a border of watercress and serve the rest of the sauce in a sauceboat.

YIELD: 8 TO 10 SERVINGS

COLD ROAST CHICKEN WITH LIME AND TARRAGON

This is an easy dish to prepare for guests, since the cooking is done ahead of time. The chicken meat is imbued with the flavors of lime and fresh tarragon, and so while it is a simple dish, it is not ordinary. It is best to roast the chickens whole so that they retain their juices. Do not refrigerate them after cooking (unless you have leftovers), as refrigeration spoils their flavor and texture. If they are intended for the evening meal, cook them in mid- to late afternoon and keep at room temperature until serving.

Two 3-pound chickens
½ cup lime juice
5 tablespoons chopped fresh
 tarragon

6 tablespoons (¾ stick) un-
 salted butter, softened
Salt
Fresh-ground pepper

FOR THE GARNISH

Fresh parsley sprigs

Early in the day, rinse the chickens, removing any loose fat, and dry with paper towels. Put them in an enameled roasting pan and pour the lime juice over the birds and inside their cavities. Marinate all day in the refrigerator, and turn them once or twice in the lime juice.

Late in the afternoon (3:00 to 5:00—this depends on serving time), pour off the marinade and reserve. Preheat the oven to 375°. Pat the chickens dry and return to the roasting pan. Combine the chopped tarragon with 4 tablespoons of the softened butter. Put about a teaspoon of the mixture into the cavity of each chicken. Insert the rest underneath the skin, spreading it with a blunt knife or your fingers to cover as large an area as possible. Truss the birds and rub with the remaining 2 tablespoons of butter. Sprinkle with salt and pepper and place each bird on its side. Roast for 30 minutes on one side and then 25 minutes on the other side, and baste with the reserved lime juice and the pan juices after the birds start to brown. Turn breast side up and roast 5 to 10 minutes longer to complete browning. The birds are done when the thigh juices run clear. Remove from the oven and let cool to room temperature, basting occasionally with the pan juices as they cool. Let stand at room temperature until ready to serve.

To serve, carve the chickens or cut them into quarters; remove the backbone. Place on a platter, garnished with sprigs of parsley. Skim the fat from the pan juices and serve the juices in a small pitcher, at room temperature or slightly warmed.

YIELD: 6 TO 8 SERVINGS

COUNTRY PIE

This is a good dish to put in a picnic basket with a wedge of Cheddar, wine or beer, and fruit and cookies. Inside the pastry casing are layers of eggplant, spinach, and onions, all with distinct but complementary flavors.

FOR THE PIE CRUST

3 cups flour
3/4 teaspoon salt
10 tablespoons cold unsalted
    butter, cut into small
    pieces

1/3 cup chilled vegetable
    shortening
Approximately 1/3 cup cold
    dry white wine or cold
    water

FOR THE EGGPLANT LAYER

1 small eggplant (3/4 to 1
    pound)

Salt

FOR THE SPINACH LAYER

Two 10-ounce packages fresh   *Salt*
    or frozen chopped   *Fresh-ground pepper*
    spinach
1 cup (4 ounces) grated
    Jarlsberg cheese

FOR THE ONION LAYER

2 pounds yellow onions,   *1 egg, lightly beaten*
    peeled and chopped   *5 slices bacon, fried until*
    coarse   *crisp and crumbled*
2 to 3 tablespoons vegetable
    oil
1 tablespoon flour

FOR THE GLAZE

1 egg white beaten with 1 tablespoon water

TO MAKE THE PIE CRUST

Mix the flour and salt in a large mixing bowl, preferably one with a flat bottom. With the tips of your fingers, rub the butter and shortening into the flour until the mixture resembles coarse meal. Add just enough cold wine or water to bind. Knead one or two turns, cover with waxed paper, and refrigerate until firm enough to roll out.

TO MAKE THE EGGPLANT LAYER

Wash the eggplant, slice it crosswise into ¼-inch-thick pieces, and put it in a colander. Sprinkle heavily with salt, and place a heavy weight directly on top of the eggplant. Leave it to drain for ½ hour or longer, then rinse well and dry. Preheat the oven to 400°. Lightly oil a baking sheet and place the eggplant slices on the sheet. Bake for 20 to 30 minutes or until tender, turning over once during cooking. Chop into 1-inch pieces.

TO MAKE THE SPINACH LAYER

Wash and stem the spinach, if you are using fresh, and chop coarse. Cook in the water clinging to the leaves in a large covered pot, or cook frozen spinach according to package directions. Drain in a colander, pressing out as much water as possible with a wooden spoon. Combine with the grated cheese and add salt and pepper to taste.

TO MAKE THE ONION LAYER

Sauté the chopped onions in the oil, sprinkle with the flour, stir to combine, and continue cooking until soft but not brown. Turn into a bowl and stir in the egg and bacon.

Preheat the oven to 375°. Roll out half the dough into a circle large enough to line a 9-inch pie dish. Fit the dough into the pan and brush the bottom with the egg-white glaze. Arrange the eggplant inside the shell; spread the spinach on top; and end with a layer of onions. Roll out the remaining dough for the top crust and place it over the pie, crimping the edges to seal. Decorate with leaves cut from scraps of dough. Cut slits in the top for air vents and brush with egg-white glaze. Bake on the lowest shelf of the oven for 45 to 55 minutes, or until lightly browned. Cool on a wire rack and serve the pie at room temperature.

YIELD: 6 TO 8 SERVINGS

FILLET OF BEEF IN ASPIC

This is a spectacular-looking dish: sliced rare beef tenderloin, garnished with lemon slices and surrounded by ripe red tomatoes, under a glistening aspic.

A 4-pound tenderloin of beef　　*Fresh-ground black pepper*
Salt　　*Ground allspice*

FOR THE ASPIC

2 quarts beef stock or broth　　*1 bay leaf*
½ cup dry white vermouth　　*Crushed shells of 4 eggs*
3 tablespoons lemon juice　　*4 egg whites, lightly beaten*
2 tablespoons lime juice　　*3 to 4 envelopes unflavored*
1 teaspoon dried tarragon　　　　*gelatin*

FOR THE GARNISH

2 very large ripe tomatoes,　　*5 capers*
　　sliced thin　　*Diced aspic*
Approximately 12 basil　　*Sprigs of parsley or water-*
　　leaves　　　　*cress*
1 lemon, sliced thin with
　　edges scalloped

TO COOK THE BEEF

Preheat the oven to 500°.

Season the beef by rubbing it with salt, pepper, and a little allspice. Turn the oven down to 225° and roast the beef for 1 hour to 1 hour 15 minutes, or until a meat thermometer registers 140°. The meat will be rare and evenly colored all the way through to the outside edges, rather than brown toward the edges and bloody in the middle. Let the meat stand until cool.

TO MAKE THE ASPIC

Place the beef stock in a large saucepan. Add to it any juices that accumulated in the pan the beef was roasted in. Add the vermouth, lemon juice, lime juice, tarragon and bay leaf, and the crushed egg-shells and egg whites. Heat the mixture slowly until it boils, stirring constantly. As soon as the egg whites froth up at the surface, remove from the heat. Dampen a clean cotton dish towel and secure it to cover the inside of a sieve or large strainer. Slowly strain the broth through the lined sieve into a deep bowl, allowing plenty of time for the liquid to drip through. Do not let the egg whites come in contact with the clarified strained broth. You should have approximately 6½ cups clarified stock.

Remove 1 cup of the clarified broth to a clean saucepan and allow it to cool completely. Soften 3 envelopes of gelatin in the cool stock (or approximately 1 envelope for every pint of liquid), and then stir it over medium heat until it dissolves. Stir this into the rest of the clarified stock.

Pour approximately 2 cups of clarified stock, to a depth of ¼ inch, in a shallow, flat-bottomed 9-by-13-inch pan for the diced aspic; refrigerate and score into dice when set.

Select a serving platter large enough to hold the sliced beef and tomatoes and pour a layer of aspic into it, to a depth of about ¼ inch; refrigerate to set. Slice the beef ⅛ to 3/16 inch thick. Arrange, overlapping, down the center of the platter over the set aspic. Place the sliced tomatoes in 2 overlapping rows on either side of the beef. Tuck a basil leaf between each slice of tomato. Place the lemon slices over the top of the row of sliced beef, with a caper in the center of each slice.

Stir the aspic over a large bowl filled with ice cubes until it appears soupy and is just about to set. Spoon it carefully over the beef and tomatoes, covering all exposed surfaces. Refrigerate.

Before serving, decorate the edges of the platter with diced aspic and a few sprigs of parsley or watercress.

YIELD: 10 SERVINGS

GINGERED SHRIMP WITH LIME AND COCONUT RICE

Shrimp marinated in a piquant, gingery sauce are served over a Middle Eastern–style rice salad. A cooling and exotic dish for sultry evenings.

FOR THE SHRIMP

*1½ pounds large unshelled
   shrimp
3 tablespoons peeled and
   grated fresh gingerroot
¼ cup chopped scallions*

*¾ teaspoon sugar
A large pinch of salt
3 tablespoons lime juice
¾ cup vegetable oil, heated*

FOR THE RICE

*¾ cup raw rice
Salt
1½ tablespoons butter
1 teaspoon yellow mustard
   seeds
⅔ cup raw cashews or
   blanched, slivered
   almonds
1 teaspoon ground coriander,
   preferably fresh-grated*

*½ teaspoon ground ginger
¼ cup currants
4 chopped scallions
3 tablespoons minced fresh
   parsley, packed
1 cup grated fresh coconut*
¼ cup lime juice
Grated rind of 1 lime
3 tablespoons olive oil*

* If using packaged, sweetened coconut, soak it in water to cover for 30 minutes or longer, drain well, and pat dry.

FOR THE GARNISH

   1 bunch of watercress

TO PREPARE THE SHRIMP

Peel, devein, and wash the shrimp. Bring a large pot of salted water to a boil, add the shrimp, and cook for 2 or 3 minutes, or until pink and firm. Drain well. In a large, wide-bottomed mixing bowl, combine the grated gingerroot, scallions, sugar, salt, lime juice, and hot vegetable oil and toss with the shrimp. Allow to marinate in the refrigerator for several hours, stirring occasionally.

TO MAKE THE RICE MIXTURE

Cook the rice in a large pot of boiling, salted water for 15 to 20 minutes, or until tender but firm. Empty into a colander, rinse with cold water, and drain well.

Heat the butter in a large skillet and add the mustard seeds. Cook, stirring occasionally, for about 5 minutes or until they begin to pop. Add the cashews or almonds and sauté gently until they begin to color but do not let them brown. Add the coriander, ginger, and cooked rice; remove from the heat and stir to combine. Turn into a mixing bowl.

Place the currants in a small saucepan with water to cover, bring to a boil, and simmer for a few minutes until softened. Drain and add to the rice mixture with the remaining ingredients, tossing to combine. Taste and season with a little salt, if necessary.

Serve the rice at room temperature with a portion of the shrimp and marinade over each serving. Garnish with watercress.

YIELD: 4 SERVINGS

HERB-ROASTED CHICKEN WITH RATATOUILLE

This simple cold roast chicken is imbued with the flavor of its marinade. It goes particularly well with cold ratatouille. Or, for a simpler accompaniment, Pasta Salad Primavera (page 78) is a good choice.

One 3-to-3 1/2-pound roasting chicken, cut up

FOR THE MARINADE

1/4 cup dry white wine

2 tablespoons olive oil

2 tablespoons lemon juice

*2 large garlic cloves, peeled
    and crushed*

1/2 teaspoon dried tarragon

1/2 teaspoon dried basil

1/2 teaspoon dried rosemary

2 tablespoons unsalted butter

Salt

Fresh-ground pepper

1 recipe Ratatouille Vinaigrette (page 82)

FOR THE GARNISH

1 bunch of parsley or watercress

Wash the chicken, remove any visible fat, and pat dry. Place the chicken pieces in a nonmetallic, shallow pan or bowl. Combine the ingredients for the marinade and pour over the chicken. Cover, refrigerate, and allow to marinate all day or overnight, turning the pieces occasionally.

Preheat the oven to 375°.

Drain the chicken, reserving the marinade, and dry thoroughly with paper towels. Put the chicken in a roasting pan, rub under and over the skin with softened butter, and sprinkle with salt and pepper. Roast for 50 minutes to 1 hour, basting occasionally with the pan juices, and with the reserved marinade after the chicken starts to brown. Remove from the oven and cool. Set the chicken pieces on a platter, cover, and refrigerate if you are not serving within a few hours.

Remove the chicken from the refrigerator at least 1 hour before serving to return to room temperature. To serve, arrange the chicken around the outside of a large platter and mound the Ratatouille Vinaigrette in the center. Garnish the edges of the platter with parsley or watercress.

YIELD: 4 SERVINGS

LAKE TROUT WITH HERB STUFFING

The pink-fleshed lake trout is similar in flavor and texture to brook or mountain trout, but it is larger. Its delicate flavor and color are enhanced by a simple stuffing of fresh green herbs.

One 2¼-to-2½-pound lake trout, cleaned, scaled, and boned, with head and tail intact
Salt
Fresh-ground pepper
Juice of 1 large lime
3 tablespoons minced fresh basil leaves
3 tablespoons minced fresh dill weed

3 tablespoons minced fresh parsley sprigs
2½ tablespoons minced fresh chives
2 tablespoons minced fresh tarragon leaves
½ cup dry white wine
1 tablespoon butter, softened
Sorrel Sauce (page 264) or Green Mayonnaise (page 261)

FOR THE GARNISH

1 large bunch of watercress   *1 lemon, cut into wedges*

Oil the bottom of a baking dish large enough to hold the trout. Wash and dry the fish and sprinkle inside and out with salt and pepper; rub the inside of the fish with half the lime juice and stuff it with the herbs. Tie with kitchen string at 2-inch intervals. Put the fish in the baking dish, pour on the remaining lime juice and the wine, and marinate for 1 to 1½ hours at room temperature.

Preheat the oven to 375°. Rub the top of the fish with the butter and bake it, basting occasionally, for 25 minutes or until it flakes easily with a fork.

Skin the fish and remove the string. Serve at room temperature on a platter, surrounded with the watercress and lemon wedges. Serve the Sorrel Sauce or Green Mayonnaise on the side.

YIELD: 4 SERVINGS

LEMON DUCK IN ASPIC

This dish looks quite elaborate, but it is not very difficult to make. Crisp-roasted duck is garnished with slivered lemon peel and green grapes and glazed under a shimmering topaz jelly. It is served with a lemony Mousseline Sauce.

1 lemon	*Duck giblets and necks*
Two 5-to-6-pound ducks,	*1 bay leaf*
quartered	*Several sprigs of parsley*
Salt	*1 small onion, peeled and*
Fresh-ground black pepper	*cut in half*

FOR THE ASPIC

Reserved duck stock and
  cooking juices
9 to 9½ cups chicken stock
  or broth
6 tablespoons lemon juice
½ cup dry white vermouth

⅔ cup orange juice
1 scant teaspoon thyme
5 egg whites, lightly beaten
Crushed shells of 5 eggs
5 envelopes unflavored gelatin

FOR THE GARNISH

Reserved strips of lemon peel
Several small bunches of
  seedless green grapes

Diced aspic
Mousseline Sauce (page 265)

TO PREPARE THE DUCK

Preheat the oven to 350°.

With a small paring knife, peel the yellow zest from around the circumference of the lemon in wide, circular strips. Cut the strips into slivers, as long and narrow as possible. Cover with plastic wrap and reserve for the garnish. Cut the lemon in half and rub it all over the skin and flesh of the duck quarters, squeezing out the juice as you do so. Season with salt and pepper and place on a rack in a roasting pan. Cook for approximately 2 hours or until the juices run clear, the skin has browned, and the layer of fat under the skin has melted. Pierce the skin with a fork as the duck cooks to help render the fat, and drain it into a large glass jar as it accumulates. As the fat cools, it will rise to the surface of the jar. Pour it off and reserve the cooking juices, which settle at the bottom of the jar, for the aspic.

While the duck is cooking, put the giblets and neck in a saucepan with 1 cup water, the bay leaf, parsley, and onion and simmer, uncovered, for about 1 hour. Drain off the stock, skim and discard the fat from the surface, and reserve for the aspic.

TO MAKE THE ASPIC

Measure the cooking juices and the duck stock; you should have about ¾ cup. Add enough chicken stock to make 10 cups. Stir in all the remaining aspic ingredients except the gelatin, and put the mixture in a very large saucepan. Heat it slowly, stirring constantly, until the mixture boils up and the egg whites froth up at the surface. Remove from the heat. Dampen a clean cotton dish towel and secure it around the inside surface of a large strainer or sieve. Allow the stock to drain slowly through the lined sieve into a deep bowl, and do not let the egg whites come in contact with the clarified stock.

Remove 1 cup of the clarified stock to a clean saucepan and allow it to cool. Sprinkle the gelatin over the cooled stock to soften it and then dissolve it over medium heat, stirring constantly. Stir this into the rest of the clarified stock.

Pour approximately 2 cups of aspic into a shallow 9-by-13-inch pan to a depth of ¼ inch and refrigerate. When set, score it into cubes for the diced aspic.

Pour a shallow layer of liquid aspic over the bottom of a large serving platter and refrigerate until set. Arrange the duck quarters on the platter with the slivered lemon zest scattered over them. Tuck a few of the small bunches of grapes here and there among the duck. Stir the aspic over a large bowl filled with ice cubes until it appears thick and viscous and is on the verge of setting. Spoon the aspic quickly over all the exposed surfaces of the duck and the grapes. Refrigerate until set.

Before serving, decorate the edges of the platter with diced aspic and additional bunches of grapes. Serve the Mousseline Sauce on the side.

YIELD: 8 SERVINGS

MOLLY'S COLD CURRIED CHICKEN

This is a simple mixture of white-meat chicken and a little sweet red pepper, dressed in a superb creamy tomato-curry sauce. The sauce, a finely balanced medley of flavors, has just enough curry to give it distinction without sharpness. The recipe comes from a good friend and good cook, Molly Stern.

2 large whole chicken
 breasts, split
2 cups chicken broth or water

1 medium-size sweet red
 pepper

FOR THE TOMATO-CURRY SAUCE

2 tablespoons minced onion
1 large garlic clove, peeled
 and crushed
2 tablespoons olive oil
2 teaspoons curry powder
1 teaspoon tomato paste
1/2 cup tomato juice

2 teaspoons lime or lemon
 juice
1 tablespoon sieved apricot
 jam
1/2 cup mayonnaise
1/2 cup sour cream

FOR THE GARNISH

Lettuce leaves

Minced parsley

Poach the chicken, partially covered, in simmering broth for 20 minutes, or just until cooked. Be careful not to overcook, or the chicken will be dry. Drain and, when cool enough to handle, strip off the skin and bones and cut the chicken into julienne strips, about inches long and 1/2 inch wide, following the grain of the meat.

Seed and core the pepper and cut it into matchstick slivers. Place the pepper and chicken breast in a mixing bowl and reserve.

TO MAKE THE TOMATO-CURRY SAUCE

Sauté the onion and garlic in the olive oil until slightly softened but do not brown. Add the curry powder and cook briefly. Stir in the tomato paste, tomato juice, lime or lemon juice, and apricot jam and cook at a low simmer for 10 minutes. Cool to room temperature and combine with the mayonnaise and sour cream. Mix the sauce with the chicken and pepper just before serving.

Serve on a bed of lettuce leaves and sprinkle with minced parsley.

YIELD: 4 SERVINGS

PICNIC PÂTÉ

Unlike most country pâtés, this one does not include liver. The effect is a less dense mixture, more suitable for hot-weather dining. Prosciutto, sautéed mushrooms, and pistachio nuts add flavor and texture. It is easy to make, and excellent picnic fare.

6 ounces mushrooms

2 tablespoons unsalted butter

2 eggs

3/4 pound ground veal
    shoulder

1/2 pound ground pork
    shoulder

2 ounces ground pork fat

1/4 pound sliced prosciutto,
    cut into 1/2-inch squares

1/3 cup pistachio nuts

1/4 cup minced fresh parsley

3 tablespoons minced shallot

2 teaspoons fresh thyme or 1/4
    teaspoon dried leaf
    thyme

1 garlic clove, peeled and
    minced

1/4 teaspoon salt

Fresh-ground pepper

1/2 cup heavy cream

3 tablespoons brandy

3/4 pound thin-sliced pork fat
    for larding

Wash, dry, trim, and chop the mushrooms. Sauté gently in the butter until the moisture evaporates. Remove from the heat and reserve.

Beat the eggs lightly in a large mixing bowl. Stir in the mushrooms and all the remaining ingredients, except the larding fat, and combine well. Sauté a spoonful of the mixture and taste for seasoning. Add more salt, if necessary.

Preheat the oven to 375°. Line a 1½-quart terrine or loaf pan with the pork fat, reserving some for the top. Pack in the pâté and cover with the remaining fat. Cover the terrine tightly with a double thickness of aluminum foil and a lid, if available. Place it inside a large pan half filled with hot water and bake for approximately 2 hours 15 minutes, or until the juices are a clear yellow and a meat thermometer registers 170°. Pour the water out of the large pan, place the terrine inside it, and weight the pâté by placing large, heavy cans or filled jars directly on top of the aluminum foil. Let stand until cool. Unmold and serve chilled or at room temperature.

YIELD: 8 SERVINGS

POACHED SALMON IN ASPIC

This is a beautiful and elegant entrée. The salmon has a simple stuffing of sliced cucumbers and dill and is accompanied by a home-made Green Mayonnaise, Cucumber Sauce, or Sorrel Sauce. Serve it with asparagus vinaigrette or a salad of Bibb lettuce, arugola or watercress, and Belgian endive.

1 whole 4½-to-5-pound salmon

FOR THE COURT BOUILLON

6 cups water
5 cups fish stock or bottled clam juice
4 cups dry white wine
2 carrots, scraped and sliced thin

3 medium onions, peeled and sliced thin
2 celery stalks, sliced thin
1 large bay leaf
2 teaspoons salt
Several bruised peppercorns

FOR THE STUFFING

1 medium cucumber, peeled and sliced thin
Salt

Fresh-ground pepper
Several sprigs of fresh dill or about 1 teaspoon dried

FOR THE ASPIC

Approximately 12 cups reserved poaching liquid
6 egg whites, lightly beaten (or 1 white for every pint of stock)

Crushed shells of 6 eggs
Dry vermouth to taste
Salt
4 to 5 envelopes unflavored gelatin

FOR THE GARNISH

1 lemon, sliced thin, with   *2 hard-boiled eggs, sliced*
    the edges scalloped   *into rounds*
Capers   *3 or 4 pitted black olives,*
Chives   *sliced crosswise*
2 cornichons, sliced crosswise   *Chopped aspic*

1 recipe Green Mayonnaise (page 261), Cucumber Sauce
    (page 266), or Sorrel Sauce (page 264)

Have the salmon cleaned and scaled and the head and backbone removed at the fish store. If you do not have a fish poacher or covered kettle large enough to hold the fish, have the tail section cut off and freeze it for another use. Or buy a 4-to-4½-pound center cut of salmon.

TO COOK THE SALMON

Place the ingredients for the court bouillon in the fish poacher or kettle in which you will cook the salmon, bring to a boil, and simmer gently, covered, for about ½ hour.

Meanwhile, rinse and dry the salmon. Fill the cavity with the sliced cucumber and sprinkle with salt and pepper. Scatter the dill weed over and under the cucumbers. Tie the fish with string at 2-inch intervals and wrap it in cheesecloth. Place the salmon on an oiled rack to fit inside the fish poacher or kettle and lower it into the simmering court bouillon. Adjust the heat to keep the liquid at a low simmer. Cover the kettle and cook gently for 7 minutes to the pound. Do not let the stock boil. If the court bouillon does not cover the fish, turn the salmon over halfway through cooking. The fish is done when it flakes easily at the center. Remove from the broth to cool. Take off the cheesecloth and string and skin the fish. Strain and reserve the poaching liquid.

TO MAKE THE ASPIC

Combine the reserved poaching liquid, the beaten egg whites, and the crushed shells in a large, heavy saucepan. Slowly bring to a boil while whisking constantly back and forth. When the liquid boils up and the egg whites froth at the surface, remove from the heat and let stand for 10 minutes. Wring out a cotton dish towel in cold water and secure it as a lining for a sieve or large strainer. Set this over a large, deep bowl and pour in as much stock as the strainer will hold. As it drips through, pour in the remaining stock. Do not disturb the egg white crust and allow plenty of time for all the liquid to drain through. Discard the egg whites and measure the clarified stock. You should have about 8 to 9 cups. Taste and flavor with salt, if necessary, and a little dry vermouth. Use 1 envelope of gelatin for every pint (2 cups) of liquid. Cool 1½ cups of the clarified stock and soften the gelatin in it. Dissolve over low heat, stirring constantly. Stir the dissolved gelatin into the rest of the stock.

Pour a thin layer of liquid aspic into the bottom of a serving platter large enough to hold the fish. Refrigerate until firm. Lay the fish on top of the layer of aspic. Place a row of lemon slices down the center of the fish with a caper in the middle of each slice. Arrange a few long strips of chives on either side of the lemons. Add 2 rows of cornichon slices along the outside edges of the fish. Arrange the egg slices, topped with pieces of black olive, on the bed of aspic surrounding the fish.

Set the remaining liquid aspic over a bowl filled with ice cubes and stir until it becomes syrupy. Carefully spoon the aspic over the fish and the decorations, coating everything completely. Refrigerate. Any remaining aspic should now be quite thick since it has been standing over ice cubes. Reheat it until it liquefies and pour in a shallow layer into a large pan. Refrigerate to set. When firm, score into ½-inch cubes and use the chopped aspic to make a decorative border around the edges of the fish platter.

Serve with Green Mayonnaise, Cucumber Sauce, or Sorrel Sauce on the side.

YIELD: 8 SERVINGS

Variation

Instead of the cucumber stuffing, the cavity of the salmon can be filled with several sprigs of fresh tarragon. Serve with Green Mayonnaise, adding 1 tablespoon minced fresh tarragon to the recipe on page 261.

RUSSIAN CHICKEN IN ASPIC

This dish consists of bite-size pieces of chicken and ground walnuts with just enough spicy aspic to bind the mixture together. It is a most unusual, cooling, and satisfying dish, and it has a long history. Our friends Marion and Harry Fulbright first had it in Poland and were so admiring that their hostess gave them the recipe and a bottle of the Russian spice mixture used to flavor the aspic. The list of ingredients, clearly printed on the label in Russian, was, for a long time, a matter for our serious speculation. We knew it had hot red pepper and something sour; the rest was mysterious. But it tasted good, whatever it was. Joseph Brodsky finally came to our rescue with a translation, which he confirmed with a phone call to London. The following are the authoritative ingredients for a genuine Russian jellied chicken.

One 3-to-3½-pound chicken,
    quartered
6 cups water, or enough to
    cover
2 medium carrots, scraped
    and sliced
2 medium celery stalks,
    sliced
Several celery leaves
2 medium yellow onions,
    peeled and sliced
Several sprigs of parsley
6 to 8 peppercorns

1 teaspoon salt
1¼ cups walnuts, ground
¾ teaspoon ground coriander
¼ teaspoon (scant) ground
    red pepper
1 garlic clove, peeled and
    pressed
A pinch of dill weed
1 teaspoon white wine vine-
    gar
⅛ teaspoon monosodium glu-
    tamate (optional)
½ teaspoon salt or to taste

Wash the chicken pieces and put them in a large, heavy kettle with
the neck and giblets. Add the water, carrots, celery stalks and
leaves, the onions, parsley, peppercorns, and 1 teaspoon salt. Bring
to a boil and simmer, partially covered, for 15 minutes, or just until
the chicken is done. Remove the chicken from the stock and, when
it is cool enough to handle, strip off the skin and bones. Cut the
meat into bite-size pieces, cover, and reserve. Return the skin,
bones, and any scraps of meat to the stock and boil it down to 3 cups
liquid. (This will take between 1 and 2 hours.) Strain, cool, and
degrease the stock. If it has jelled, heat it until liquid. Remove from
the heat and stir in the ground walnuts and all the remaining
ingredients. Add the chicken, cover, and refrigerate until syrupy.
Stir and refrigerate until firm. If desired, serve with Sour Cream-
Horseradish Sauce (page 267).

YIELD: 4 SERVINGS

SALMON FILLETS

Salmon fillets are a fine lunch or dinner entrée, requiring little preparation. They can be served with any one (or two) of a number of interesting sauces, as described below. When shopping for salmon, try to get Norwegian or Scottish, which are superior in flavor and texture to Alaskan king salmon.

> *Olive oil*
> *2 tablespoons minced shallot*
> *2½–3 pounds salmon fillets*
> *¼ cup dry white wine or*
>   *lemon juice*
>
> *1 tablespoon minced fresh*
>   *herbs, such as dill,*
>   *tarragon, or basil*
> *Fresh-ground pepper*
> *Sauce (see below)*

FOR THE GARNISH

> *Sprigs of fresh dill, parsley, tarragon, or watercress*

Preheat the oven to 375°. Oil the bottom of a large baking pan and sprinkle with half the minced shallot. Put in the fish in one layer, skin side down, and rub a little oil into the flesh of each fillet. Sprinkle with the wine or lemon juice, the remaining shallot, and the herbs and seasoning. Cover the pan tightly with aluminum foil, and bake for about 20 minutes, or just until cooked through. Remove from the oven and skin the fillets.

To accompany the salmon, prepare one of the following sauces found on pages 259 to 267: Green Mayonnaise, Herb and Caper Mayonnaise, Lime and Mint Mayonnaise, Provençal Sauce, Sorrel Sauce, Piquant Sauce, a double quantity of Cucumber Sauce, or Salsa Verde. Serve the salmon at room temperature, garnished with fresh herbs.

YIELD: 6 TO 8 SERVINGS

SHRIMP IN PARSLEYED ASPIC

Shrimp, avocado, and cucumber suspended in a flavorful fish aspic offer an appealing variety of textures and colors.

1 *pound unshelled shrimp*	1 *tablespoon lemon juice*

FOR THE ASPIC

4 1/2 *cups fish stock or bottled clam juice*
1/3 *cup lime juice*
1/2 *cup dry white wine*
3 *egg whites*
Crushed shells of 3 eggs
2 *envelopes plus 1/2 teaspoon unflavored gelatin*
1 *large sweet red pepper*

1 *large avocado*
3/4 *cup sliced cucumber*
1/4 *cup minced fresh parsley*
2 *teaspoons minced fresh dill or 1/4 teaspoon dried*
Salt
Sour Cream–Horseradish Sauce (page 267)

Shell and devein the shrimp. Heat a large pot of salted water to boiling, add the shrimp, and cook for 2 to 3 minutes or just until they are pink and firm. Drain and toss with the lemon juice.

TO MAKE THE ASPIC

Combine the fish stock, lime juice, and wine in a large, heavy saucepan. Lightly beat the egg whites and add them to the stock with the crushed shells. Heat to boiling, whisking back and forth continuously. When the whites froth up to the surface, remove immediately from the heat and let stand 10 minutes. Wring out a cotton dish towel and secure it as lining inside a large sieve. Set the sieve over a deep bowl, pour in the stock, and do not disturb until it has dripped completely through. You should have a little less than 4 cups of clarified stock. Soften the gelatin in 1/2 cup of this stock and dissolve over low heat, stirring constantly. Mix the dissolved gelatin into the rest of the clarified stock. Pour about ½ cup into a small bowl and refrigerate until it is syrupy.

Core and seed the red pepper and slice it crosswise into several rings. Coat the pepper rings with the thickened aspic and press them against the sides of a 6-to-8-cup glass bowl. Refrigerate until they are set.

Peel and halve the avocado and slice it lengthwise. Combine the shrimp, avocado, cucumber, parsley, and dill and place them in the glass bowl, being careful not to dislodge the pepper rings. Season the liquid aspic with a little salt, if necessary, and pour it into the bowl. Cover with plastic wrap and refrigerate until firm. Serve from the bowl, with the Sour Cream–Horseradish Sauce on the side.

YIELD: 4 TO 6 SERVINGS

SLICED STEAK WITH BASIL SAUCE

This dish is composed of alternating slices of rare steak, roasted red pepper, a mild goat cheese, and tomato, the whole moistened with vinaigrette and flavored with a thick basil sauce. It is a good choice for a dinner party, as it looks and tastes terrific and is easy to make.

FOR THE STEAK COMPOSITION

1¾–2 pounds lean sirloin,
    cut 1½ inches thick
    and trimmed of fat*
Salt
1 tablespoon olive oil
    (optional)

3 medium-size sweet red
    peppers
8–10 ounces of Montrachet
    goat cheese
3 medium-size, ripe farm
    tomatoes

* You may substitute a two-pound section of beef tenderloin. Cook according to the method on page 129. A meat thermometer should register 140°. Start checking after 40 minutes.

FOR THE BASIL SAUCE

> 2 cups fresh basil leaves,   2 small anchovies, rinsed
>   lightly packed   and patted dry
> 1 small garlic clove, peeled   ½ tablespoon lemon juice
> An 8-inch section of a   ⅔ cup light olive oil, or
>   French baguette, 2–2½   half olive and half
>   inches in diameter   vegetable oil

FOR THE VINAIGRETTE

> 2 teaspoons Dijon mustard   ⅓ cup olive oil
> 1½ tablespoons lemon juice   1 tablespoon capers

FOR THE GARNISH

> Watercress   Niçoise olives

Dry the steak with paper towels, lightly salt it, and cook over medium-high heat in a large skillet with a tablespoon of olive oil for 4 to 5 minutes on each side, or until browned but rare. Or brown under a broiler or on a charcoal grill. Remove from the heat and cool to room temperature.

Place the peppers in a pan in the broiler, 4 inches below the heat source, and cook, turning, until blackened on all sides. Peel under cold running water, core, seed, and cut into 1½-inch-wide strips.

TO MAKE THE BASIL SAUCE

Mince the basil and garlic in a food processor. Trim the crusts off the bread, tear it into bite-size pieces, and add it to the processor bowl, along with the anchovies and lemon juice. With the motor running, add the olive oil in a thin stream. The sauce should be about as thick as mayonnaise. Place it in a small container and refrigerate until needed.

TO MAKE THE VINAIGRETTE

Whisk together the mustard and lemon juice and gradually add the olive oil. Stir in the capers.

Shortly before serving, slice the steak ⅛ inch thick. Slice the goat cheese and tomatoes about ¼ inch thick. Alternate overlapping slices of steak, red pepper, goat cheese, and tomato on 6 dinner plates, allowing 3 or 4 slices of each per serving. Spoon the vinaigrette evenly over the steak arrangement on each plate. Then spoon an inch-wide strip of basil sauce down the center of each row of slices. Garnish the plates with watercress and Niçoise olives.

YIELD: 6 SERVINGS

SLICED VEAL WITH FUNGHI TRIFOLATI IN ASPIC

Mushrooms sautéed in a classic style are sandwiched between thin slices of veal under an aspic flavored with white wine and lemon juice. If you like, serve with Salsa Verde (page 267) or Provençal Sauce (page 263) on the side.

FOR THE MARINADE

1 cup dry white wine
2 tablespoons olive oil
Several sprigs of fresh parsley
1 garlic clove, peeled and crushed

1 bay leaf
6 black peppercorns, cracked
8 juniper berries, crushed
½ teaspoon thyme
Peel from ½ lemon

FOR THE ROAST VEAL

One 4½–5-pound leg of veal, boned and tied

½ pound pork fat, sliced

FOR THE FUNGHI TRIFOLATI

2 1/4 pounds firm white
    mushrooms
5 tablespoons unsalted butter
5 anchovy fillets
10 scallions, chopped
2 garlic cloves, peeled and
    crushed

1/3 cup minced fresh parsley,
    packed
1/2 cup dry white wine
3 tablespoons lemon juice
Fresh-ground pepper

FOR THE ASPIC

Approximately 1/2 cup veal
    pan juices
8 cups chicken stock or broth
1 cup dry white wine
1/3 cup lemon juice

1/4 cup dry white vermouth
1 teaspoon thyme
6 egg whites, lightly beaten
Crushed shells of 6 eggs
4 envelopes unflavored gelatin

FOR THE GARNISH

5 thin slices of lemon with
    edges scalloped
5 capers

Diced aspic
Several sprigs of fresh parsley

TO COOK THE VEAL

Combine the ingredients for the marinade. Place the veal in an enameled or glass pan and pour the marinade over it. Let stand for several hours at room temperature or overnight in the refrigerator. Turn the veal every now and then to coat with the marinade.

Preheat the oven to 325°. Remove the veal from the marinade, dry it, and cover the top with slices of pork fat. Place the veal in a heavy casserole or roasting pan, pour the marinade into the pan, and cover tightly. Cook for approximately 2 hours, depending on the thickness of the veal, basting frequently with the pan juices. It is done when a meat thermometer registers 170° to 175° and the juices are a clear yellow. The meat should be a whitish color and not pink.

Remove to a platter and let the veal stand until it cools to room temperature.

TO MAKE THE FUNGHI TRIFOLATI

While the veal is cooking, clean the mushrooms by wiping with a damp towel or rinsing briefly under cold water. Trim the ends and slice. Melt the butter in a very large skillet; add the anchovy fillets and mash them with the back of a spoon to dissolve. Add the mushrooms, scallions, garlic, and parsley to the pan and cook gently for a few minutes. Sprinkle with the wine and lemon juice, turn up the heat, and cook until the liquid evaporates, stirring to prevent scorching. Remove from the heat and season to taste with fresh-ground black pepper.

TO MAKE THE ASPIC

Scrape off the surface layer of fat that has congealed over the veal pan juices. Empty the pan juices into a large saucepan and add the chicken stock, white wine, lemon juice, vermouth, thyme, egg whites, and crushed shells. Cook over medium heat, stirring constantly, until the mixture boils and the egg whites froth up at the surface. Remove from the heat immediately. Dampen a clean cotton dish towel and secure it as a lining for a sieve or large strainer. Set the sieve over a large bowl. Slowly pour the stock into the lined sieve, allowing plenty of time for the liquid to drip through into the bowl. You should have approximately 8½ cups clarified stock.

Remove 1 cup of the clarified stock to a clean saucepan and allow it to cool to room temperature. Sprinkle the gelatin over the surface and then stir over medium heat until dissolved. Stir this into the rest of the clarified stock.

Pour approximately 2 cups of the liquid aspic, to a depth of ¼ inch, into a shallow, flat-bottomed 9-by-13-inch pan and refrigerate to set. When firm, score into dice.

Pour a shallow layer of aspic onto a serving platter and refrigerate until set. Slice the veal about ⅛ inch thick. Pour about ½ cup of liquid aspic into a small bowl or saucer and dip one side of each slice of veal in it. Spread a layer of mushrooms on the moistened side of each slice, and set the slices, overlapping closely, on the serving platter over the set aspic. Arrange a row of lemon slices, with a caper in the center of each, over the top of the veal. Anchor the capers with toothpicks to hold them in place while coating with aspic.

Stir the liquid aspic over a large bowl filled with ice cubes until it appears thick and is about to set. Quickly spoon the aspic over the veal, covering all exposed surfaces. Refrigerate.

Before serving, decorate the platter with diced aspic and a few sprigs of parsley.

YIELD: 12 SERVINGS

SOLE IN FENNEL ASPIC

Fillets of sole wrapped around sautéed shrimp and herbs are set in a splendid aspic made from Cream of Fennel Soup.

24 large raw shrimp in the shell (approximately 1 pound)
Butter
6 tablespoons dry white wine
Salt
Fresh-ground pepper

12 small fillets of sole or flounder or 6 large, wide fillets cut in half lengthwise
2 tablespoons chopped fresh fennel ferns
3 tablespoons chopped fresh chives

FOR THE ASPIC

3 envelopes unflavored gelatin
¾ cup cold water

6 cups Cream of Fennel Soup (page 14), at room temperature

FOR THE GARNISH

Fennel ferns   *Chives*

Peel and devein the shrimp. Melt 1 tablespoon of butter in a large skillet. Add the shrimp, sprinkling them with 2 tablespoons of the wine and salt and pepper. Sauté until the shrimp turn pink and reserve with the pan juices.

Preheat the oven to 350°. Generously butter a 9-inch-square baking dish. Sprinkle one side of each fish fillet with equal amounts of the fennel ferns and chives and a little salt. Place 2 shrimp, slightly overlapping, in the center of each fillet and roll up tightly, securing with a toothpick. Place the rolled fillets in the buttered baking dish and dot each one with a small piece of butter. Pour the juices reserved from cooking the shrimp over the fish. Bake for 20 minutes or until just done, basting with the remaining 4 tablespoons white wine. Cool on a wire rack and drain.

Soften the gelatin in the cold water and dissolve over low heat, stirring constantly. Cool slightly, then stir into the Cream of Fennel Soup. Lightly oil a 2-quart decorative mold or shallow bowl. Place 12 small sprays of fennel and the chives, evenly spaced, around the bottom of the mold to indicate where the fish fillets will be placed. Spoon in a thin layer of the liquid aspic and refrigerate until set. Place a fish fillet on top of each spray of garnish. (The garnish will be a guide to judging portions because the aspic is opaque.) Pour the remaining aspic over the fish and refrigerate until firmly set. Serve unmolded on a platter.

YIELD: 6 SERVINGS

STEAK TARTARE CASANOVA

On a recent trip to Italy, I had a splendid lunch in the Casanova Grill at the Palace Hotel in Milan—steak tartare, arugola salad, fresh raspberries, and a delicious Antinori wine. The waiter prepared the steak tartare at the table, and it was the best version of that dish I've had. A close reproduction of his recipe follows.

2 egg yolks
1 tablespoon Düsseldorf or
    Dijon mustard
1 tablespoon lemon juice
1 teaspoon Worcestershire
    sauce
1/3 cup olive oil
1 1/2 pounds fresh-ground
    lean top round, flank,
    or sirloin steak

1 1/2 tablespoons fine-minced
    fresh parsley
1 1/2 tablespoons chopped
    capers
1 1/2 tablespoons fine-minced
    onion
2 small anchovy fillets,
    minced fine
Salt
Fresh-ground pepper

FOR THE GARNISH

Fresh parsley sprigs

Lemon wedges

In a small bowl, whisk together the egg yolks, mustard, lemon juice, and Worcestershire sauce. Add the olive oil, whisking to blend. (Do not make a mayonnaise; just combine the ingredients.)

Put the ground beef into a large bowl, pour the sauce over it, add the remaining ingredients, and combine well. (This is most easily done with a large 2-pronged fork from a carving set.) Cover tightly with plastic wrap and refrigerate until serving.

Garnish each portion with parsley sprigs and a lemon wedge and serve toasted, thin-sliced French bread on the side.

YIELD: 4 SERVINGS

SUMMER PORK WITH APPLE, MINT, AND GINGER CONSERVE

A boned loin of pork is marinated and cooked with lime juice, wine, fresh mint leaves, and grated gingerroot. It is served in thin slices with a conserve of apple, mint, and fresh ginger. The pork is kept moist by cooking it in a plastic cooking bag.

A 5½–6-pound boned pork loin, rolled and tied
⅓ cup lime juice
⅔ cup peeled and grated fresh gingerroot
½ cup chopped scallions
1 cup chopped mint leaves
½ cup dry white wine
Salt
One 14-by-20-inch plastic "brown-in-bag" cooking bag

FOR THE CONSERVE

3 cups chunky applesauce
1 tablespoon grated fresh gingerroot
¼ cup chopped mint leaves, loosely packed
5 teaspoons lime juice

FOR THE GARNISH

A large bunch of fresh mint
Cherry tomatoes

Untie the loin of pork and place the two halves side by side, fat side down, in a large bowl. Rub the lime juice all over the cut surfaces and spread the uppermost surface of each half with the gingerroot, scallions, and mint leaves. Pour the wine over the pork and refrigerate overnight. The next day, reassemble the two halves, sandwiching all the ginger, scallions, and mint leaves between them, and retie securely with kitchen string. Sprinkle all over with salt.

Preheat the oven to 325°. Proceed according to the directions on the cooking bag package: put 1 tablespoon flour in the bag and shake to coat the inside. Place the bag in a large, shallow roasting pan, put the pork inside, pour in the marinade, and tie securely. With the point of a knife, make 6 half-inch slits along the top of the bag to allow steam to escape. Place in the center of the oven, allowing plenty of room around the sides so that as the bag inflates, it will not touch the oven walls. Cook for approximately 30 minutes to the pound, or 2½ to 3 hours. The pork is done when a meat thermometer registers 170°. Remove from the oven and slash the bag open along the top so that the meat does not continue cooking. Baste occasionally with the pan juices as the pork cools.

Combine the ingredients for the conserve. Serve the pork at room temperature, sliced thin and surrounded with sprigs of mint and cherry tomatoes. Pass the conserve separately.

YIELD: 10 SERVINGS

TERRINE OF SOLE AND CRABMEAT

An elegant dish for a summer luncheon. The terrine is served with cucumbers vinaigrette and Green Mayonnaise or Sorrel Sauce. Don't forget the chilled white wine.

6 ounces cooked crabmeat, fresh or frozen, thawed and
drained

FOR THE MARINADE

3 tablespoons dry white wine   *1½ tablespoons lemon juice*

FOR THE PÂTÉ

4 tablespoons unsalted butter
¼ cup flour
¼ cup reserved marinade
⅔ cup fish stock or bottled
    clam juice
1 pound sole fillets
4 eggs
1 tablespoon fresh parsley
    sprigs, packed
1½ cups light cream
2 tablespoons dry white wine

1 tablespoon lemon juice
¼ teaspoon salt
Fresh-ground white pepper
1 tablespoon minced fresh
    chives
Several sprigs of fresh dill
    weed
1 recipe Green Mayonnaise
    (page 261) or Sorrel
    Sauce (page 264)

FOR THE CUCUMBERS VINAIGRETTE

3 large cucumbers, peeled
    and sliced very thin
Salt

½ recipe Basic Vinaigrette
    (page 49)

FOR THE GARNISH

1 bunch of watercress

Marinate the crabmeat in the white wine and lemon juice for several hours. Drain, reserving the marinade, which should equal approximately ¼ cup.

TO MAKE A FISH VELOUTÉ

Melt the butter in a saucepan and stir in the flour. Gradually add the reserved marinade and the fish stock. Whisk over medium heat until the mixture comes to a boil and thickens. Remove from the heat and reserve.

TO MAKE THE PÂTÉ

Cut the fish fillets into large pieces and place in the bowl of a food processor with the eggs and parsley. Purée and, with the motor running, add the fish velouté, the light cream, white wine, lemon juice, and salt. Add fresh-ground pepper to taste and stir in the minced chives.

Preheat the oven to 350°.

Generously butter a 5-to-6-cup terrine or an 8½-by-4½-inch loaf pan. Spoon in half the fish purée. Add a layer of crabmeat, placing some fresh sprigs of dill weed above and beneath the crabmeat layer. Add the remaining fish purée and cover with a buttered double thickness of aluminum foil and the terrine lid, if available.

Place inside a large pan half filled with boiling water and bake for 1 hour 15 minutes. Remove from the water bath and cool in the terrine on a wire rack. Unmold and chill.

TO PREPARE THE CUCUMBERS

Place them in a colander, sprinkle generously with salt, and toss to distribute the salt evenly. Place a heavy weight inside the colander directly on top of the cucumbers and let stand for 1 hour. Rinse well and pat dry. Marinate in the vinaigrette dressing.

TO SERVE

Place the fish pâté on a platter surrounded by watercress. Pass the Green Mayonnaise or Sorrel Sauce in a sauceboat and serve the cucumbers as a side dish.

YIELD: 6 SERVINGS

TOMATO TART

An attractive, summery tart of ripe tomatoes studded with black olives and sprinkled with chives and basil in a cheese-flavored crust. It should be served at room temperature and is good patio or picnic fare.

FOR THE PIE CRUST

3 ounces (¾ cup) grated
extra-sharp Cheddar
cheese

1 ⅓ cups flour

3 tablespoons cold unsalted
butter, cut into small
pieces

2 tablespoons cold vegetable
shortening

3 to 4 tablespoons cold dry
white wine or cold wa-
ter

FOR THE FILLING

⅓ cup fine-crushed plain
cracker crumbs (Brem-
ner wafers or Uneeda
biscuits)

2 ounces (½ cup) grated
Jarlsberg cheese

1 ounce (¼ cup) grated
extra-sharp Cheddar
cheese

4 medium tomatoes (1 ¼
pounds), each cored and
cut into 8 wedges

Olive oil

8 anchovy fillets, rinsed well
and dried

8 pitted black olives, preferably Calamata

¼ cup chopped chives

2 tablespoons chopped fresh
basil or ¾ teaspoon
dried

Fresh-ground black pepper

TO MAKE THE PIE CRUST

Stir together the cheese and flour in a mixing bowl. With the tips of
your fingers, rub in the butter and shortening until the mixture resembles coarse meal. Add just enough cold wine or water to form a
dough. Wrap in waxed paper and refrigerate until firm enough to roll
out.

Preheat the oven to 375°. Roll the dough into a circle and fit it
into a 9-inch tart pan. Cover the unbaked pie shell with a sheet of
lightly buttered aluminum foil and fill with uncooked rice or dried

beans. Bake for 15 minutes. Remove the foil and rice or beans and bake for an additional 5 minutes. Set on a wire rack to cool.

TO MAKE THE FILLING

Lightly combine the cracker crumbs with the grated Jarlsberg and Cheddar. Scatter this mixture evenly over the bottom of the baked pie shell. Return to the oven and bake for 7 or 8 minutes at 375°. Lay the tomato wedges, slightly overlapping, in two concentric circles over the cheese mixture. Brush them very lightly with olive oil, but do not salt. Lay the anchovies on top in a radial design and place the olives between the anchovy fillets. Scatter the chives and basil over the top and add pepper to taste. Return to the oven for 15 to 20 minutes, or until the tomatoes are softened but not shriveled. Cool on a wire rack and serve at room temperature.

YIELD: 4 TO 6 SERVINGS

VEAL ROULADE WITH PROSCIUTTO AND SALSA VERDE

A large, flat piece of veal is rolled up with a layer of prosciutto and green parsley sauce inside. It is served sliced and at room temperature, with extra green sauce on the side.

FOR THE MARINADE

1 cup dry white wine
2 tablespoons olive oil
Several sprigs of parsley
1 garlic clove, peeled and crushed

1 bay leaf
6 black peppercorns, cracked
6 juniper berries, crushed
1/4 teaspoon thyme

FOR THE VEAL

> *4½ pounds veal, cut from the leg and butterflied to measure approximately 10 by 15 inches*
> *1 cup Salsa Verde (page 267), made with 4 slices of bread*

> *8 ounces very thin-sliced prosciutto*
> *8 ounces pork fat or beef suet, sliced thin*
> *⅓ cup dry white wine for basting*
> *1 cup Salsa Verde (page 267)*

FOR THE GARNISH

> *1 bunch of parsley*

Combine the ingredients for the marinade in a large nonmetallic pan or bowl. Marinate the veal in the refrigerator for several hours or overnight, turning it occasionally.

Meanwhile, make 1 cup of thickened Salsa Verde, using 4 slices of bread rather than 2. Refrigerate the sauce while the veal is marinating so that it will be firm enough to use as a filling.

After the veal has marinated, preheat the oven to 325°. Drain the meat, reserving the marinade; lay it on a flat surface, cut side up, and flatten it slightly. Cover with an even layer of prosciutto; then spread the thickened Salsa Verde evenly over the prosciutto. Roll the veal up from the long side and tie securely with string every 2 or 3 inches. Place it in a roasting pan with the reserved marinade and cover the veal with the larding fat. Roast, basting frequently with the pan juices and white wine, for approximately 2 hours, or until a meat thermometer registers 170°–175°. Remove to a platter and allow to cool thoroughly. Let the pan juices cool and scrape off the fat after it has hardened on the surface. Strain and reserve the pan juices.

When cool, cut the veal into thin slices and arrange, overlapping, in 2 rows on a platter. If the pan juices have jelled, heat to liquefy and cool until slightly thickened but not set. Spoon a little juice over each slice of veal. Decorate the platter with fresh parsley and cover tightly with plastic wrap. If you refrigerate it, return to room temperature before serving. Make another cup of Salsa Verde (using 2 slices of bread rather than 4) and serve it in a sauceboat with the veal.

YIELD: 12 SERVINGS

WAPPINGHAM PIE

This recipe, which goes back several generations in the family of George H. Ford, has generously been given for publication by his wife, Pat. It is composed of veal, pork, and aspic, covered with pastry, and baked in a deep pie dish. It is elegant in its simplicity and once you try it, it is likely to become a summer tradition in your own family. It needs little more to accompany it than a good white wine and a green salad. The cooking and preparation should be done the day before serving to allow enough time for the aspic to set.

2 ½ pounds boneless veal from the shank*
1 shank and knuckle bone, cut up
1 pound lean pork, cut into stew-size pieces
4 cups water
1 medium onion, peeled and quartered

1 celery stalk with leaves, chopped coarse
A few sprigs of parsley
1 bay leaf
½ teaspoon thyme
1 teaspoon salt
4 peppercorns

* Ask the butcher to cut the meat from 2 shanks of veal and, if necessary, add enough stewing veal to total 2 ½ pounds.

FOR THE PIE CRUST

2½ cups flour
½ teaspoon salt
10 tablespoons cold unsalted
 butter, cut into small
 pieces

4 tablespoons cold vegetable
 shortening
5 to 8 tablespoons cold water

FOR THE GARNISH

Watercress or other greens
Tomato wedges

Hard-boiled eggs, quartered

Put the veal, bones, pork, and water in a 4-quart stew pot with the meat and bones immersed, and bring to a boil. Skim off as much scum as possible, and then add the vegetables, herbs, and seasoning. Simmer, partially covered, for 1½ to 2 hours, or until the meat is tender. (There should be an opening of about 1 inch to allow the steam to escape.) Put the meat on a platter to cool. Strain the stock, discarding the vegetables, and cool to room temperature. You should have at least 2 cups of stock. Refrigerate until the fat hardens on the surface and can be removed easily and the strength of the jelly ascertained. (The stock should jell without any need for powdered gelatin.)

Meanwhile, prepare the pie crust. Combine the flour and salt in a large mixing bowl and, with the tips of your fingers, rub in the butter and shortening until the mixture resembles coarse meal. Add enough water to form the mixture into a dough. Knead 1 or 2 turns, wrap in waxed paper, and refrigerate until firm enough to roll out.

Trim all the fat and tendon from the pork and veal and cut the meats into small cubes. Roll out one-quarter of the pastry dough on a lightly floured board and cut out a circle to fit the bottom of a 6-cup soufflé dish. Roll out another quarter of the dough to make a circle of equal size for the top crust. Roll out the remaining dough into a long strip about 1 inch wider than the height of the soufflé dish. Use one circle and the strip to line the bottom and sides of the soufflé dish, pinching the seams to seal. Loosely fill the pie with the cubes of meat. Cover with the second circle of dough for the top crust. Fold over and crimp the edges of the side crust, but do not overlap the edge of the dish or it will be difficult to unmold. Cut a dime-sized circle in the top crust and decorate with leaves or flowers cut from pastry scraps.

Preheat the oven to 375°. Bake the pie for 1 hour, or until the crust is lightly browned. Remove from the oven and let stand for 15 minutes. Heat the reserved jelly in a saucepan until it is liquid. Set a funnel in the hole in the top crust and pour in as much of the liquid aspic as the pie will hold. Add the remaining aspic in about an hour, after some of the liquid has been absorbed. Cool to room temperature and then chill for at least 5 or 6 hours to make certain that the aspic is well set.

To serve, set the baking dish in hot water for a few seconds to facilitate unmolding. If necessary, loosen the sides with a knife. Unmold onto a platter and garnish with the greens, tomato wedges, and eggs.

YIELD: 8 SERVINGS

5: Desserts

TH E desserts included in this chapter are those that seem most appropriate for summer dining, beginning with a number of simple and elegant ways of preparing fresh fruits. At a time of year when there is an abundant variety of fruits and berries, most of them from local gardens, orchards, and roadsides, it almost seems a pity to serve anything else for dessert. Nothing can surpass the flavor and visual appeal of fruit desserts, which are colorful, light and refreshing, and naturally sweet.

For richer desserts, there are chilled mousses, Bavarians, and soufflés. These desserts are all light in texture, incorporating a great deal of air into their composition through beaten egg whites and whipped cream. (No one, however, ever claimed to lose any weight eating them.) Most are made with fresh fruits and have seasonal appeal; all are suitably grand conclusions to a fancy dinner party and can be prepared a day ahead of time.

The frozen desserts—ice creams, frozen soufflés or mousses, and fruit ices—can be prepared several days in advance of serving (but not more than 2 weeks), certainly an advantage when preparing for a party. Many of them, such as the Frozen Grapefruit Soufflé au Chocolat, are intended for special occasions. Being frozen, all of them are refreshing summertime fare, particularly those with a citrus or other fruit base. Since I have found that most people do not own an ice cream freezer (I among them), I have included only recipes for frozen desserts that can be made satisfactorily without one. Certain ingredients, such as honey, egg custard, and whipped cream, will prevent an ice cream from freezing into a solid, rock-like mass. Some of the frozen soufflés and mousses, however, should be moved from the freezer to the refrigerator ½ to 2 hours before serving to soften slightly. Before dinner begins, you should insert a metal skewer or knife in the dessert to judge its firmness.

There is, understandably, some confusion over dessert terminology, which I'm not sure that I can dispel. "Mousse," "soufflé," and "Bavarian" are terms often used interchangeably in describing chilled or frozen desserts, and as soon as one sets out to differentiate among them, an exception gets in the way. A soufflé was, in its original conception, a fluffy, hot dish, made by incorporating stiffly beaten egg whites into a flavored pastry cream or custard. But now we have frozen soufflés and chilled soufflés, and almost anything can qualify as long as it is served in a soufflé dish. (Rather like a "casserole": is it the ceramic pot or the stew?) Bavarians or mousses, however, can be served out of any sort of dish or molded into fancy shapes.

A proper Bavarian always has a custard base of egg yolks and milk or cream. A mousse or soufflé may or may not have this base. All three contain whipped cream and/or stiffly beaten egg whites. If they are not frozen, these desserts are usually held firm by the addition of gelatin. An exception would be a chocolate mousse, which contains a sufficient proportion of chocolate and butter to harden when chilled. Mousses with a puréed fruit base are sometimes made without gelatin; they are softer in texture and should be served within a few hours after they are made.

To add to the confusion, ice cream, which is basically cream and a flavoring, can also contain custard, gelatin, and egg whites. But it is always a much denser mixture, and few of us will have trouble recognizing it.

Certain techniques are used repeatedly in this chapter and require some explanatory notes:

Making custards: A custard is a liquid, usually milk, cooked with beaten egg yolks or whole eggs until thickened. The process is speeded up by scalding the milk first, then slowly beating it into the eggs. The mixture is then placed over simmering water or directly over a low flame and stirred constantly until the eggs have poached and thickened the liquid. Use a wooden spoon and keep it moving all over the bottom of the pan. Never stop stirring and do not allow the custard to overheat or the eggs will curdle. It should not approach a simmer; when fully cooked, the mixture will be from 160° to 170°. This should be accomplished within 5 to 15 minutes, depending on the intensity of the heat. The consistency will vary according to the proportion of eggs to liquid. A zabaglione will become very thick, like a fluffy pudding, while other custards will only coat the spoon. When a custard is made with a little flour, it becomes a pastry cream and thickens more readily. When thickened, remove the custard from the heat and stir for a minute to stop the cooking. Put it on a wire rack and cool to room temperature; then cover and chill. Do not cover it while warm or the evaporating moisture will not escape and will thin the custard. A custard should always be cooled before incorporating it into beaten egg whites or whipped cream; a hot custard will deflate and liquefy the whipped ingredients.

Beating egg whites: Egg whites should be at room temperature to separate and whip properly. If you have just taken eggs out of the refrigerator, immerse them in hot tap water for a few minutes before breaking them open. If sugar is to be beaten into the egg whites, do not begin to add it until they hold definite peaks when the beater is raised. At this point they will have reached their maximum volume but will still be moist enough to allow the sugar to melt. Once the sugar is added, they will not increase further in volume. Add the sugar slowly, while beating, until you have a stiff and shiny meringue.

Whipping cream: Cream should be ice-cold to be whipped properly. Beat it only until it holds soft peaks and no liquid remains in the bowl. It should be slightly glossy. When it begins to look dull and lumpy, it has been overwhipped and will make a frozen dessert heavy and buttery and a chilled mousse rather woolly and spongy in texture.

Folding: Care should be taken in folding whipped cream and beaten egg whites into a custard base or a fruit purée. Do not overmix or you will deflate the air beaten into the mixture and lose volume as well as lightness. To fold, use a plastic or rubber spatula and scrape the mixture from the bottom of the bowl to the top, turning it over in broad strokes and rotating the bowl as you work. A wide, flat-bottomed bowl will enable you to do this most easily.

For directions on dissolving and using gelatin and on unmolding mousses and Bavarians, refer to Chapter 3, Entrée Mousses.

Fruit Desserts

FRUIT SALADS

You don't really need a recipe for a fruit salad; any combination of fresh, seasonal fruits will make an excellent light summer dessert. You may add a little sugar or honey, some mint leaves, lemon juice or liqueur, according to the mixture of fruit and your own taste. But do not add the sweetener or liqueur until just before serving, as it will draw out the juice from the fruit. Nor should you add particularly juicy fruit, such as watermelon, until shortly before serving. The following are combinations I particularly like, but you can, of course, substitute according to what is on hand and in season. Any of the thin, crisp cookies in Chapter 6 would go well with a fruit salad.

Sliced peaches and raspberries with peach brandy or almond liqueur
Seedless green grapes, blueberries, and honeydew melon balls
Blueberries with Fluffy Lemon Sauce (page 238)
Grapefruit sections with honey and mint leaves
Pineapple shells filled with pineapple, strawberries, and kirsch
Nectarines, strawberries, blueberries, seedless green grapes, orange
    sections, and bananas with Cointreau
Oranges and strawberries with Cointreau
Raspberries with Crème Fraîche (page 237)

ALMOND PEACHES

These peaches are baked with an almond paste filling and served
plain or with Vanilla Custard Sauce.

One 8-ounce can almond
    paste (not "marzipan")
2 tablespoons unsalted but-
    ter, softened
1 egg, lightly beaten

2 tablespoons brandy
8 large ripe freestone peaches
Vanilla Custard Sauce (page
    239), optional

Preheat oven to 350°.

Cream together the almond paste, butter, egg, and brandy with
a wooden spoon or in a food processor or blender.

Immerse the peaches in boiling water for about 20 seconds to
facilitate peeling. Peel, halve, and stone them and fill the cavity of
each half with a spoonful of the almond mixture. Place in a shallow
baking dish, cover, and bake for 15 minutes. Baste well with the
juices that accumulate in the pan. Cool. If desired, serve with
Vanilla Custard Sauce.

YIELD: 8 SERVINGS

BLUEBERRY AND GREEN GRAPE TART

Because blueberries and green grapes make a delicious and pretty fruit salad, they seemed to me a promising combination for a dessert tart. This one consists of a base of cooked blueberries studded with whole green grapes glazed to a gem-like sheen.

FOR THE TART CRUST

1½ cups flour
2 tablespoons sugar
Grated rind of 1 small
    lemon
5 tablespoons unsalted but-
    ter, chilled and cut into
    small pieces

3 tablespoons vegetable short-
    ening, chilled
2 to 3 tablespoons cold water

FOR THE FILLING

1 pint blueberries, washed
1½ tablespoons lime juice
½ cup sugar

A pinch of salt
1¼ pounds seedless green
    grapes, washed and
    dried

FOR THE GLAZE

⅓ cup apple jelly

TO MAKE THE TART CRUST

Combine the flour, sugar, and lemon rind in a large mixing bowl. Rub in the butter and vegetable shortening with the tips of you fingers, combining until the mixture resembles coarse meal. Ad just enough cold water to hold the dough together. Knead one o two turns, form into a ball, wrap in waxed paper, and refrigerate until firm enough to roll out.

Preheat the oven to 375°.

Between 2 sheets of lightly floured waxed paper, roll out the dough into a circle large enough to line a 9-inch tart pan. Fit the dough into the pan, doubling it around the sides to a thickness of about ⅜ inch. Line the inside of the tart shell with aluminum foil and fill with uncooked rice or beans to keep the dough from bubbling. Bake in the middle of the oven for 20 minutes. Remove the foil and rice, prick the bottom of the crust with a fork in several places, and bake for an additional 10 to 15 minutes, or until lightly browned. Cool on a wire rack before filling.

TO MAKE THE FILLING

Combine the blueberries, lime juice, sugar, and salt in a large, heavy saucepan. Cook gently, stirring until the sugar is melted. Turn up the heat and boil for 10 to 15 minutes, stirring as the mixture thickens, until it is as thick as jam. Remove from the heat and allow to cool thoroughly. Then spread it evenly inside the tart shell and refrigerate for about 30 minutes, or until the filling is firm. Starting at the center of the tart, place the grapes upright, side by side, in concentric circles to completely cover the surface of the tart.

TO MAKE THE GLAZE

Melt the apple jelly in a small saucepan and simmer for 4 or 5 minutes until slightly reduced. With a pastry brush, carefully paint all the grapes and the top edge of the tart crust with the jelly glaze.

Note: This tart can be made a day ahead of serving. Set several toothpicks around the outside edge of the tart to keep the covering from touching the glaze and then cover with plastic wrap. Store at room temperature.

YIELD: 6 TO 8 SERVINGS

CARIBBEAN GRAPES

———

*1 ½ pounds black grapes,
    washed, dried, halved,
    and seeded*
1 cup sour cream

1 tablespoon light rum
2 tablespoons sugar
*A scant ¼ teaspoon cinna-
    mon*

Combine all the ingredients, chill, and serve.

YIELD: 4 OR 5 SERVINGS

CHOCOLATE PEARS WITH ZABAGLIONE

———

This is a rather whimsical dessert—cored and peeled pears dipped in a chocolate coating and filled with a thick port-wine custard. They may seem a nuisance to make, but are not really difficult.

FOR THE CUSTARD

8 egg yolks
½ cup sugar
½ cup white port

*6 medium Bartlett or Anjou
    pears*

FOR THE CHOCOLATE COATING

*6 ounces Baker's semi-sweet
    baking chocolate*

2 tablespoons unsalted butter

TO MAKE THE CUSTARD

Beat the egg yolks in the top of a non-aluminum double boiler or a heatproof mixing bowl. Gradually add the sugar and port. Place over simmering water and stir constantly with a wooden spoon until the custard is thick. This will take about 10 minutes. Do not let the custard boil. Cool to room temperature, then chill.

Dip the pears in boiling water for about 30 seconds so that they can be peeled easily. Peel, and cut ½-inch off the stem end. Carefully scoop out the core, using a small serrated knife and a spoon. If necessary, level the bottom of the pear by shaving off a thin slice to make it stand upright.

TO MAKE THE CHOCOLATE COATING

Cut the chocolate and butter into small pieces and place over hot, not simmering, water and stir constantly until melted. Keep the chocolate over warm water, but remove from the stove while dipping the pears.

TO COAT THE PEARS

Dry each pear thoroughly with paper towels. Grasp the pear carefully but firmly with kitchen tongs and swirl it in the melted chocolate; be careful not to let any chocolate run into the cavity. If there are any uncovered spots, spoon a little chocolate over them. Place the coated pears on a wire rack set on top of a large platter and put them in the refrigerator to harden.

Spoon the custard into the pears and refrigerate until serving.
YIELD: 6 SERVINGS

GRAPEFRUIT SNOW

A very light gelatin and fruit dessert suitable for an informal summer lunch or supper.

1 envelope unflavored gelatin
1/4 cup cold water
1 1/2 cups fresh grapefruit
    juice
2 tablespoons Curaçao
1/2 teaspoon vanilla extract

1/4 cup plus 2 tablespoons
    sugar
1 cup grapefruit sections
3/4 cup seedless green grapes
1 egg white

FOR THE GARNISH

Frosted Grapes (page 256)

Soften the gelatin in the cold water and dissolve over low heat, stirring constantly. Combine the grapefruit juice, Curaçao, vanilla, and 1/4 cup of sugar, and stir until the sugar is dissolved. Mix in the dissolved gelatin and chill until thickened. Stir in the grapefruit sections and the grapes. Beat the egg whites until stiff and continue beating while gradually adding the remaining 2 tablespoons of sugar. Fold into the grapefruit mixture. Turn into a lightly oiled 4-cup mold or glass serving bowl and chill until set.

Serve unmolded or from the glass bowl and garnish with Frosted Grapes.

YIELD: 4 SERVINGS

GREEN GRAPE DESSERT

---

*1 pound seedless green
  grapes, washed and
  dried*
*1 cup Crème Fraîche (page
  237) or sour cream*

2 tablespoons light honey

Combine all the ingredients, chill, and serve.
YIELD: 4 SERVINGS

PEACH BOWLER

This is my husband's recipe, taught to him by his father at an early
age. He attempted to introduce it to the American Academy in
Rome in 1950, only to find that members had already been en-
lightened by Madame Rostovtzeff. It is a delicious and intoxicating
dessert and we have several photographs to prove it.

Peel and slice fresh peaches. Put them into a Mason jar with
enough brandy to cover and let stand in warm sunlight all day.
Drain the peaches and reserve the brandy for another use. Place
them in a crystal bowl and chill. Before serving, add *fraises des bois*
and iced champagne.

PEACH COMPOTE

Serve this compote with Lemon-Coconut Wafers (page 272).

6 *large, ripe, unblemished*
   peaches
1 ½ *cups sugar*
1 ½ *cups water*
Rind of 1 large lemon (no
   white pith), cut into
   long, narrow julienne
   strips

1 *cinnamon stick*
8 *whole cloves*
3 *tablespoons peach brandy*
   or brandy

Peel the peaches after immersing them in boiling water for about 20 seconds. Leave whole and set aside.

Combine the sugar, water, lemon rind, cinnamon stick, and cloves in a heavy saucepan, large enough to hold the peaches in one layer. Boil for 5 minutes. Add the peaches and simmer for an additional 5 minutes, or just until tender. With a slotted spoon, transfer the peaches to individual glass compotes or bowls. Boil the syrup a few minutes longer until slightly thickened. Remove from the heat, stir in the brandy, and strain over the peaches. Discard the cinnamon stick and cloves and strew the lemon rind on top of the peaches.

YIELD: 6 SERVINGS

PEACHES AND STRAWBERRIES IN WINE JELLY

A simple and light dessert that looks particularly attractive in small glass dessert bowls.

4 *medium-size ripe peaches*   1 *pint strawberries*

FOR THE JELLY

1 *cup strained orange juice*   ¼ *cup light honey*
6 *tablespoons strained lime*   2 *tablespoons Curaçao*
   juice   1 *envelope unflavored gelatin*
½ *cup dry white wine*   3 *tablespoons cold water*

Peel the peaches after immersing in boiling water for about 20 seconds. Slice them into 4 individual glass dessert bowls. Wash, hull, and dry the strawberries and cut in half any large ones. Divide them among the bowls.

Combine the orange juice, lime juice, white wine, honey, and Curaçao in a mixing bowl. Soften the gelatin in the cold water and dissolve over low heat, stirring constantly. Cool slightly and stir into the wine and juice mixture, combining well. Ladle the liquid jelly into the 4 dessert bowls, cover, and refrigerate until firm.

YIELD: 4 SERVINGS

RASPBERRY TART

For this tart, fresh raspberries are set on a base of crème fraîche and glazed with a kirsch-flavored fruit jelly. Strawberries or blackberries can be substituted for the raspberries. Plan ahead, as it takes about 24 hours to make the crème fraîche.

2 pints raspberries (or straw-berries or blackberries)
1 fully baked 9-inch tart shell (page 176)
1 tablespoon red raspberry jelly or apple jelly

1 tablespoon confectioners' sugar
1 recipe Crème Fraîche (page 237)

FOR THE GLAZE

⅓ cup red raspberry jelly or apple jelly

1 tablespoon kirsch

Wash and hull the berries and let stand, upside down, on several thicknesses of paper towels for at least 30 minutes to drain. Melt 1 tablespoon red raspberry or apple jelly and spread it inside the baked tart shell. Allow to set.

Stir the confectioners' sugar into the crème fraîche and spread it evenly inside the cooled tart shell.

Refrigerate for 30 minutes to firm.

Starting at the center of the tart, set the berries closely side by side in concentric circles on top of the crème fraîche.

TO MAKE THE GLAZE

Melt the jelly in a small saucepan, stir in the kirsch, and simmer for 5 minutes. With a pastry brush, carefully paint each berry with the glaze. If you are using apple jelly, brush the glaze over the top edge of the tart crust as well. Refrigerate until serving.

YIELD: 6 TO 8 SERVINGS

Chilled Desserts

ANOTHER BIRTHDAY CAKE FOR TONY

After the recipe for Tony's original birthday cake appeared in my first cookbook, friends, casual acquaintances, and even a few strangers asked me the date of his birthday. I took this to be a sign that generous admirers were eager to present us with his cake—and perhaps other gifts—on that occasion, and I always replied readily. But, alas, the best intentions go astray and for some reason, that never happened. Perhaps it was only idle curiosity. In any case, I found myself on his very next birthday in need of a cake. And so, from the same wife who brought you Tony's original stupendous birthday cake, here is Another Birthday Cake for Tony, to be served on the 16th of January and, of course, throughout the summer. It is a sponge cake filled with apricot-orange mousse and covered with a thin coating of apricot jam and chocolate icing.

This cake appeared in the original edition of *Cold Cuisine*. See page 201 for the birthday cake created for this new and expanded edition.

FOR THE SPONGE CAKE

3 eggs, at room temperature
6 tablespoons sugar
1 teaspoon vanilla extract

½ cup plus 1 tablespoon
flour

FOR THE APRICOT-ORANGE FILLING

2 teaspoons unflavored
  gelatin
2 tablespoons cold water
½ cup plus 2 tablespoons
  apricot jam
½ cup orange juice

1 tablespoon plus 2 tea-
  spoons orange liqueur
1 cup heavy cream

Additional orange liqueur
2 to 3 tablespoons sieved
  apricot jam

FOR THE CHOCOLATE ICING

6 ounces Baker's semi-sweet baking chocolate
3 tablespoons unsalted butter
1 tablespoon orange liqueur

TO MAKE SPONGE CAKE

Preheat the oven to 350°. Butter and lightly flour a round of waxed paper to fit the bottom of one round 9-inch cake pan.

Combine the eggs and sugar in a large mixing bowl and set the bowl over a pan of barely simmering water. Stir continuously until the eggs are quite warm, being careful not to let the water boil. Remove from the heat, stir in the vanilla, and beat the mixture with an electric mixer until it is thick, light, and tripled in volume. This will take 12 to 15 minutes. Sift the flour over the beaten eggs and fold together gently but thoroughly. Turn into the prepared pan, spread evenly with a spatula, and bake in the center of the preheated oven for 20 to 25 minutes, or until the cake springs back when pressed lightly and a toothpick tests clean. Cool in the pan on a wire rack.

TO MAKE THE FILLING

Soften the gelatin in the cold water and dissolve over low heat, stirring constantly. Purée the apricot jam in a blender or food processor. Add the orange juice and orange liqueur and blend. With the motor running, pour in the dissolved gelatin in a thin stream. Whip the cream and fold it into the apricot mixture.

With a long-bladed serrated knife, carefully cut the sponge cake horizontally into two layers. Sprinkle the cut side of each layer very lightly with a little orange liqueur. Wash and dry the pan in which the cake was baked. Return the bottom half of the cake to the pan, cut side up. Spread the apricot filling evenly over the cake layer. It should be approximately 1½ inches deep and just reach the top of the pan. Cover with plastic wrap and refrigerate until firm. When the mousse is firm, place the top half of the cake over it, invert, and unmold onto a cake platter. Spread a thin layer of sieved apricot jam over the surface of the cake, and return it to the refrigerator while you prepare the chocolate icing.

TO MAKE THE ICING

Cut up the chocolate into very small pieces. Put it in the top of a double boiler with the butter and orange liqueur and melt it over hot, not simmering, water, stirring constantly. When the chocolate has melted, remove from the heat and stir vigorously until the icing is shiny and of spreading consistency. Remove the cake from the refrigerator. Pour the icing over the top all at once and spread evenly with the blade of a knife, allowing the icing to drip a little over the edges. Refrigerate until serving. To serve, hold a serrated knife perpendicular to the cake and cut with a sawing motion, beginning at the outside edge.

YIELD: 8 SERVINGS

APPLE-PRALINE MOUSSE

Fresh apples, puréed in a food processor or blender, not cooked and sweetened applesauce, should be used in this mousse. The dessert is laced with coarse-crushed almond praline.

4 eggs, separated
3/4 cup sugar
1 cup light cream or half-
    and-half, scalded
2 cups fresh apple purée
Grated rind of 1 small
    lemon
3 tablespoons Calvados or
    applejack

2 envelopes unflavored gelatin
1/2 cup cold apple juice
A pinch of cream of tartar
1 cup heavy cream
1 cup coarse-crushed almond
    praline (page 238)

FOR THE GARNISH

1/2 cup lightly sweetened whipped cream
2 to 3 tablespoons crushed almond praline (page 238)

Beat the egg yolks with 1/4 cup of the sugar until light and thick. Gradually add the scalded light cream or half-and-half and cook over a low flame or in the top of a double boiler over simmering water, stirring constantly, for 5 to 10 minutes, or until thickened. Remove from the heat and add the apple purée, lemon rind, and Calvados or applejack.

Soften the gelatin in the apple juice and dissolve over low heat, stirring constantly. Stir it into the apple custard.

Beat the egg whites until frothy. Add the cream of tartar and continue beating until the egg whites begin to stiffen. Gradually add the remaining 1/2 cup sugar, beating until you have a stiff meringue. Whip the cream until it holds soft peaks.

Stir a little of the beaten egg whites into the apple custard. Fold in the remaining whites, the whipped cream, and 1 cup crushed praline. Turn into a serving bowl and chill until set.

Before serving, decorate with a border of sweetened whipped cream sprinkled with crushed praline.

YIELD: 8 SERVINGS

APRICOT-ORANGE MOUSSE WITH STRAWBERRIES

A colorful, summery dessert, this mousse is set in a decorative mold with a center tube and, when unmolded, the cavity is filled with fresh strawberries.

FOR THE MOUSSE

8 ounces dried apricots
1 cup plus 3 tablespoons
    sugar
1 cup orange juice
3 1/2 tablespoons curaçao or
    other orange liqueur

1 envelope plus 1 teaspoon
    unflavored gelatin
1/3 cup cold water
4 egg whites
1 1/4 cups heavy cream

FOR THE STRAWBERRY MIXTURE

2 cups strawberries
Sugar

Curaçao or other orange
    liqueur (optional)

Lightly oil a 6-cup decorative mold with a center tube. Or invert a tall, narrow drinking glass or jar in the center of a mold to create a well and oil the sides of the glass as well as the mold.

Put the apricots in a large bowl filled with cold water and let them soak for 1 or 2 hours to remove the sulfur. Drain well, put them in a saucepan with 3 tablespoons of the sugar, and cover with fresh water. Simmer gently for about 5 minutes, or until the skins are soft. Drain, and purée in a food processor or blender with ¼ cup sugar, adding the orange juice and orange liqueur in a thin stream.

Soften the gelatin in the cold water and dissolve over low heat, stirring constantly. With the motor running, add the dissolved gelatin to the apricot purée.

Beat the egg whites until almost stiff. Gradually add ½ cup of the sugar, beating until you have a stiff, shiny meringue. Whip the cream with the remaining ¼ cup sugar until it holds soft peaks. Fold together the apricot purée, the cream, and the egg whites, combining gently but thoroughly. Turn into the prepared mold, holding the drinking glass in place if you are using one.

Wash, hull, and dry the strawberries. Refrigerate but do not add sugar or liqueur until serving time.

To serve, unmold the mousse onto a serving plate. Combine the strawberries with a little sugar and, if desired, orange liqueur, and fill the center cavity of the mousse with the fruit.

YIELD: 8 SERVINGS

COFFEE INFUSION

This is an old family recipe from the kitchen of our friend and neighbor Vee Angle. Known alternatively to members of her family as "coffee confusion," it forms itself, while cooling and setting, into 3 layers ranging from a clear coffee jelly of intense flavor to a light, foamy surface. It is quickly and easily made and should confound your guests with pleasure.

½ cup sugar
1¾ cups boiling water
¼ cup instant coffee
3 eggs, separated

1 envelope unflavored gelatin
¼ cup cold water
1 tablespoon vanilla extract

Combine the sugar, boiling water, and coffee in the top of a double boiler or a heavy saucepan. Lightly beat the egg yolks and stir in a little of the coffee mixture. Then pour the yolks back into the pan and cook over moderate heat, stirring constantly, for about 10 minutes or until the mixture coats a spoon.

Soften the gelatin in the cold water and dissolve over low heat, stirring constantly. Stir the dissolved gelatin and the vanilla into the coffee custard. Cool. Beat the egg whites until stiff but not dry and fold in. Rinse a 4-to-5-cup ring mold in cold water and turn in the coffee mixture. Chill until set and unmold. If desired, serve with lightly whipped cream flavored with a little sugar and vanilla extract.

YIELD: 6 SERVINGS

COFFEE MOUSSE

This mousse is delicate in flavor and remarkably light, fluffy, and creamy in texture.

6 eggs, separated
1 ¼ cups sugar
1 cup half-and-half or light
    cream
2 tablespoons plus 1 teaspoon
    instant espresso coffee
    powder

2 envelopes unflavored gelatin
½ cup cold water
2 tablespoons white crème de
    cacao
1 teaspoon vanilla extract
A pinch of cream of tartar
2 cups heavy cream

Beat the egg yolks with ¼ cup of the sugar until light and thick. Beat in the half-and-half or light cream and the instant espresso. Cook in the top of a double boiler over simmering water, stirring constantly, for 5 to 10 minutes, or until slightly thickened. Sprinkle the gelatin over ½ cup cold water to soften and stir constantly over low heat until dissolved. Stir into the coffee custard, add the crème de cacao and vanilla, and cool to room temperature.

Beat the egg whites until foamy. Add the cream of tartar and continue beating until almost stiff. Gradually add ¾ cup sugar and beat until you have a stiff meringue.

Whip the cream with the remaining ¼ cup sugar until it holds soft peaks. Place the coffee custard over a bowl filled with ice cubes and stir until it begins to thicken but take care that it does not begin to set. Fold it into the whipped cream and the beaten egg whites. Turn into a glass serving bowl and chill until set. Serve with Chocolate Fudge Sauce (page 237), if desired.

YIELD: 10 SERVINGS

HONEY-HAZELNUT BLANCMANGE

This smooth, velvety dessert is an interesting variation on the traditional almond-flavored blancmange. Serve it with Chocolate Hazelnut Cookies (page 269), which provide both a perfect accompaniment to the blancmange and a use for the leftover ground nuts.

2 cups hazelnuts	⅔ cup light honey
2¾ cups cold milk	2 tablespoons brandy
2 envelopes unflavored gelatin	1 teaspoon vanilla extract
½ cup cold water	1½ cups heavy cream

FOR THE GARNISH

10 to 12 whole, unblanched hazelnuts	Honey

Preheat the oven to 350°.

Spread the hazelnuts on a baking sheet and heat them for 5 to 6 minutes. Pile them onto a large coarse linen dish towel and, while they are still hot, rub them vigorously to remove the skins. Do not be concerned if you have only partial success, as a few skins will not make any difference.

In batches, grind the nuts in a food processor or blender, adding the milk in a thin stream. Line a sieve with a damp cotton dish towel, set it over a bowl, and strain the hazelnut milk through it, ⅓ at a time. As each batch is strained, wring the nuts in the towel over the bowl to squeeze out as much liquid as possible. After straining and wringing, you should have 2½ cups liquid.

Soften the gelatin in the cold water and dissolve over low heat, stirring constantly. Stir the dissolved gelatin into the hazelnut milk. Add the honey, brandy, and vanilla extract, stirring well to combine. Whip the cream until it holds soft peaks.

Stir the hazelnut milk mixture over a bowl of ice cubes until it becomes syrupy but does not start to set. Fold in the whipped cream. Turn into a lightly oiled 8-cup decorative mold, preferably one with a funneled center. Cover and refrigerate until set.

Before serving, unmold onto a platter. Roll each whole hazelnut in a little honey and press them around the top of the blancmange.
YIELD: 8 SERVINGS

LEMON-KIWI MOUSSE
(or Lime-Kiwi Mousse)

This fluffy, light-textured mousse has a pleasantly tart flavor—cool refreshment for a sweltering day. Garnished with slices of jade-green kiwi fruit, it looks decorative and inviting.

¾ cup plus 2 tablespoons sugar	¼ cup cold water
4 eggs, separated	Grated rind of 1 lemon (or lime)
½ cup lemon (or lime) juice	1 cup heavy cream
2 teaspoons unflavored gelatin	1½ tablespoons light rum*

* Do not substitute dark rum, as the flavor is too strong.

FOR THE GARNISH

2 kiwi berries, peeled and cut crosswise into ¼-inch slices

In the top of a double boiler, whisk together ¼ cup of the sugar, the egg yolks, and the lemon juice. Place over simmering water and cook, stirring with a wooden spoon, for about 10 minutes, or until thick. Do not boil. Remove from the heat. Soften the gelatin in the cold water and dissolve over low heat, stirring constantly. Stir the dissolved gelatin and the grated rind into the lemon custard. Cool to room temperature.

Beat the egg whites until they hold firm peaks; continue beating as you gradually add ½ cup sugar. Whip the cream with the rum and the remaining 2 tablespoons sugar until it holds soft peaks.

Fold the cream and then the egg whites into the cooled lemon custard. Turn into a 4-to-5-cup glass serving dish and chill until firm.

Before serving, decorate the top of the mousse with a border of kiwi slices.

YIELD: 6 SERVINGS

LEMON PUDDING

This is an old-fashioned recipe composed of a sponge cake topping and a custard base. It is light, tart, and just the right dessert for an informal summer supper.

1 tablespoon unsalted butter, softened	*2 tablespoons flour*
¾ cup sugar	*¼ cup lemon juice*
2 eggs, separated	*Grated rind of 1 lemon*
	1 cup milk

Preheat the oven to 350°. Butter a 1-quart baking dish.

Cream the butter and blend in the sugar. With an electric mixer, beat in the egg yolks, then the flour, and then the lemon juice. Stir in the lemon rind and milk. Beat the egg whites until stiffened but not dry and fold them into the batter. Turn into the prepared baking dish and place in a pan half filled with hot water. Bake for 40 minutes or until the pudding shrinks from the sides of the pan and is lightly browned on top.

YIELD: 3 OR 4 SERVINGS

PEAR-AMARETTI TRIFLE

When our friend Cyrus Hoy had completed 10 years of scholarly labor on a multivolume, complete edition of the works of Thomas Dekker, we asked him to have a celebratory dinner with us. Entertaining just one guest was an unaccustomed luxury, involving none of the logistical problems I often face in preparing dinner for 10 or 12. We began simply with a chilled Lemon-Mint Soup (page 27) served with small wedges of Toasted Syrian Bread (page 253); roast duck and steamed asparagus followed; then a salad of greens and avocado with a garlicky vinaigrette. My husband poured a 1966 Pommard in tribute to Cyrus's scholarship and my cooking. After this, a pure unadulterated dessert of, say, strawberries sprinkled with Cointreau would have been appropriate and elegant. But, challenged by the significance of the occasion, I was willing to sacrifice those virtues for an unabashedly rich, multilayered, festive-looking composition I call Pear-Amaretti Trifle. A traditional English trifle with an Italian accent, it is made of sponge cake, pear jam, white-port zabaglione, crumbled *amaretti* (Italian macaroons), and whipped cream, all blended into a congenial mass.

Here is the recipe. If you don't want to make the pear jam, a store-bought apricot or peach jam would substitute nicely, but it may be necessary to thin it to spreading consistency with a few teaspoons of hot water. You will need about 1½ cups.

One 9-inch sponge cake layer (page 185)

FOR THE CUSTARD

12 egg yolks	*¾ cup white port*
¾ cup sugar	*¾ cup heavy cream, whipped*

FOR THE PEAR JAM

1½ pounds pears
3 tablespoons lemon juice
1 cup sugar
A 2-inch piece of vanilla bean
2 to 3 tablespoons white port
12 amaretti, crumbled into coarse bits

¾ cup heavy cream
1 tablespoon sugar
¼ teaspoon vanilla extract
2 tablespoons sliced almonds

TO MAKE THE CUSTARD

Beat the egg yolks in the top of a non-aluminum double boiler or a heatproof mixing bowl, gradually adding the sugar and port. Place over simmering water and stir constantly with a wooden spoon until the custard is thick. This will take 10 to 15 minutes; do not let the custard boil. Cool to room temperature and chill. When the custard is chilled, fold in the whipped cream.

TO MAKE THE PEAR JAM

Peel and core the pears, chop them into small pieces, and, as they are chopped, combine them with the lemon juice in a heavy pot. Add the sugar and vanilla bean, and slowly bring the mixture to a boil. Simmer, stirring frequently, for about 30 minutes, or until the jam looks almost as thick as applesauce. It should remain very pale in color. Remove from the heat and test the consistency by placing a small amount on a saucer and chilling it in the freezer for a few minutes. It should be rather thick and not runny. Allow the jam to cool to room temperature before using in the dessert.

TO ASSEMBLE THE DESSERT

Cut the sponge layer in half horizontally, and cut the halves into ½-inch cubes. Place half the cubes in the bottom of a large, round flat-bottomed bowl, preferably glass. Sprinkle the cake cubes with a little white port. Spread with half the pear jam; cover the jam with half the custard; sprinkle the custard with half of the crumbled *amaretti*. Repeat with a second layer of cake cubes; sprinkle again with port; spread with the remaining pear jam; cover with the remaining custard; and scatter the remaining crumbled *amaretti* over the custard. Whip ¾ cup cream with 1 tablespoon sugar and ½ teaspoon vanilla extract and spread it over the top of the dessert. Refrigerate until serving.

Before serving scatter the sliced almonds over the whipped cream.

YIELD: 10 SERVINGS

PEAR MOUSSE

This is a welcome hot-weather dessert, so light it is almost immaterial. It may be served with Fluffy Lemon Sauce (page 238) or stand on its own, as you will.

5 eggs, separated	Grated rind of 1 lemon
1 cup sugar	1 teaspoon vanilla extract
1 cup light cream or half-and-half	¼ cup white port
	2 envelopes unflavored gelatin
2 cups pear purée (2 pounds whole fresh Bartlett pears)	½ cup cold water
	A pinch of cream of tartar
	1 cup heavy cream

Beat the egg yolks with ¼ cup of the sugar until light and thick. Stir in the light cream or half-and-half and cook in the top of a double boiler over simmering water, stirring constantly, for 5 to 10 minutes, or until slightly thickened. Remove from the heat and add the pear purée, lemon rind, vanilla, and white port, and allow to cool.

Soften the gelatin in the cold water and dissolve over low heat, stirring constantly. Stir it into the pear custard.

Beat the egg whites until frothy. Add the cream of tartar and continue beating until they begin to stiffen. Gradually add ½ cup sugar, beating until you have a stiff meringue. Whip the cream with the remaining ¼ cup sugar until it holds soft peaks.

Stir ¼ of the beaten egg whites into the pear custard. Fold in the remaining whites and the whipped cream. Turn into a serving bowl and chill until set.

YIELD: 8 SERVINGS

RASPBERRY BAVARIAN

A classic, smooth, creamy Bavarian with a custard base. The recipe can be adapted to almost any berry flavor. If desired, serve it with Raspberry Sauce (page 239).

2 pints fresh raspberries,
    washed and dried
4 egg yolks
¾ cup sugar
¾ cup milk, scalded

2 tablespoons kirsch
1 envelope plus 1¼ teaspoons
    unflavored gelatin
⅓ cup cold water
¾ cup heavy cream

FOR THE GARNISH

Reserved raspberries

Purée enough of the berries to make 2 cups, setting aside a few for garnish. Strain through a fine sieve, pressing through as much pulp as possible. You should have 1⅔ cups.

Beat the egg yolks with ½ cup of the sugar until thick and light.

Gradually beat in the scalded milk and cook over a medium flame, stirring constantly, for about 5 minutes, or until thickened. Do not boil. Remove from the heat and stir vigorously to stop the cooking. Add the raspberry purée and kirsch.

Soften the gelatin in the cold water and dissolve over low heat, stirring constantly. Cool slightly and add the dissolved gelatin to the raspberry custard, stirring until thoroughly combined.

Whip the cream with the remaining ¼ cup sugar until it holds soft peaks.

Place the raspberry custard over a bowl filled with ice cubes and stir until it starts to thicken, but do not let it begin to set. Fold in the whipped cream. Turn into a lightly oiled 6-cup decorative mold and chill until firm.

To serve, unmold and garnish with the reserved raspberries. Serve the Raspberry Sauce on the side, if desired.

YIELD: 6 SERVINGS

STRAWBERRIES AND CREAM MOUSSE

A light and creamy mixture laced with marinated strawberries. This mousse is rather soft in texture, with just enough gelatin to stabilize it, and is not firm enough to unmold.

> 1 pint fresh ripe strawberries
> ¼ cup plus 2 teaspoons sugar
> 1½ tablespoons orange liqueur
>
> 1¼ teaspoons unflavored gelatin
> 2 tablespoons cold water
> 1 cup heavy cream

Wash, hull, and dry the strawberries. In a food processor or blender purée about half of them, or enough to yield 1 cup purée. Add tablespoons of the sugar and blend. Slice the remaining berries and combine in a shallow bowl with the orange liqueur and 2 teaspoons sugar, or to taste. Let stand for about 30 minutes.

Soften the gelatin in the cold water and dissolve over low heat, stirring constantly. Stir into the strawberry purée.

Whip the cream with the remaining 2 tablespoons sugar until it holds soft peaks. Fold the strawberry purée and the sliced strawberries with their juice into the cream. Turn into a glass serving dish and chill until firm.

YIELD: APPROXIMATELY 4 CUPS

Peaches and Cream Mousse

Follow the recipe above, substituting 1 pound peaches, peeled and pitted, for the strawberries, and Madeira or cognac for the orange liqueur.

TONY'S FIFTH BIRTHDAY CAKE

Every January, when it is time to make my husband a birthday cake, I ask him what he would like. "Linzertorte," he invariably replies, and then I make him something else. Linzertorte is a rather sweet tart made of almond pastry and raspberry jam. He only thinks he likes it, I reason to myself; what he really likes is raspberries. His birthday cake this year is the closest I've come to a linzertorte. It is composed of two hazelnut cake layers with a raspberry mousse filling and chocolate icing. It is the fifth in a series of birthday cakes for Tony that appear in each of my cookbooks.

FOR THE CAKE LAYERS

½ pound hazelnuts (generous 1½ cups)
4 eggs, lightly beaten
½ cup plus 1 tablespoon sugar
1 teaspoon vanilla extract

4 tablespoons unsalted butter, melted
Approximately 3 tablespoons curaçao

FOR THE RASPBERRY MOUSSE FILLING

¾ cup seedless raspberry jam
1 teaspoon unflavored gelatin
1 tablespoon curaçao

1 tablespoon cold water
½ cup heavy cream

FOR THE ICING

4 ounces Baker's German's sweet chocolate
2½ tablespoons unsalted butter

1½ tablespoons heavy cream

TO MAKE THE CAKE

Preheat the oven to 350°. Spread the hazelnuts in a baking pan and cook for 5 minutes. Do not turn off the oven. Put them, a handful at a time, in a coarse linen towel and rub vigorously to remove as much of the skins as possible. (Don't expect to get them perfectly clean; about half the skins will remain.) Grind the nuts in a food processor, using an off-on motion, so that they are partly pulverized and partly chopped fine. Reserve.

Butter and lightly flour 2 pieces of wax paper to fit the bottom of 2 round 9-inch cake pans.

Mix the eggs and sugar in a large mixing bowl and set over a pan of boiling water. Stir until the eggs are quite warm, but do not let them cook. Remove from the heat, add the vanilla, and beat with an electric mixer for 5 to 8 minutes, until the eggs are very pale in color, tripled in volume, and have the consistency of lightly whipped cream. Fold in the ground nuts, and then the melted butter, combining thoroughly but taking care not to deflate the eggs. Turn into the prepared cake pans and bake for about 20 minutes, or until a toothpick tests clean. Loosen the edges of the cakes with a knife and invert onto a wire rack. Peel off the wax paper and cool to room temperature. When cool, sprinkle the bottom of each layer with a little curaçao.

TO MAKE THE FILLING

Warm the raspberry jam in a saucepan or in a Pyrex measuring cup in a microwave oven. Soften the gelatin in the cold water and curaçao, and dissolve over very low heat, stirring constantly. (This is most easily done in a stainless steel measuring cup.) Stir into the warm raspberry jam, and let the mixture cool to room temperature. Then whip the cream until it holds firm peaks and fold into the raspberry jam. Place the mousse in the refrigerator until it becomes firm.

TO ASSEMBLE THE CAKE

Place one layer on a serving plate and spread the raspberry mousse on top, to within ½ inch of the edge. Cover with the other layer.

TO MAKE THE ICING

Break the chocolate into very small pieces and put it in the top of a double boiler, or in an enamelled iron saucepan over a simmer pad, with the butter and cream. Stir constantly over hot water or low heat until the chocolate has melted. Be careful not to overheat it. Pour the melted chocolate over the top of the cake, and spread evenly with a knife, allowing a little to drip down the sides of the cake. Refrigerate until shortly before serving.

YIELD: 8 TO 10 SERVINGS

ZABAGLIONE

Served in small goblets and accompanied by crisp cookies, this is a fine dessert in itself. It can also be used (without the sliced strawberries) as a sauce for fresh fruit.

> 12 egg yolks
> ½ cup plus 2 tablespoons
>   sugar
>
> ⅓ cup Marsala
> ¾ cup sliced strawberries
>   (optional)

In a heatproof mixing bowl or the top of a double boiler, beat the egg yolks until lemon-colored. Gradually beat in the sugar and the Marsala. Place over simmering water and beat constantly with a wire whisk until the mixture thickens and foams up. This will take about 15 minutes. Cool to room temperature and, if desired, fold in the strawberries.

YIELD: 2 CUPS

Frozen Desserts

BISCUIT TORTONI

Flavored with honey and kirsch, this dessert is an unusual version of a biscuit tortoni. The honey both contributes flavor and creates a smoother texture by preventing the mixture from freezing too firm.

1 cup heavy cream

2½ tablespoons light honey

1 egg white

2 teaspoons kirsch

½ cup fine-crushed amaretti

Beat the cream until it begins to thicken. Continue beating while adding the honey, until it holds soft peaks. Beat the egg white until stiff. Fold the egg white, kirsch, and *amaretti* into the cream, reserving approximately 1 tablespoon of the *amaretti*. Turn into 4 custard cups, sprinkle the top of each with the reserved *amaretti* crumbs, and freeze.

YIELD: 4 SERVINGS

BLUEBERRY ICE CREAM

A very smooth ice cream with an intense blueberry flavor and color.

1 pint fresh blueberries (2½ cups)

2 tablespoons lime juice

¾ cup plus 1 tablespoon sugar

½ cup half-and-half

6 egg yolks, lightly beaten

1 cup heavy cream

1½ teaspoons vanilla extract

Wash the blueberries, discarding any that are soft or green. Put them in a heavy pot with the lime juice and ¾ cup sugar. Bring slowly to a boil and boil, stirring occasionally, for 20 to 25 minutes or until quite syrupy. Remove from the heat and cool to room temperature.

Heat the half-and-half to almost simmering and beat into the egg yolks. Return the mixture to the saucepan and cook, stirring constantly over medium heat, until thickened. Remove and cool to room temperature.

Whip the cream with the remaining tablespoon sugar and the vanilla until it holds soft peaks. Fold in the cooled blueberry mix-

ture and the cooled custard, combining thoroughly. Turn into a
serving bowl, cover, and freeze for a few hours until thickened. Stir
and freeze until firm.

YIELD: APPROXIMATELY 1 QUART

BOMBE FAVORITE

This splendid concoction is a specialty of our friend Miggie Baum,
adapted from a London Cordon Bleu recipe. The crumbled meringues melt into the cream, preventing it from freezing too hard
and creating a texture that is smooth and mellow. It is served with
Raspberry Sauce.

FOR THE MERINGUES

*4 egg whites, at room
   temperature
⅛ teaspoon cream of tartar*

*1 cup sugar
1 teaspoon vanilla extract*

FOR THE CREAM MIXTURE

2 cups heavy cream

2 tablespoons kirsch

1 recipe Raspberry Sauce (page 239)

Preheat the oven to 250°. Line a very large baking sheet with brown
paper.

Beat the egg whites until frothy. Add the cream of tartar and
continue beating until the egg whites hold definite peaks. Continue
beating while gradually adding the sugar and the vanilla extract.
Shape into 5 or 6 large meringues, each about ½ inch thick, on the
prepared baking sheet. Bake for approximately 1 hour 15 minutes.

or until dry in the center. Leave the meringues to cool in the turned-off oven with the door ajar.

Whip the cream with the kirsch until it holds very soft peaks. Do not overbeat. It should have the consistency of crème Chantilly.

Break up the cooled meringues into pieces roughly 1 inch square and fold them into the whipped cream. Turn into a 2-quart serving dish or a decorative mold and freeze.

Serve with the Raspberry Sauce, which should be passed in a sauceboat.

YIELD: 8 SERVINGS

Coffee Bombe Favorite

Follow the preceding recipe with these changes: Stir 1 teaspoon instant coffee dissolved in 1 teaspoon hot water into the beaten egg whites when making the meringues. Omit the kirsch and flavor the whipped cream with 1½ teaspoons instant coffee dissolved in 1½ teaspoons hot water. Omit the Raspberry Sauce.

CHOCOLATE GÂTEAU FAVORITE

This chocolate version of Bombe Favorite, frozen between thin chocolate-nut cake layers, was first made when I was entertaining 40 people for my mother's birthday. The recipe below is given in less alarming quantity, sufficient for 8 to 10 servings. As the crumbled meringues prevent the filling from freezing too hard, it should not be necessary to remove the cake from the freezer in advance of serving.

FOR THE CAKE LAYERS

3 eggs
½ cup plus 2 tablespoons
  sugar

3 tablespoons unsweetened
  cocoa
1 cup fine-chopped walnuts
  or pecans

FOR THE MERINGUES

4 egg whites, at room
  temperature
⅛ teaspoon cream of tartar

1 cup sugar
2 tablespoons plus 2 tea-
  spoons unsweetened cocoa

FOR THE CREAM FILLING

2⅓ cups heavy cream
¼ cup sugar
2 tablespoons plus 1 teaspoon
  unsweetened cocoa

2 tablespoons crème de cacao,
  preferably white

FOR THE CHOCOLATE ICING

4 ounces German's sweet
  baking chocolate
2 tablespoons unsalted butter

1 tablespoon crème de cacao,
  preferably white

TO MAKE THE CAKE LAYERS

Preheat the oven to 350°. Line two 9-inch round cake pans with buttered and floured waxed paper. Combine the eggs and sugar in a mixing bowl. Set over a pan of barely simmering water and heat stirring constantly, until the eggs feel quite warm, but do not let them cook. Remove from the heat and beat with an electric mixer for about 10 minutes, or until very light, thick, and tripled in volume. Sift the cocoa over the egg mixture and sprinkle with the chopped nuts. Fold all together gently but thoroughly. Turn into the prepared cake pans and bake for 20 minutes, or until the cake springs back when pressed lightly and a toothpick tests clean. Loosen the edges with a knife and invert onto a cake rack. Carefully peel off the waxed paper and cool.

TO MAKE THE MERINGUES

Lower the oven temperature to 250°. Line one very large or two smaller baking sheets with brown paper. Beat the egg whites until foamy. Add the cream of tartar and beat until they hold definite peaks. Continue beating while gradually adding the sugar. Sift the cocoa over the whites and mix in, using the lowest speed of the electric mixer. Spread into 5 or 6 large rounds, each about ½ inch thick, on the prepared baking sheet. Bake for 1 hour to 1 hour 15 minutes, or until dry. Leave in the turned-off oven with the door ajar to cool.

TO MAKE THE CREAM FILLING

Whip the cream, adding the sugar gradually, until it holds soft peaks. Do not overbeat; it should have the consistency of crème Chantilly. Sift the cocoa over the cream, add the crème de cacao, and fold all together using the lowest speed of the electric beater. Break up the cooled meringues into approximately 1-inch pieces and fold into the cream mixture with a spatula.

TO ASSEMBLE THE CAKE

Place one cake layer, smooth side down, inside a round 9-inch spring-form pan or deep, straight-sided saucepan, or a cake pan fitted with a 3-inch heavy foil collar. Spread the cream filling on top and cover with the remaining cake layer, smooth side up. Cover and freeze until firm. Loosen the sides with a knife, unmold onto a cake plate, and return to the freezer.

TO MAKE THE ICING

Break up the chocolate into small pieces and put it in the top of a double boiler with the butter and crème de cacao. Melt over hot, not simmering, water, stirring constantly until smooth and shiny. Remove from the heat, take the cake out of the freezer, and pour all the melted chocolate over the top, spreading it out with a knife and allowing a little to drip over the edges of the cake. Return to the freezer until serving. (Note: the cake can be covered with plastic wrap after the icing has hardened.)

YIELD: 8 TO 10 SERVINGS

COCONUT ICE CREAM

A very agreeable blend of coconut, honey, and kirsch.

> 3 eggs, separated
> 6 tablespoons light honey
> 1/2 cup grated, unsweetened
>   coconut*
> A pinch of cream of tartar
>
> 1 cup heavy cream
> 2 to 3 teaspoons kirsch
> Frosted Grapes (page 256)
>   (optional)

* If using packaged, sweetened coconut, soak it in water to cover for 15 minutes. Drain and pat dry with paper towels.

Beat the egg yolks and honey with a wire whisk in the top of a double boiler. Add the coconut, place over simmering water, and cook, stirring slowly but steadily with a wooden spoon for 8 to 10 minutes or until slightly thickened. Do not let the mixture boil. Remove from the heat, cool, and chill.

Beat the egg whites until frothy. Add the cream of tartar and beat until stiff. Whip the cream until it holds soft peaks. Stir the kirsch into the chilled custard; then fold in the whipped cream and beaten egg whites. Freeze until firm. If desired, garnish with Frosted Grapes.

YIELD: APPROXIMATELY 1 QUART

FROZEN CAPPUCCINO

In this reinterpretation of the Italian beverage, coffee, chocolate, brandy, cinnamon, and cream are transformed into a memorable frozen dessert.

6 egg yolks
¾ cup plus 2 tablespoons sugar
½ cup milk
1 tablespoon plus 1 teaspoon powdered instant espresso coffee

1 ounce unsweetened chocolate, broken into several small pieces
1 tablespoon brandy
¼ teaspoon cinnamon
1 cup heavy cream
4 egg whites

FOR THE GARNISH

Grated unsweetened or semi-sweet chocolate

In the top of a double boiler, whisk together the egg yolks, 2 tablespoons of the sugar, and the milk. Place over simmering water and stir with a wooden spoon until the mixture is warm. Add the coffee and chocolate pieces and continue stirring until the custard is thick. Do not allow it to boil. Remove from the heat, stir in the brandy and cinnamon, and let cool to room temperature.

Whip the cream until it holds soft peaks. Beat the egg whites until almost stiff and continue beating as you gradually add the remaining ¾ cup sugar. Fold the cream and the beaten whites into the cooled custard. Turn into a 6-cup soufflé or other freezer-proof serving dish and freeze until firm.

Ten minutes before serving, remove the Cappuccino from the freezer to soften slightly at room temperature. Garnish with grated chocolate.

YIELD: 6 TO 8 SERVINGS

FROZEN CHOCOLATE MOUSSE
WITH NUT CRUNCH

———————————

A smooth, rich-tasting chocolate mousse that is made without butter. It is laced with a crumbled walnut mixture, which is not a brittle but, in fact, a baked pie crust.

F O R   T H E   N U T   C R U N C H

> 4 tablespoons unsalted but-
>   ter, softened
> 1/4 cup sugar
> 1 tablespoon flour

> 1 cup coarse-chopped walnuts
>   (chopped by hand, not
>   in a blender or food
>   processor)

F O R   T H E   C H O C O L A T E   M O U S S E

> 1 1/2 cups heavy cream
> 8 ounces German's sweet or
>   semi-sweet baking
>   chocolate

> 6 eggs, separated and at
>   room temperature
> 1 1/2 teaspoons vanilla extract
> 2/3 cup sugar

Preheat the oven to 325°.

T O   M A K E   T H E   N U T   C R U N C H

Mix all the ingredients and press into the bottom of an 8-inch square or 9-inch round baking pan. Bake for about 30 minutes, or until dry and very slightly browned. Cool on a wire rack.

T O   M A K E   T H E   M O U S S E

Whip 1 1/4 cups of the cream until it holds soft peaks and set aside. Break up the chocolate into small pieces and combine it with the remaining 1/4 cup cream in the top of a double boiler. Melt over hot, not simmering, water, stirring constantly. Remove the double boiler from the stove, but leave the chocolate over the hot water.

Beat the egg yolks until they are pale and thick. Beat in the vanilla and the melted chocolate. Add this mixture to the whipped cream, beating, if necessary, to combine thoroughly.

Beat the egg whites until they are almost stiff. Continue beating while gradually adding the sugar, until you have a stiff meringue. Carefully fold the egg whites into the chocolate mixture. Break up the nut crunch into coarse pieces and fold it into the mousse. Turn into a 6-to-8-cup freezer-proof serving bowl and freeze.

YIELD: 8 SERVINGS

Chocolate Mousse with Zabaglione Sauce

Follow the preceding recipe, omitting the nut crunch. Serve with Zabaglione sauce (page 204).

FROZEN GRAPEFRUIT SOUFFLÉ AU CHOCOLAT

The surface of this unusual and elegant soufflé is coated with a hard chocolate glaze for a striking and delicious effect.

²/₃ cup milk
4 egg yolks
1 ¹/₃ cups sugar
3 tablespoons flour
1 ¹/₃ cups grapefruit juice
4 egg whites, at room
    temperature

A pinch of cream of tartar
1 ¹/₃ cups heavy cream
²/₃ cup fine-diced candied
    grapefruit peel*

* Available at fine confectioners.

FOR THE CHOCOLATE COATING

4 ounces German's sweet
baking chocolate

1 tablespoon unsalted butter

Tape a heavy foil collar, of double or triple thickness and 3 inches high, around the outside of a 6-cup soufflé dish.

Scald the milk in the top of a double boiler. Beat the egg yolks with ⅓ cup of the sugar until very thick and light. Beat in the flour and then gradually stir in the scalded milk. Return the mixture to the top of the double boiler and cook over simmering water, or directly over medium heat, stirring constantly for 10 to 15 minutes, or until the custard has thickened. Remove from the heat, cool to room temperature, cover, and chill. Stir in the grapefruit juice.

Beat the egg whites until frothy. Add the cream of tartar and continue beating until they begin to stiffen. Gradually beat in ⅔ cup of the remaining sugar. Whip the cream with the remaining ⅓ cup sugar until it holds soft peaks. In a large mixing bowl, fold together the grapefruit custard, the whipped cream, the beaten egg whites, and the candied grapefruit peel. Turn the soufflé into the prepared mold and freeze until firm.

TO MAKE THE CHOCOLATE COATING

Break the chocolate into small pieces. Melt it with the butter in the top of a double boiler over hot, not simmering, water, stirring constantly. Take the frozen soufflé out of the freezer and remove the foil collar. Pour the melted chocolate over the top of the soufflé, spreading it quickly and evenly with a knife, and allowing a little to drip over the raised edges of the soufflé. Return to the freezer.

Approximately ½ hour before serving, move the soufflé from the freezer to the refrigerator to soften slightly.

YIELD: 8 SERVINGS

FROZEN HONEY AND ALMOND CREAM

The flavor of this dessert is rich and mellow, and the texture as smooth as a fine ice cream, punctuated by bits of chopped praline.

3 eggs, separated	*½ teaspoon almond extract*
6 tablespoons light honey	*⅓ cup chopped almond pra-*
A pinch of cream of tartar	*line (page 238) or*
1 cup heavy cream	*toasted slivered almonds*

Beat the egg yolks and the honey with a wire whisk in the top of a double boiler. Place over simmering water and cook, stirring slowly but steadily with a wooden spoon for 8 to 10 minutes, or until slightly thickened. Do not let the mixture boil. Remove from the heat, cool, and chill.

Beat the egg whites until frothy. Add the cream of tartar and beat until stiff. Whip the cream until it holds soft peaks. Stir the almond extract into the chilled custard; then fold in the whipped cream, egg whites, and chopped praline or almonds. Freeze until firm.

YIELD: APPROXIMATELY 1 QUART

FROZEN LIME SOUFFLÉ

A light and refreshing conclusion for almost any meal.

1 cup milk	*½ cup lime juice*
3 egg yolks	*7 egg whites, at room*
1¼ cups sugar	*temperature*
3 tablespoons flour	*A pinch of cream of tartar*
2 tablespoons light rum	*2 cups heavy cream, whipped*
Grated rind of 4 limes	

FOR THE GARNISH

Frosted Grapes (page 256)

Heat the milk slowly in the top of a double boiler until scalded. Beat the egg yolks with ¼ cup of the sugar until thick and lemon-colored. Stir in the flour. Gradually add the hot milk and then return the mixture to the double boiler and cook over hot water, stirring constantly for 15 minutes or until the mixture has thickened and coats a spoon. Remove from the heat, cool to room temperature, cover, and chill. Stir in the rum, lime rind, and lime juice.

Beat the egg whites until foamy; add the cream of tartar and continue beating until they begin to stiffen. Gradually beat in the remaining cup of sugar. The whites should be stiff and glossy. Fold in the chilled lime custard and the whipped cream. Turn into an 8-cup soufflé dish and freeze until firm.

One hour before serving, move the soufflé from the freezer to the refrigerator to soften slightly. To serve, place the soufflé dish on a platter and surround with clusters of Frosted Grapes.

YIELD: 10 SERVINGS

FROZEN MAPLE-PECAN CREAM

5 egg yolks	3 egg whites
6 tablespoons pure maple syrup	A pinch of cream of tartar
	1 cup heavy cream
2 teaspoons dark rum (optional)	½ cup chopped pecans

Combine the egg yolks and maple syrup in the top of a double boiler. Cook over simmering water, stirring slowly but steadily

with a wooden spoon for 8 to 10 minutes or until very thick. Cool
to room temperature, cover, and chill. Stir in the rum, if desired.

Beat the egg whites until frothy. Add the cream of tartar and
continue beating until stiff. Whip the cream until it holds soft
peaks. Fold the whipped cream, egg whites, and chopped pecans
into the maple custard and freeze until firm.

YIELD: APPROXIMATELY 1 QUART

FROZEN ORANGE SOUFFLÉ

Like the Frozen Grapefruit Soufflé (page 213), this dessert can be
made with a chocolate coating.

4 eggs, separated	*A pinch of cream of tartar*
1 cup sugar	*1 1/3 cups heavy cream*
3 tablespoons flour	*2/3 cup fine-diced, good-*
2/3 cup milk, scalded	*quality candied orange*
1 1/2 cups fresh orange juice	*peel or 2 teaspoons*
3 tablespoons orange liqueur	*grated orange rind*

Fit a 6-cup soufflé dish with a 3-inch-high foil collar, or use an
8-cup soufflé dish.

Beat the egg yolks with 1/3 cup of the sugar until thick and light.
Beat in the flour and gradually add the scalded milk. Pour the
mixture into a saucepan and cook over low heat, stirring constantly,
until thick. Remove from the heat, cool to room temperature,
cover, and chill. Stir in the orange juice and orange liqueur.

Beat the egg whites until frothy. Add the cream of tartar and
continue beating until they begin to stiffen. Gradually add 1/3 cup
sugar, beating until the meringue is stiff. Whip the cream with the
remaining 1/3 cup sugar until it holds soft peaks. Fold together the

chilled orange custard, the whipped cream, egg whites, and candied orange peel or orange rind, combining the ingredients gently but thoroughly. Turn into the soufflé dish and freeze until firm.

Approximately 1 hour before serving, move the soufflé from the freezer to the refrigerator to soften slightly.

YIELD: 8 TO 10 SERVINGS

FROZEN PEACH MOUSSE WITH AMARETTI

Two pounds of peaches are used in this mousse to produce a very pronounced fresh peach flavor. Crumbled *amaretti* (Italian macaroons) are folded in to give it texture and a barely detectable almond flavor. Serve it with a plate of Lime-Lace Cookies (page 273) or *amaretti*.

> 2 pounds peaches (6 to 7
>   medium)
> 2 tablespoons lemon juice
> 6 egg yolks
> 1 cup sugar
> 2 tablespoons flour
> 4 egg whites, at room
>   temperature
>
> A pinch of cream of tartar
> 3 tablespoons peach brandy
>   or cognac
> 1 cup heavy cream, whipped
> 1 1/2 cups coarse-crumbled
>   amaretti

To prepare the peaches for peeling, immerse them in rapidly boiling water for 20 to 30 seconds. Peel, remove the pits, and chop them coarsely. Purée the peaches with the lemon juice in a food processor or blender, a little at a time.

Beat the egg yolks with 1/4 cup of the sugar until they are thick and lemon-colored. Beat in the flour and combine this mixture with the peach purée. Heat the mixture in a double boiler or over low heat, stirring constantly with a large wooden spoon or rubber spatula for about 15 minutes or until it is quite hot and has thickened. Remove and cool partially at room temperature and then place in the refrigerator to complete cooling. Or stir the peach custard over a large bowl filled with ice cubes to cool rapidly.

When the custard has cooled, beat the egg whites in a very large bowl until they are foamy. Add the cream of tartar and continue beating until they begin to stiffen. Add the remaining ¾ cup sugar gradually, beating until you have a stiff meringue.

Stir the peach brandy or cognac into the peach custard. Fold the custard into the beaten egg whites. Then fold in the whipped cream and the crumbled *amaretti*. Turn into an 8-cup soufflé dish and freeze. About 2 hours before serving, remove from the freezer and place in the refrigerator to soften a bit.

YIELD: 10 TO 12 SERVINGS

FROZEN PEAR-PRALINE SOUFFLÉ

A creamy pear mixture speckled with bits of hazelnut praline.

2½ pounds Bartlett pears (5 large pears), peeled, cored, and chopped fine
2 tablespoons lemon juice
½ cup light cream
A 2-inch piece of vanilla bean
4 eggs, separated

A pinch of cream of tartar
1 cup sugar
⅓ cup water
1 cup heavy cream, whipped
1 cup coarse-chopped hazelnut praline (page 238)

Tape or tie a 3-inch-high heavy foil collar around the outside of an 8-cup soufflé dish.

Cook the pears with the lemon juice in a large, heavy pot at a low boil for 20 to 25 minutes, stirring frequently, until they are as thick as applesauce. Cool to room temperature and reserve.

Scald the light cream in the top of a double boiler with the vanilla bean. Beat the egg yolks until thick and light in color. Stir in a little of the hot cream and then pour the mixture back into the pan and cook over hot water, stirring constantly, for about 15 minutes or until thickened. Cool, cover, and chill.

Beat the egg whites until frothy. Add the cream of tartar and continue beating until stiff but not dry. Combine the sugar and water in a small, heavy saucepan and boil for 5 minutes, or until a little of the syrup can be formed into a soft ball when dropped in a glass of ice water. Pour the syrup in a thin stream over the egg whites while beating constantly with an electric mixer.

Remove the vanilla bean from the cooled custard and discard. Stir the custard into the pear purée. Then, in a very large bowl, fold together the custard-pear mixture, the beaten whites, the whipped cream, and the chopped praline. Turn into the prepared soufflé dish and freeze.

Approximately 2 hours before serving, move the soufflé from the freezer to the refrigerator to soften slightly.

YIELD: 10 TO 12 SERVINGS

GINGER ICE CREAM

This ice cream has a very soft and creamy texture. It is flavored with bits of preserved ginger stem and a little brandy.

2 cups heavy cream
3 tablespoons brandy
3 tablespoons syrup from the preserved ginger stem
1 teaspoon vanilla extract
⅓ cup fine-diced preserved ginger stem
3 egg whites
⅔ cup sugar

Whip the cream with the brandy, syrup, and vanilla until it holds soft peaks. Fold in the ginger stem. Set aside. Wash the beaters thoroughly and beat the egg whites until they hold firm peaks. Continue beating while gradually adding the sugar. Fold the whites into the cream mixture. Turn into a serving bowl, cover with plastic wrap, and freeze until firm.

YIELD: 6 TO 8 SERVINGS

LEMON SHERBET

²/₃ *cup sugar*
²/₃ *cup water*

½ *cup lemon juice*
1 *cup heavy cream*

Combine the sugar and water in a small, heavy saucepan. Boil for about 10 minutes or until a little of the syrup can be formed into a soft ball when dropped into a glass of ice water. Remove from the heat, cool to room temperature, and stir in the lemon juice. Whip the cream until it holds soft peaks and fold into the lemon syrup. Freeze.

YIELD: APPROXIMATELY 3 CUPS

LIME AND HONEY ICE CREAM

This is a simple dessert, but I find it a rather exotic combination of flavors. The honey creates a wonderfully smooth texture.

1½ cups heavy cream	*6 tablespoons lime juice*
¾ cup light honey	*Grated rind of 1 small lime*

Whip the cream until it holds soft peaks. Beat in the honey and the lime juice and rind. Freeze until firm.

YIELD: APPROXIMATELY 1 QUART

MOCHA ICE CREAM

This is a fine dessert, creamy in texture and delicately flavored. Serve it as it is or, for elaborate dinners, accompanied by Chocolate Fudge Sauce (page 237) and Chocolate Hazelnut Cookies (page 269) or Mocha Hazelnut Crescents (page 274).

5 egg whites, at room	*2 tablespoons instant coffee*
temperature	*powder or granules*
A pinch of cream of tartar	*1 tablespoon unsweetened*
1 cup plus 3 tablespoons	*cocoa, sifted*
sugar	*2½ cups heavy cream*
⅔ cup water	

FOR THE TOPPING

*Grated semi-sweet chocolate or Chocolate Fudge Sauce
(page 237)*

Beat the egg whites until frothy. Add the cream of tartar and continue beating until stiffened but not dry. In a small, heavy saucepan, stir together the sugar and water. Set over medium-high heat and bring to a boil. Boil without stirring for about 5 minutes or until a little of the syrup can be formed into a soft ball when dropped in a glass of ice water. Pour the syrup over the egg whites in a very thin stream while beating constantly with an electric beater.

If the instant coffee is powdered, beat it into the egg-white mixture. If it is freeze-dried, dissolve the granules in 1 tablespoon hot water and cool slightly before beating into the egg whites.

Add the sifted cocoa to the heavy cream and whip the cream until it holds soft peaks. Fold into the egg-white mixture. Freeze until firm in a 7-to-8-cup serving dish.

To serve, garnish with grated chocolate or serve Chocolate Fudge Sauce on the side.

YIELD: APPROXIMATELY 7 CUPS

PEACH ICE CREAM

A smooth, mellow ice cream with a subtle brandy flavor. It is laced with chopped peaches, which are precooked so that they will not turn "icy."

½ cup half-and-half or light cream	*¾ cup sugar*
6 egg yolks, lightly beaten	*1 cinnamon stick*
1 pound peaches (3 or 4 large)	*2½ tablespoons brandy*
	2 teaspoons vanilla extract
	1 cup heavy cream

Heat the half-and-half in the top of a double boiler or in a small, heavy saucepan. Stir it gradually into the beaten egg yolks and then return the mixture to the pan and heat over barely simmering water or a low flame, stirring constantly, until thickened. Cool to room temperature.

Immerse the peaches in boiling water for 20 seconds and then peel them. Chop into fairly small pieces and put them in a heavy saucepan with ½ cup of the sugar and the cinnamon stick. Slowly bring the mixture to a boil and simmer, stirring frequently, for about 20 minutes or until the syrup is reduced to a thick sauce. Remove from the heat and cool. Remove the cinnamon stick and stir in the brandy and vanilla.

Whip the cream with the remaining sugar until it holds soft peaks. Combine the cooled peach mixture with the custard and fold it all into the whipped cream. Cover and freeze for a few hours until thickened; stir and freeze until firm.

YIELD: APPROXIMATELY 1 QUART

PEAR-HONEY SORBET

An unusual and delicately flavored sorbet.

1½ pounds ripe Bartlett or Anjou pears (4 or 5 medium)	*¼ cup light honey*
	½ cup milk
	2 tablespoons white port
2 tablespoons lemon juice	*A small pinch of salt*
2 tablespoons sugar	*1 cup heavy cream*

Immerse the pears, one at a time, in boiling water for about 30 seconds so that they can be peeled easily. Peel, core, and chop them coarse. Drop the pears into a food processor or blender with the lemon juice and purée. Add the sugar, honey, milk, port, and salt and blend. Turn into a mixing bowl and freeze for a few hours until firm around the edges. Then remove from the freezer and beat with an electric mixer until smooth and light. Whip the cream until it holds soft peaks and fold it into the pear mixture. Freeze until firm.

If the sorbet seems too firm, remove it from the freezer about 30 minutes before serving to soften slightly.

YIELD: 4 TO 5 CUPS

RHUBARB SHERBET WITH STRAWBERRIES

An unusual sherbet combining rhubarb and cassis.

> *3 pounds rhubarb, washed*
> *and chopped*
> *1 3/4 cups sugar*
> *Grated zest of 1 lemon*
> *6 tablespoons crème de cassis*
> *liqueur or 8 tablespoons*
> *cassis syrup*

> *1/2 cup reserved rhubarb juice*
> *1 cup heavy cream*

FOR THE GARNISH

> *2 pints fresh strawberries*
> *Sugar*

> *Crème de cassis or cassis*
> *syrup*

Preheat the oven to 325°. Put the rhubarb, 1 1/2 cups sugar, and the lemon zest in a heavy casserole, cover, and bake until soft (30 to 40 minutes.) Drain, reserving the juice, and purée the rhubarb in a food processor. Stir in the cassis.

Boil down 1/2 cup of the reserved rhubarb juice to 1/4 cup and stir it into the rhubarb purée. Freeze until firm.

Whip the cream with the remaining 1/4 cup sugar. Break the

frozen rhubarb into chunks and purée it, in small batches, in a food processor until smooth. The mixture should have the consistency of frozen juice concentrate. Turn into a mixing bowl and fold in the whipped cream. Cover with plastic wrap and refreeze immediately.

Rinse, hull, and slice the strawberries. Just before serving, mix them with a little sugar and cassis. Spoon some of the berries over each serving of sherbet.

YIELD: 6 CUPS OF SHERBET OR 8 SERVINGS

STRAWBERRY AND HONEY ICE CREAM

1 pint strawberries	*1 cup heavy cream*
2 teaspoons vanilla extract	*⅓ cup light honey*

Wash and hull the berries, discarding any that are soft or yellow. Purée enough to make 1 cup. Stir in the vanilla.

Whip the cream until it holds soft peaks. Fold the strawberry purée and the honey into the whipped cream. Freeze until frozen around the edges. Stir and freeze until firm.

YIELD: APPROXIMATELY 3 CUPS

Quick Fruit Ice Creams

In making fruit-based ice creams over the past several years, I have found that cooking the fruit with sugar, rather than simply purée-ing it, produces a smooth and soft ice cream without any icy bits of fruit and with a more intense flavor. Since I was, in fact, making a jam, it occurred to me that the same results could be achieved by substituting bottled jam or preserves for the fresh fruit and sugar in my recipes. This is a much quicker method, and you are not limited to fruits in season. Recipes follow for black cherry, peach, raspberry, and strawberry ice creams. You can, of course, experiment with other fruit preserves. Be sure to use a good-quality commercially prepared jam, one not too stiff or sweet (better still are homemade preserves, if you have them). The proportions may have to be altered slightly in each recipe, according to the jam you are using, as some brands will be sweeter than others. In calling these "quick" ice creams, I refer to the time invested by the cook; once they are put into your freezer, they will require the usual 4 to 6 hours to become firm.

QUICK BLACK CHERRY ICE CREAM

Black cherry preserves are not easy to find, except in specialty stores. If you are successful in locating a jar, this ice cream is well worth trying. Two excellent brands are imported from Switzerland: Hero and Fischlin. If you use the latter, which contains kirsch, do not add the kirsch called for in the recipe.

> 2 cups heavy cream
> ⅔ cup Hero or ¾ cup
>   Fischlin black cherry
>   preserves

> 2½ tablespoons kirsch
>   (optional)

Using an electric mixer, whip the cream with the preserves and kirsch, if you are using it, until the mixture holds soft peaks. Turn into a serving bowl, cover with plastic wrap, and freeze until firm.
YIELD: APPROXIMATELY I QUART

QUICK PEACH ICE CREAM

2 *cups heavy cream*   2 *to 3 tablespoons brandy*
1 *cup peach preserves or jam*
   (*such as Smucker's*)

Using an electric mixer, whip the cream and the peach jam until the mixture holds soft peaks. Fold in the brandy, according to taste. Turn into a serving bowl, cover with plastic wrap, and freeze until firm.

YIELD: APPROXIMATELY 1 QUART

QUICK RASPBERRY ICE CREAM

This ice cream has a pure, fresh, raspberry flavor and is best without the addition of any liqueur. Seedless blackberry preserves may be substituted for the raspberry.

2 *cups heavy cream*
¾ *cup seedless red raspberry preserves* (*preferably Trappist*
   brand)

Using an electric mixer, whip the cream with the raspberry preserves until the mixture holds soft peaks. Turn into a serving bowl, cover with plastic wrap, and freeze until firm. Remove from the freezer and let stand at room temperature for 15 to 30 minutes before serving.

YIELD: APPROXIMATELY 1 QUART

QUICK STRAWBERRY ICE CREAM

2 cups heavy cream
*¾ cup plus 1 tablespoon
    strawberry jam or
    preserves*

*2 tablespoons curaçao
    (optional)*

Using an electric mixer, whip the cream with the jam and curaçao
until the mixture holds soft peaks. Turn into a serving bowl, cover
with plastic wrap, and freeze until firm.

YIELD: APPROXIMATELY 1 QUART

Ices

The following fruit ices are perfect summer desserts. They are simple, light, and refreshing; and each has a crisp and distinctive flavor.
Although they seem rather creamy, like milk sherbets, they are
composed of little more than a sweetened fruit purée or juice.

None of these recipes requires an ice cream freezer, and yet all are
smooth-textured and will not crystallize and harden after freezing.
After many experiments, I found a combination of methods to
ensure success: using a boiled sugar syrup or honey as a sweetener;
adding dissolved gelatin; and puréeing the ice, after freezing, in a
food processor or blender. With these factors in mind, you will be
able to vary and adapt the recipes to almost any fruit base. They are
so easy to make that I often serve two scoops of different flavored ices
for dessert, such as Honeydew and Tangerine, Blackberry and
Lemon, or Grapefruit and Strawberry.

BLUEBERRY ICE

The flavor of the white rum cannot be detected in this recipe, but it has a distinct effect on the blueberries, which, without it, tend to be rather flat. Do not substitute dark rum, which is too strong and cloying; if white rum is not available, use cognac or a good brandy.

1 pint blueberries	*A pinch of salt*
½ cup sugar	*1 teaspoon unflavored gelatin*
¼ cup water	*3 tablespoons cold water*
1½ tablespoons lime juice	*2 tablespoons white rum*
1 cinnamon stick	

Wash the blueberries, discarding any that are soft or green. Put them in a large, heavy saucepan with the sugar, ¼ cup water, the lime juice, cinnamon stick, and salt. Stir and bring slowly to a boil. Boil gently for 15 minutes, stirring occasionally. Remove from the heat, discard the cinnamon stick, and purée in a food processor or blender.

Soften the gelatin in 3 tablespoons cold water and dissolve over low heat, stirring constantly. Stir into the blueberry mixture. Add the rum and freeze until firm. Break the ice into chunks and purée in a food processor or blender until smooth but not liquefied. It should remain very thick. Refreeze immediately.

YIELD: APPROXIMATELY 2¾ CUPS

CANTALOUPE ICE

This sherbet is made distinctive by the unexpected combination of cantaloupe and Pernod. The taste is subtle and memorable.

1 medium-size cantaloupe	*1 tablespoon lime or lemon*
¼ cup sugar	*juice*
⅓ cup water	*1 tablespoon light honey*
1 envelope unflavored gelatin	*1 tablespoon Pernod*
2 tablespoons cold water	

Cut the melon in half, discard the seeds, and scoop out the flesh. Purée it in a food processor or blender. You should have about 2 cups of purée.

In a small saucepan, stir together the sugar and ⅓ cup water. Slowly bring the mixture to a boil and boil 3 to 5 minutes or until the syrup spins a thread when a little is dropped into a glass of ice water. Cool slightly. With the motor running, add the syrup to the melon purée in the food processor.

Soften the gelatin in 2 tablespoons water and the lime or lemon juice and dissolve over low heat, stirring constantly. Cool and blend thoroughly with the melon mixture. Blend in the honey and Pernod. Freeze until firm. Break the ice into chunks and purée in a food processor or, in batches, in a blender until smooth but not liquefied. It should remain very thick and cold but without ice crystals. Refreeze immediately.

YIELD: APPROXIMATELY 1 PINT

GRAPEFRUIT-HONEY ICE

An interesting, rather tart flavor. Serve with thin, crisp cookies or chocolate-dipped candied grapefruit peel.

1 envelope unflavored gelatin   *6 tablespoons light honey*
2¼ cups grapefruit juice   *1½ tablespoons light rum*

Soften the gelatin in ¼ cup of the grapefruit juice and dissolve over low heat, stirring constantly. Cool slightly and then stir into the remaining grapefruit juice. Mix in the honey and rum and freeze until firm. Break into chunks and purée in a food processor or, in batches, in a blender until smooth but not liquefied. It should be cold and thick but without ice crystals. Refreeze immediately.

YIELD: APPROXIMATELY 2½ CUPS

HONEYDEW ICE

A cooling summer dessert with a wonderfully delicate flavor.

1 small honeydew melon (5   *1 envelope unflavored gelatin*
    inches in diameter)   *2 tablespoons cold water*
¼ cup light honey   *1½ tablespoons lime juice*

Cut the melon in half, scoop out and discard the seeds, and cut th flesh of the melon from the rind. Purée it in a food processor o blender. You should have 2 generous cups of purée. Stir in th honey.

Soften the gelatin in the water and lime juice and dissolve ove low heat, stirring constantly. Stir off the heat for a minute to cool. Then stir into the melon purée, combining thoroughly.

Freeze until firm. Break up into chunks and purée until smooth but not liquefied, in a food processor or, in batches, in a blender. The mixture should remain very cold and thick but free from ice crystals. Refreeze immediately.

YIELD: APPROXIMATELY I PINT

LEMON ICE

One of the most popular and refreshing of summer desserts. Garnish each serving with a sprig of fresh mint or make the candied lemon peel described below.

F O R   T H E   I C E

> *1 cup sugar*
> *2¼ cups water*
>
> *¾ cup lemon juice*

F O R   T H E   C A N D I E D   P E E L

> *3 large lemons*
> *1 cup sugar*
>
> *1 cup water*

T O   M A K E   T H E   I C E

Stir together the sugar and water in a small, heavy saucepan. Heat to boiling and boil for 2 minutes. Cool and stir in the lemon juice. Freeze until firm. Purée in a food processor or blender until smooth but do not liquefy. The ice should remain very thick. Refreeze immediately.

T O   M A K E   T H E   C A N D I E D   P E E L

Peel the rind from the lemons with a vegetable parer from top to bottom in long strips, taking care to cut off only the yellow zest and none of the white pith. Cut each strip into narrow julienne strips. Combine the sugar and water in a saucepan, add the rind, and bring to a boil. Boil for about 15 to 20 minutes or until the rind is transparent and has absorbed some of the syrup. Drain and use the rind as a garnish for the lemon ice.

YIELD: 3 CUPS

Lime Ice

Follow the preceding recipe for Lemon Ice, substituting lime juice and peel for lemon. If desired, add 1 tablespoon white rum.

RASPBERRY-ALMOND ICE

4 pints raspberries   ½ cup almond paste (not
1 cup sugar   marzipan)

Wash the berries and drain well. Put them in a large, heavy kettle with the sugar. Slowly bring to a simmer, stirring occasionally. Cook for 1 or 2 minutes. Remove from the heat and strain through a fine sieve to remove the seeds, pressing through as much pulp as possible.

Put the almond paste in a food processor and, with the motor running, add the raspberry purée in a thin stream. Freeze until firm. Break into chunks and purée, in batches, in a food processor until smooth but not liquefied. Refreeze immediately.

YIELD: APPROXIMATELY 1 QUART OR 6 SERVINGS

STRAWBERRY-CASSIS ICE

4 pints strawberries   6 tablespoons cassis syrup
⅔ cup sugar

Rinse and dry the strawberries. Hull them and cut each in half. Put the berries and sugar in a large kettle and slowly bring to a simmer. Cook gently, stirring frequently, for 5 or 6 minutes, or until the berries are soft. Purée in a food processor, reserving the juice. Turn into a bowl or freezer container and stir in the reserved strawberry juice and the cassis syrup. Freeze until firm. Break into chunks and purée, in four batches, in a food processor until smooth but not liquefied. As each batch is puréed, return it to the freezer before it has a chance to melt. Freeze until firm.

YIELD: 5½ CUPS OR 6 TO 8 SERVINGS

TANGERINE ICE

3 tablespoons sugar
¼ cup water
2 cups tangerine juice (9
    medium-size tangerines)

1 envelope unflavored gelatin
3 tablespoons cold water
2 tablespoons curaçao or
    other orange liqueur

Combine the sugar with ¼ cup water in a small saucepan. Slowly bring to a boil and boil for 3 to 5 minutes or until the syrup spins a thread when a little is dropped into a glass of ice water. Cool slightly and stir into the tangerine juice.

Soften the gelatin in 3 tablespoons cold water and dissolve over low heat, stirring constantly. Stir to cool and combine thoroughly with the tangerine mixture. Add the curaçao and freeze until firm. Break the ice into chunks and purée in a food processor or, in batches, in a blender until smooth but not liquefied. It should remain cold and thick but without ice crystals. Refreeze immediately.

YIELD: APPROXIMATELY 1 PINT

WATERMELON-CASSIS ICE

Cassis is the perfect complementary flavor for watermelon; it adds character without overpowering the delicate melon taste.

1 wedge watermelon, approx-
imately 10 by 6 inches,
or enough to make 4
cups purée
1 cup sugar

½ cup water
2 envelopes unflavored gelatin
⅓ cup cold water
⅓ cup crème de cassis

Remove the rind and seeds from the watermelon. In a food processor or blender, in batches, purée enough to make 4 cups.

Combine the sugar and ½ cup water in a small, heavy saucepan and slowly bring to a boil. Boil for 7 to 8 minutes or until a little of the syrup can be formed into a soft ball when dropped into a glass of ice water. Allow to cool while you dissolve the gelatin.

Soften the gelatin in ⅓ cup cold water and dissolve over low heat, stirring constantly. Stir the dissolved gelatin into the sugar syrup; cool slightly and stir into the watermelon liquid, combining thoroughly. Stir in the crème de cassis and freeze until firm. Break into chunks and purée, in batches, in a food processor or blender until the ice is smooth but not liquefied. Refreeze immediately.

YIELD: APPROXIMATELY 6 CUPS

Dessert Sauces and Toppings

CHOCOLATE FUDGE SAUCE

3 ounces unsweetened chocolate, broken into very
   small pieces
1 tablespoon unsalted butter

3 tablespoons milk
7 tablespoons sugar
1/2 cup heavy cream
1 1/2 teaspoons vanilla extract

Put the chocolate in the top of a double boiler with the butter, milk, and sugar. Stir constantly over hot, not simmering, water until smooth. Remove from the heat and stir in the cream and vanilla extract.

Serve at room temperature. If refrigerated, heat gently, stirring until melted, in the top of a double boiler.

YIELD: APPROXIMATELY 1 CUP

CRÈME FRAÎCHE

A thickened, soured cream to serve with fresh berries or other fruit.

1 cup heavy cream
2 teaspoons buttermilk or 1/3 cup sour cream

Put the cream and buttermilk or sour cream in a lidded glass jar and shake vigorously. Unscrew the lid, leave loosely covered, and let stand in a warm place until the mixture is very thick. (This will take between 12 hours and 2 days, depending on the temperature.) After it has thickened, the crème fraîche should be refrigerated. It will keep well for several days.

YIELD: APPROXIMATELY 1 CUP

FLUFFY LEMON SAUCE

—————————◆—————————

2 egg yolks, *lightly beaten*
1/4 cup lemon juice (1 *large*
      lemon)
Grated rind of 1 *large*
      lemon

1/4 cup sugar
2 egg whites
A pinch of cream of tartar

Combine the egg yolks, lemon juice and rind, and the sugar in a small, heavy saucepan. Place over medium-low heat and cook, stirring constantly, until thickened (about 5 minutes). Remove from the heat.

Beat the egg whites until frothy. Add the cream of tartar and beat until stiff. Continue beating as you gradually add the lemon custard. Cool. This sauce is at its best the day it is made. If kept longer, it will still taste good, but the whites will deflate and the sauce will be more liquefied.

YIELD: APPROXIMATELY 2 CUPS

PRALINE

—————————◆—————————

This is a hard, clear brittle that is crushed and used to add flavor and texture to many desserts.

1/3 cup hot water
1 tablespoon honey
1 cup sugar

1/2 cup blanched, slivered
      almonds, lightly
      toasted, or 1/2 cup
      blanched, chopped
      hazelnuts

In a heavy saucepan, pour hot water over the honey and sugar and stir, off the heat, until dissolved. Place over heat and gradually bring to a boil. Then let the mixture boil until it reaches 300° to 305° on a candy thermometer and is a light caramel color. Stir in the chopped nuts and pour the mixture onto a well-oiled marble slab or baking sheet. When cold, remove from the sheet and break into coarse pieces with a hammer. The praline will keep indefinitely in a closed jar.

YIELD: 1½ CUPS CRUSHED PRALINE

RASPBERRY SAUCE

Two 10-ounce packages fro-
zen raspberries in syrup

4 teaspoons lemon juice
1 tablespoon kirsch

Heat the berries in their syrup and strain through a fine sieve. Add the lemon juice and kirsch.

YIELD: APPROXIMATELY 2 CUPS

VANILLA CUSTARD SAUCE

1 cup milk
¾ cup half-and-half or
light cream
4 egg yolks, lightly beaten

6 tablespoons sugar
1½ teaspoons vanilla extract

Rinse a heavy saucepan or the top of a double boiler in cold water and pour in the milk and half-and-half or cream. Heat until almost simmering. Combine the egg yolks and sugar and stir in a little of the hot liquid. Then pour this mixture into the rest of the liquid and heat, stirring constantly, over barely simmering water or medium-low heat for about 5 minutes, until the custard is slightly thickened and coats a metal spoon. Remove from the heat, strain into a bowl, and stir in the vanilla extract.

YIELD: APPROXIMATELY 2 CUPS

ZABAGLIONE

See page 204.

6: Accompaniments

Breads and Crackers

BISCUITS

These crisp and flaky biscuits go well with any of the entrée mousses or salads.

2 cups sifted flour
2¼ teaspoons baking powder
¾ teaspoon salt
5 tablespoons unsalted butter, chilled and cut into small pieces

1 tablespoon vegetable shortening, chilled
A scant ⅔ cup milk

Preheat the oven to 450°.

Resift the flour with the baking powder and salt into a mixing bowl. With the tips of your fingers, rub in the butter and shortening until the mixture resembles oatmeal in texture. Stir in the milk, mixing only until combined. Knead for 1 or 2 turns on a lightly floured board, being careful not to overwork the dough.

Roll out the dough to a thickness of ⅜ to ½ inch. Using a floured biscuit cutter or the rim of a glass, cut into rounds 1¾ to 2 inches in diameter. When cutting the biscuits, press straight down and lift the cutter up without twisting, as twisting seals the edges together and prevents the biscuits from rising fully. Place about 1 inch apart on an ungreased baking sheet. Brush the tops with milk if a slight sheen is desired. Bake for about 12 minutes or until lightly browned. Cool on a wire rack.

YIELD: APPROXIMATELY 2 DOZEN

CHEESE TWISTS

Flaky, Cheddar-flavored strips are made from pastry dough. They are good served with salads or as an hors d'oeuvre.

1 ½ cups flour
5 ounces grated Cheddar cheese (1 ¼ cups)
3 tablespoons vegetable shortening, chilled
1 tablespoon unsalted butter, chilled
2 to 3 tablespoons dry white wine or water, chilled
Fresh-grated Parmesan cheese

Preheat the oven to 400°.

Stir together the flour and Cheddar cheese. With the tips of your fingers, rub the butter and vegetable shortening into the flour, just until the fat is broken down into small bits. Add a little white wine or water to form a dough. Roll out on a lightly floured board to a thickness of ⅛ inch. Sprinkle on a little Parmesan cheese and press it in lightly with the rolling pin. Cut the dough into strips ½ by 4½ inches and twist each strip into a corkscrew shape. Place on ungreased cookie sheets and bake for about 10 minutes or until dry but not browned. Cool on a wire rack.

YIELD: APPROXIMATELY 5 ½ DOZEN

CORN MUFFINS

1 cup flour
1 tablespoon sugar
2 teaspoons baking powder
1/2 teaspoon baking soda
3/4 teaspoon salt
1 cup yellow cornmeal

1 egg, *lightly beaten*
2 tablespoons *light honey*
1 cup buttermilk
4 tablespoons unsalted butter, melted

Preheat the oven to 425°. Generously grease a set of muffin tins.

Sift the flour, sugar, baking powder, baking soda, and salt together into a mixing bowl, and stir in the cornmeal. Beat the egg
and honey together in a separate bowl and mix in the buttermilk.
Add this to the flour mixture with the melted butter and stir only
until combined. The batter should be lumpy. Fill the prepared
muffin tins to 3/4 capacity and bake for 15 to 20 minutes or until
lightly browned and a toothpick tests clean.

YIELD: 12 MUFFINS

CROUTONS

Use these to garnish soups or salads.

3 slices of firm white bread
 (such as Pepperidge
 Farm)
1 tablespoon butter

2 tablespoons vegetable oil or
 olive oil
1 large garlic clove, peeled
 and crushed (optional)

Spread the bread on a rack and let it dry for a few hours. Trim off
the crusts and cut into small cubes.

Heat the butter, oil, and garlic, if desired, in a large skillet. When it begins to sizzle, add the bread cubes and sauté over medium heat, stirring constantly, for 3 to 5 minutes or until lightly browned on all sides. Store in an airtight container.

YIELD: 1 CUP

Herb-Parmesan Croutons

Combine the following in a small mixing bowl.

2 ½ tablespoons grated Parmesan cheese	¼ teaspoon dried basil
¼ teaspoon dried marjoram	¼ teaspoon dried thyme

Follow the preceding recipe for croutons. After sautéing the bread cubes, toss them, while still warm, in the bowl with the herbs and Parmesan.

CUBAN BREAD

This bread is much like a French *baguette,* with one important difference—it is not difficult to make. Moreover, it can be made with relative speed as yeast breads go, because the second rising takes place in the oven. This type of bread does not keep well. If you do not use it the day it is made, store in the freezer.

2 packages active dry yeast	Approximately 5 cups un-
2¼ cups lukewarm water	bleached white flour,
(110°–115°)	preferably bread flour
2 teaspoons sugar	¼ cup cornmeal
2 teaspoons salt	

Stir the yeast into the warm water, add the sugar, and let stand for 10 minutes to proof. Transfer the mixture to a very large, flat-bottomed mixing bowl. Add the salt and gradually add 3 cups of the flour, beating well with a wooden spoon after each addition. Let the dough rest for 10 minutes. With your hands, work in enough of the remaining flour to make a very moist but workable dough. Knead on a lightly floured board, dusting with a little additional flour as necessary to prevent sticking, for about 5 minutes or until smooth and elastic. Oil a bowl, put in the dough, and turn it over so that the top surface is oiled. Cover with plastic wrap and set in a warm, draft-free place to rise until more than doubled in bulk. This will take 1 hour or longer.

Punch down and divide the dough into thirds. On a lightly floured board, roll each with the palms of your hands into a long, narrow loaf approximately 2 inches by 14 inches. Dust a large baking sheet with the cornmeal and place the loaves on the sheet. With a very sharp knife, make diagonal slashes on the top of each loaf in 3 or 4 places. Brush with water and let rest for 5 minutes. Set the loaves in the middle of a cold oven. Turn the oven temperature to 400° and bake for 35 to 40 minutes or until the loaves are browned and sound hollow when tapped.

YIELD: 3 LONG LOAVES

Whole Wheat Cuban Bread

Follow the preceding recipe for Cuban Bread, but use half whole wheat flour and half unbleached white flour.

GEORGIAN CHEESE-FILLED BREAD

A cross between a bread and a pie, this is made from a yeast dough that encases a cheese mixture. It would make a splendid accompaniment to many of the salads in Chapter 2, particularly the green salads. Serve it at room temperature or reheat just before serving.

FOR THE DOUGH

1 package active dry yeast
2 teaspoons sugar
½ cup warm water (105°–
    115°)

1 teaspoon salt
4 tablespoons unsalted but-
    ter, softened
1½ to 1¾ cups flour

FOR THE CHEESE FILLING

1 egg, *lightly beaten*
1 pound grated Gruyère or
    Muenster cheese
2 tablespoons minced parsley
    (optional)

⅓ cup minced chives
    (optional)

F O R   T H E   G L A Z E

1 egg yolk beaten with 1 tablespoon water

Stir the yeast and sugar into the warm water and allow to proof.

Combine the yeast mixture, salt, and butter in a mixing bowl. Stir in enough of the flour to make a firm but moist dough. Knead for 3 to 4 minutes on a lightly floured board. Place the dough in an oiled bowl, turn it over so that the surface is oiled, cover the bowl with plastic wrap, and set it in a warm place to rise for 2 to 3 hours. (Because of the high proportion of fat, this dough will not rise as much as most bread doughs.)

While the bread is rising, prepare the cheese filling. In a mixing bowl, thoroughly combine the egg and cheese and, if desired, the parsley and chives. Cover and reserve.

When the dough is almost twice its original bulk, punch it down and roll it out on a lightly floured board into a circle 16 inches in diameter. Drape the dough over an 8- or 9-inch pie tin and fill it with the cheese mixture. Pull up the excess dough that hangs over the edges of the tin in overlapping folds, stretching if necessary, to meet in the center and form a top crust. Brush with the glaze and preheat the oven to 375°. Let the dough rest for 15 or 20 minutes before baking. Bake for 50 minutes or until lightly browned. Cool on a wire rack. Serve at room temperature or reheat before serving.

YIELD: 8 SERVINGS

GOUGÈRE

This light, crisp, airy ring, made from cream puff pastry, or *pâté à chou,* and flavored with cheese, is a good accompaniment to any of the entrée salads.

1 cup flour
¼ teaspoon salt
4 tablespoons unsalted but-
    ter, cut into several
    pieces
¾ cup boiling water

4 eggs, at room temperature
⅓ cup grated extra-sharp
    Cheddar or Parmesan
    cheese

Generously butter and chill a large baking sheet. Preheat the oven to 425°.

Combine the flour and salt and set it next to the stove.

Put the butter and boiling water in a heavy 1-quart saucepan and return to a boil. When the butter has melted, remove the pan from the heat and add the flour all at once, stirring vigorously to combine. Return to the heat and cook for a few minutes, stirring with a wooden spoon, until the mixture is formed into a ball and does not stick to the sides of the pan. Remove from the heat and beat in the eggs, one at a time, incorporating each thoroughly before adding another. Then stir in the grated cheese, reserving about 1 tablespoon.

Spoon onto the baking sheet in 8 connecting mounds to form a ring, and sprinkle with the reserved cheese. Bake for 15 minutes or until lightly browned. Lower the temperature to 350° and continue baking for 30 to 40 minutes longer or until the Gougère is hollow and dry in the center. Serve immediately or cool on a wire rack and reheat before serving.

YIELD: 8 SERVINGS

MELBA TOAST

Preheat the oven to 250°.

Using a knife with a long serrated blade, cut slices as thin as possible from an uncut loaf of firm, fine-grained white bread. One-eighth inch thick is fine; ¼ inch is too thick and will taste more like stale bread than melba toast. Trim off the crusts and cut each slice in half diagonally. Place on an ungreased baking sheet and bake for 15 to 20 minutes or until very lightly browned.

MUSHROOM TOASTS

Small, savory toasts made from Syrian bread, which can be served with salads or as hors d'oeuvres.

Two 8-inch or eight 4-inch loaves of Syrian bread
12 ounces mushrooms, cleaned, trimmed, and minced
3 tablespoons unsalted butter
¼ cup dry white wine
1 tablespoon lemon juice
2 anchovy fillets
1½ tablespoons flour
Salt
Fresh-ground pepper

Put the minced mushrooms in a large skillet with the butter, wine, lemon juice, and anchovies and sauté gently until the mushrooms begin to render their juice. Sprinkle with the flour and stir to combine. Turn up the heat and cook, stirring, until the moisture evaporates and the mixture is slightly thickened. Season to taste with salt and pepper.

Split the Syrian bread in half and cut each circle into small wedges or triangles. Spread the cut side of each wedge with the mushroom mixture. Place on baking sheets, cover with plastic wrap, and let stand until serving or refrigerate if you are making them a day ahead.

Before serving, preheat the oven to 400°. Bake for 5 minutes or until the bread is lightly toasted.

YIELD: 5 TO 6 DOZEN 2-INCH WEDGES

OATMEAL BREAD

———————————◆———————————

1 *package active dry yeast*
1/4 *cup warm water (105°–115°)*
1/2 *teaspoon sugar*
1 *cup milk*
1 *cup rolled oats (not instant)*
1 *cup cracked wheat*
3 *tablespoons unsalted butter, softened*

3 *tablespoons light honey*
2 *teaspoons molasses*
1 *teaspoon salt*
1 *egg, lightly beaten*
2½ *to 2¾ cups unbleached white flour, preferably bread flour*

Dissolve the yeast in the warm water; stir in the sugar and allow to proof. Heat the milk to scalding. Combine the oats, cracked wheat, butter, honey, molasses, and salt in a large mixing bowl and stir in the scalded milk. Cool slightly and beat in the egg and the yeast mixture. Slowly add enough flour to make a firm but quite moist dough. Cover with a towel and let the dough rest for 10 minutes. Knead on a lightly floured board for 3 to 5 minutes or until smooth, dusting with additional flour as needed to prevent sticking.

Place the dough in a greased mixing bowl, turn over to grease the top surface, cover with plastic wrap, and set in a warm place to rise until doubled—approximately 1½ hours. Punch down, then roll or pat the dough into a rectangle approximately 12 by 8 inches. Roll up from the short side, so that you have a loaf 8 inches long, and pinch the seams to seal. Put the loaf, seam side down, in a buttered and lightly floured 9-by-5-inch loaf pan. Lightly oil the surface of the loaf, cover with plastic wrap, and let rise in a warm place until the top just crests over the rim of the pan. Preheat the oven to 350° and bake for 45 to 55 minutes or until the loaf sounds hollow when tapped and a skewer tests clean. Remove from the pan and cool on a wire rack.

YIELD: 1 LOAF

OATMEAL CRACKERS

These crackers are easy to make and can be served with any of the soups or salads.

½ cup rolled oats (not instant)
⅔ cup flour
1 teaspoon baking powder

½ teaspoon salt
1½ tablespoons melted butter
⅓ cup sour cream

Preheat the oven to 350°. Lightly butter a large baking sheet.

Combine the oats, flour, baking powder, and salt in a mixing bowl. Stir in the melted butter and sour cream and knead briefly to combine. Divide the dough in half and roll out each half on a lightly floured board into a paper-thin rectangle approximately 10 inches by 13 inches. Place one rectangle on the prepared baking sheet and pat it with your fingers to even it out. Score deeply with a knife into squares or rectangles. Bake for 10 to 15 minutes or until dry and very lightly browned. If the outside sections brown more quickly, break them off and return the rest to the oven to continue baking. Repeat with the second rectangle of dough. Cool the crackers on a rack and then break into sections.

YIELD: APPROXIMATELY 4½ DOZEN 1½-INCH-SQUARE CRACKERS

SCONES

This is a flaky scone, which is not sweet, and is therefore appropriate to serve with any of the entrée mousses or salads.

2 cups flour, preferably
   unbleached
½ teaspoon baking soda
½ teaspoon baking powder
1 tablespoon sugar

A pinch of salt
6 tablespoons unsalted but-
   ter, chilled and cut into
   small pieces
¾ cup buttermilk (or less)

Preheat the oven to 400°.

Sift the flour, baking soda, baking powder, sugar, and salt together into a mixing bowl. Rub in the butter with the tips of your fingers. Mixing with your hands, add the buttermilk gradually until a soft dough is formed. Knead it lightly for a few turns on a floured board. Roll the dough into a circle 7 inches in diameter and ¾ inch thick and cut it into 8 wedges. Place the wedges about 1 inch apart on a lightly greased baking sheet and bake for 15 minutes or until lightly browned.

Store in an airtight container. These may be reheated before serving by wrapping them in aluminum foil and putting them for 5 to 10 minutes in a 350° oven.

YIELD: 8 SCONES

TOASTED SYRIAN BREAD

Known variously as "Sahara Bread," "Sandwich Pockets," and "Lebanese Bread," these flat loaves are easily made into an excellent hors d'oeuvre or toast to accompany a soup, salad, or any entrée. The thinner the bread, the better. Avoid doughy varieties and, if possible, buy them at Near Eastern grocery stores. They can be prepared in a variety of ways, as described below.

Using the point of a sharp knife, cut around the edges of four 4-inch loaves or one 8-inch loaf of Syrian bread and split each in half. Spread the cut side of each round with softened, unsalted butter (approximately 4 tablespoons) or brush with 4 tablespoons olive oil or unsalted butter that has been melted with 1 small clove of crushed garlic. Cut these rounds into small wedges or triangles and sprinkle with one of the following toppings, if desired:

1. sesame seeds
2. Spice Islands Lemon-Pepper Marinade
3. a mixture of:
     ¼ cup grated Parmesan cheese
     ¼ teaspoon dried thyme
     ¼ teaspoon dried basil
     ¼ teaspoon dried tarragon

Place on a baking sheet under a preheated broiler and broil them very briefly, just until they begin to brown. Watch carefully so that they do not burn.

YIELD: APPROXIMATELY 2½ DOZEN 2-INCH WEDGES

Hors d'oeuvres and Garnishes

CAVIAR MUSHROOMS

Use to garnish a salad or as an hors d'oeuvre.

*3 ounces cream cheese,
    softened*
3 tablespoons sour cream
1 teaspoon lemon juice
2 drops Tabasco sauce

½ pound fresh mushrooms
*1 small jar red caviar,
    lumpfish or salmon roe*

Clean the mushrooms with a damp towel or rinse briefly under cold running water and dry. Remove the stems and reserve them for another use.

Combine the cream cheese, sour cream, lemon juice, and Tabasco. Fill the cavity of each mushroom with this mixture and spoon about ⅛ teaspoon of red caviar on top.

YIELD: APPROXIMATELY 1 ½ DOZEN STUFFED MUSHROOMS

COLD STUFFED MUSHROOMS

These make a nice summer hors d'oeuvre as well as a delicious garnish for a mousse or an entrée salad.

12 ounces medium-size mushrooms (cleaned and stemmed)

8 ounces cream cheese, at room temperature

2 tablespoons sour cream

1 small garlic clove, peeled and crushed

1 tablespoon minced fresh parsley

1 teaspoon lemon juice

Fresh-ground black pepper

2 tablespoons capers, drained

Beat the cream cheese with a fork or wooden spoon until it is light. Stir in the sour cream, crushed garlic, minced parsley, and lemon juice. Season generously with fresh-ground black pepper. Fold in the capers. Stuff each mushroom cap with the mixture, mounding it in the center.

YIELD: 2 TO 2½ DOZEN STUFFED MUSHROOMS

DEVILED EGGS

This is a creamy, highly flavored formula for deviled eggs. I prefer to use the smaller-size eggs, classified as "medium," since they are less filling. If you use large eggs, you may have to increase the other ingredients slightly and boil them a minute longer.

6 *medium-size eggs*
3 *tablespoons mayonnaise*
1 *tablespoon plus 2 teaspoons*
  sour cream
1 *teaspoon Dijon mustard*
¼ *teaspoon Worcestershire*
  sauce

A pinch of dried dill weed,
  or ¼ teaspoon fresh
1 *tablespoon capers*
  (optional)
Fresh-ground black pepper to
  taste

Place the eggs in a saucepan, cover with water, bring to a boil, and boil gently for 9 minutes. Remove from the heat, drain, and run ice-cold water over them until they are cool. Gently crack the shell of each egg and peel. Slice in half lengthwise and empty the yolks into a mixing bowl. Mash the yolks thoroughly with a fork until smooth and then mix in the remaining ingredients. Mound this mixture into the egg-white halves, cover with plastic wrap, and refrigerate. Serve on a platter decorated with fresh parsley.

YIELD: 12 DEVILED EGG HALVES

FROSTED GRAPES

These pale green sugar-frosted grapes make a beautiful garnish for summer desserts or salad platters.

Coat clusters of seedless green grapes with lightly beaten egg white and roll in granulated sugar. Dry on a wire rack.

HAM CORNUCOPIAS

Make as a salad garnish or an hors d'oeuvre.

*3 large round slices of baked
    ham, ⅛ to ¹/₁₆ inch
    thick (approximately ¼
    pound)*

*3 to 4 tablespoons Rondelé or
    Boursin cheese*

Cut each round of ham into 4 quarters. Spread one side of each quarter with a thin layer of cheese and roll up into a cone shape. Place them seam side down on a platter, cover, and refrigerate until serving.

YIELD: 12 CORNUCOPIAS

STUFFED BELGIAN ENDIVE

A good summer hors d'oeuvre or garnish for cold meat or fish.

Spread the inside of each endive stalk with a thin layer of Rondelé or Boursin cheese. Arrange in a radial design on a serving plate and sprinkle with minced parsley or chives.

STUFFED CHERRY TOMATOES

Slice off the stem end of each cherry tomato and scoop out the pulp. Stuff with Salsa Verde (page 267) or with rolled anchovy fillets.

Savory Sauces

AVOCADO SAUCE

A creamy, delicately flavored sauce that can accompany many dishes, such as a fish mousse or a seafood salad.

½ large avocado, peeled　　　*Salt*
2 teaspoons lime juice　　　*Fresh-ground white pepper*
6 tablespoons mayonnaise　*A pinch of ginger*
¼ cup sour cream
4 teaspoons minced fresh
　　mint leaves

Purée the avocado in a food processor or blender. Add the lime juice, mayonnaise, sour cream, and mint leaves and blend. Season to taste with salt, pepper, and a little ginger.

YIELD: APPROXIMATELY 1 CUP

CAPPON MAGRO SAUCE

This is a tart version of an Italian green sauce, to be used as an accompaniment to fish, fowl, beef, or raw vegetables.

1 cup parsley sprigs, packed
1 garlic clove, peeled
2 teaspoons capers
2 anchovy fillets
2 hard-boiled egg yolks
4 pitted green olives
1 tablespoon green fennel fern
  or fresh tarragon, or ½
  teaspoon dried tarragon

1 slice of white bread
1 tablespoon white wine
  vinegar
½ cup olive oil

Purée the parsley, garlic, capers, anchovies, egg yolks, olives, and fennel or tarragon in a food processor or blender. Crumble the bread, combine it with the vinegar, add to the purée, and blend. With the motor running, pour in the olive oil in a thin stream.
YIELD: APPROXIMATELY 1 CUP

MAYONNAISE AND VARIATIONS

Various kinds of homemade mayonnaise add a distinctive, often opulent, touch to a number of chilled foods. Serve them with the entrée mousses, particularly those with a fish or seafood base; with raw vegetables; with cold meat, fish, or fowl. Even a homely platter of cold cuts will be more appetizing when served with 2 or 3 different kinds of homemade mayonnaise.

With a food processor or blender, mayonnaise can be made very quickly and easily. Before starting, make sure your ingredients are all at room temperature. Warm the eggs, if necessary, under hot tap water. The only caution is to add the oil very slowly, almost drop by drop, particularly at the beginning. If you forget to do this and your mayonnaise separates, start again with 2 more egg yolks and add the curdled mayonnaise bit by bit, as with the oil. When using a machine, do not attempt to make mayonnaise with only 1 egg yolk; it will not absorb the oil, although 1 yolk will work when making mayonnaise by hand.

For a lighter and creamier mayonnaise, add 2 tablespoons tepid water after half the oil has been absorbed. It is important to use a very fine, fresh, delicate imported olive oil in mayonnaise. If your oil tastes strong or rancid, the mayonnaise will be no better. If you are unsure of the quality of your olive oil, substitute a good vegetable oil, all or in part.

Always refrigerate mayonnaise and do not let it stand around at room temperature for any length of time, as it is highly susceptible to spoilage. Homemade mayonnaise will keep for 1 week or longer under refrigeration.

Finally, do not attempt to make mayonnaise if a thunderstorm is threatening or under way. I cannot tell you why, but I acquired this bit of information by reading Irma Rombauer, and as one who takes her advice seriously, I pass it on to you.

BASIC MAYONNAISE

---

2 egg yolks	½ cup olive oil
1½ to 2 teaspoons Dijon mustard	2 tablespoons tepid water (optional)
3 to 4 teaspoons lemon juice	Salt
½ cup vegetable oil	Fresh-ground pepper

Put the egg yolks, 1½ teaspoons mustard, and 3 teaspoons lemon juice in the bowl of a food processor or blender, and blend. With the motor running, add the vegetable oil slowly, drop by drop, and then the olive oil in a very thin stream. If desired, blend in the tepid water. Continue to add the remaining oil in a thin stream. Season to taste with salt and pepper and add a little more mustard and lemon juice, if desired.

YIELD: 1¼ CUPS

Green Mayonnaise

There are many ways to make green mayonnaise. Spinach is often used and almost any combination of herbs is possible. The following formula produces a delicate but flavorful mayonnaise with herbs that are readily available. To the above recipe for Basic Mayonnaise, add:

1 tablespoon minced fresh parsley	1 tablespoon minced chives
1 tablespoon minced water-cress leaves	1 teaspoon fresh dill weed or ¼ teaspoon dried

The herbs may be minced in a food processor. Then add the egg yolks to the work bowl and proceed with the basic recipe.

YIELD: 1¼ CUPS

Herb and Caper Mayonnaise

Prepare the Basic Mayonnaise recipe on page 261, and then add:

2 tablespoons fine-minced parsley, packed	4 teaspoons capers
1 teaspoon fresh dill weed or ¼ teaspoon dried	

YIELD: 1¼ CUPS

Lemon or Lime Mayonnaise

In the Basic Mayonnaise recipe on page 261, increase the lemon juice to 2 tablespoons, or substitute 2 tablespoons lime juice. Stir in the grated rind of 1 lemon or lime.

YIELD: 1¼ CUPS

Lime and Mint Mayonnaise

Follow the recipe for Basic Mayonnaise on page 261, substituting 1½ tablespoons lime juice for the lemon juice. Stir in the grated zest of 1 lime and 1½ tablespoons fine-minced fresh mint leaves.

YIELD: 1¼ CUPS

Mayonnaise Collée

This mayonnaise, made firm with gelatin, is used to coat or to decorate cold fish and other foods, often under an aspic glaze.

Soften 1¼ teaspoons unflavored gelatin in 2 tablespoons chicken or fish stock and dissolve over low heat, stirring constantly. Cool

slightly and stir into 1¼ cups Basic Mayonnaise (see page 261).
Spread with a knife on the food to be coated, and chill until set.
YIELD: 1¼ CUPS

Mustard Mayonnaise

Add 3 additional tablespoons Dijon mustard to the mustard in the
Basic Mayonnaise recipe (page 261), as well as 1 teaspoon minced
fresh tarragon or ¼ teaspoon dried.
YIELD: APPROXIMATELY 1½ CUPS

Provençal Sauce

A piquant blend that goes well with fish and seafood.

2 *tablespoons fresh parsley sprigs, packed*	5 *anchovy fillets*
	A *pinch of tarragon*
1 *small garlic clove, peeled*	*Ingredients for 1 recipe Basic*
1 *large shallot, peeled, or the white part of 1 scallion*	*Mayonnaise (page 261)*
	1 *tablespoon capers*

In a food processor or blender, mince the parsley, garlic, shallot,
anchovies, and tarragon. Add the egg yolks and proceed with the
recipe for Basic Mayonnaise. After the mayonnaise is made, turn it
into a mixing bowl and fold in the capers.
YIELD: APPROXIMATELY 1⅓ CUPS

Rouille

Add 4 garlic cloves, peeled, and a dash of cayenne to the food processor or blender and proceed with the recipe for Basic Mayonnaise (page 261).

YIELD: 1¼ CUPS

Russian Dressing

To ⅔ cup Basic Mayonnaise (page 261), add 2 tablespoons ketchup, 2 tablespoons sour cream, and 1½ tablespoons well-drained capers.

YIELD: APPROXIMATELY 1 CUP

Sorrel Sauce

Make a mayonnaise (following Basic Mayonnaise recipe, page 261) using 2 egg yolks, 2 teaspoons Dijon mustard, 1 tablespoon lemon juice, and ½ cup olive oil. Stir in ⅓ cup fine-minced sorrel leaves, ½ cup sour cream, 2 tablespoons well-drained capers, and salt and pepper to taste.

YIELD: 1¼ CUPS

Tomato Mayonnaise

Stir 6 tablespoons tomato purée into 1¼ cups Basic Mayonnaise (page 261). If desired, fold in just before serving 1 small tomato, peeled, seeded, and chopped.

YIELD: APPROXIMATELY 1¾ CUPS

MOUSSELINE SAUCE

7 *egg yolks*
¼ *cup lemon juice*
½ *pound unsalted butter*

A pinch of salt
Fresh-ground white pepper
½ *cup heavy cream*

Beat the egg yolks with the lemon juice in the top of a double boiler over hot, not boiling, water until they begin to thicken. Gradually add the butter, a few tablespoons at a time, beating constantly until the sauce is thick and fluffy. Do not let it get too hot or it will separate. If it does, rehomogenize by beating in a tablespoon of boiling water. Let the sauce cool to room temperature and season with a little salt and pepper.

Before serving, whip the cream until stiff and fold into the sauce.

YIELD: APPROXIMATELY 2 CUPS

PIQUANT SAUCE

This mayonnaise-based sauce is good with swordfish, halibut, or salmon steaks, with a fish mousse, or with Tomato Aspic (page 116).

2 *egg yolks*
1 *teaspoon Dijon mustard*
2 *anchovy fillets*
½ *cup olive oil*
⅓ *cup buttermilk*
2 *teaspoons lemon juice*
1 *teaspoon white wine vinegar*

½ *teaspoon Worcestershire sauce*
2 *teaspoons minced fresh tarragon or* ½ *teaspoon dried*
Fresh-ground white pepper to taste

Place the egg yolks, mustard, and anchovies in the bowl of a food processor or blender and blend. With the motor running, add the olive oil drop by drop and then, as the mixture thickens, in a very thin stream. Blend in the remaining ingredients.

YIELD: I CUP

RÉMOULADE SAUCE

This is a good dressing for chicken, lobster, or crabmeat. It is quick and simple to make and lends itself to variations, which follow.

½ cup sour cream
2 tablespoons mayonnaise
I teaspoon Dijon mustard
I teaspoon lime or lemon juice

I scallion, chopped
A few sprigs of fresh parsley, minced
A pinch of tarragon

Combine all the ingredients and chill.

YIELD: ⅔ CUP

Cucumber Sauce

Salt ½ cup chopped, peeled cucumber and drain in a colander with a weight on top for ½ hour. Rinse well and squeeze dry with paper towels. Prepare the above recipe for Rémoulade Sauce, omitting the scallion, parsley, and tarragon. Add instead the cucumber and a few sprigs of minced fresh mint or dill weed.

YIELD: APPROXIMATELY I CUP

Sour Cream–Horseradish Sauce

Prepare the recipe on page 266 for Rémoulade Sauce, omitting the scallion, parsley, and tarragon. Add 1 tablespoon drained, prepared white horseradish and some chives or a little dill weed.

YIELD: ⅔ CUP

SALSA VERDE

A version of Italian green sauce to serve with meat, fish, and fowl.

1 cup parsley sprigs, packed
¼ cup watercress leaves,
   packed
1 small garlic clove, peeled
2 slices of white bread

1 tablespoon white wine
   vinegar
3 to 4 anchovy fillets, rinsed
   and patted dry
⅓ to ½ cup olive oil

In a food processor or blender, mince the parsley, watercress, and garlic. Crumble the bread, moisten it in the vinegar, and add this to the bowl of the food processor with the anchovies. Purée. With the motor running, add the olive oil in a thin stream until the sauce is the desired consistency.

YIELD: 1 CUP

Cookies

ALMOND MERINGUES

These cookies approximate the crisp, meringue-like almond cookies (*amaretti*) that are made in Italy, although the Italian version is more pungently flavored with bitter almonds, which are not available in this country.

1 cup blanched, slivered	*2 egg whites*
*almonds, toasted**	*A pinch of cream of tartar*
¾ cup sugar	*½ teaspoon almond extract*

* To toast the almonds, spread them on a baking sheet and bake at 350° for 5 to 6 minutes, or until lightly browned.

Preheat the oven to 300°. Line a cookie sheet with parchment or brown paper.

Grind the almonds to a powder in a food processor, adding ¼ cup of the sugar.

Beat the egg whites until foamy. Add the cream of tartar and continue beating until almost stiff. Gradually add the remaining ½ cup sugar and the almond extract while beating. Fold in the ground almonds. Drop by teaspoonfuls onto the prepared cookie sheet and bake for approximately 30 minutes or until dry in the center and lightly browned. When they have cooked enough, the cookies will lift off the paper without sticking. Cool on a wire rack.

YIELD: 2½ TO 3 DOZEN

CHOCOLATE HAZELNUT COOKIES

This is a recipe which I improvised after making the Honey-Hazelnut Blancmange (page 193), of which ground hazelnuts are the industrial waste product. Chagrined at the prospect of throwing away all those expensive, if somewhat used, ground nuts, I found a successful way to recycle them—a moist chocolate drop cookie. If it happens that you have not made a Honey-Hazelnut Blancmange and have no used nuts on hand, substitute ½ cup whole hazelnuts and grind them in a food processor or blender with 1 teaspoon cold milk.

2½ ounces unsweetened
    baking chocolate
4 tablespoons unsalted butter
1 egg
¾ cup plus 1 tablespoon
    sugar
½ teaspoon vanilla extract

½ cup ground hazelnuts,
    fresh or left over from
    the Honey-Hazelnut
    Blancmange
⅓ cup flour

Preheat the oven to 350°. Lightly butter a large cookie sheet.

Break the chocolate into small pieces and melt it with the butter in the top of a double boiler over hot, not simmering, water, stirring constantly. Beat the egg with an electric mixer, adding the sugar gradually. Stir in the vanilla extract, the melted chocolate mixture, the ground nuts, and the flour. Drop by teaspoonfuls, about 1 inch apart, on the prepared baking sheet. Bake for 8 to 10 minutes or until dry on the outside but slightly moist in the center. Cool for a minute before removing to a wire rack.

YIELD: APPROXIMATELY 2½ DOZEN

CRISP GRANOLA COOKIES

A thin granola cookie. Use any good-quality, not too sweet granola cereal, such as Nature Valley. If the cereal is in very large chunks, break them up to the size of coarse-chopped walnuts. You may vary the recipe by adding ⅓ cup of chopped nuts, dates, raisins, or chocolate chips.

¼ pound unsalted butter,
softened
½ cup light brown sugar
1 egg

½ teaspoon vanilla extract
¾ cup flour
¾ cup granola cereal

Preheat the oven to 325°. Lightly butter a large baking sheet.

With an electric beater, cream the butter until light. Beat in the brown sugar, and then the egg and vanilla extract. Stir in the flour and granola and drop by teaspoonfuls, at least 2 inches apart, on the prepared baking sheet. Bake for 10 minutes or until very lightly browned around the edges.

YIELD: APPROXIMATELY 2½ DOZEN COOKIES

FLORENTINES

A delicious combination of orange, almonds, and chocolate in a crisp and lacy cookie.

¼ pound unsalted butter
½ cup sugar
2 tablespoons light honey
2 tablespoons heavy cream
1⅓ cups blanched, slivered
almonds

⅔ cup diced candied orange
or grapefruit peel
1 cup flour
4 teaspoons orange liqueur

FOR THE CHOCOLATE COATING

> 8 ounces German's sweet   1 1/2 tablespoons unsalted
>   baking chocolate   butter

Preheat the oven to 350°. Butter well 2 or 3 cookie sheets (enough room for 3 1/2 dozen cookies).

Melt the butter with the sugar, honey, and cream in a saucepan over low heat. Mix the almonds and candied peel with the flour and stir this into the melted butter mixture. Remove from the heat and stir in the orange liqueur. Drop by teaspoonfuls onto the cookie sheets, about 2 inches apart, and flatten each cookie with the back of a spoon. Bake for 8 to 10 minutes or until lightly browned around the edges. Let stand for a few seconds and then remove to a wire rack with a spatula and allow to cool.

TO MAKE THE CHOCOLATE COATING

Break up the chocolate and put it in the top of a double boiler with the butter. Stir over hot, not boiling, water until melted. Continue stirring for a minute off the heat. Spread the flat underside of each cookie with a thin coating of chocolate and dry on a wire rack.

YIELD: APPROXIMATELY 3 1/2 DOZEN COOKIES

LEMON-COCONUT WAFERS

―――――――

2 egg whites
⅓ cup sugar
Grated rind of 1 large
    lemon
4 tablespoons unsalted but-
    ter, melted and cooled
    to room temperature

1 tablespoon lemon juice
⅓ cup plus 1 tablespoon
    flour
⅓ cup sweetened flaked
    coconut

Preheat the oven to 350°. Butter and lightly flour a large cookie
sheet.

Whisk together the egg whites and sugar until combined. Stir in
the remaining ingredients.

Drop by teaspoonfuls, at least 2 inches apart, on the prepared
baking sheet. Bake for 8 to 10 minutes or until the cookies are dry
and the edges browned. Remove from the baking sheet with a
spatula while the cookies are still warm. If any stick, return them
to the oven for a minute to soften.

YIELD: 1½ TO 2 DOZEN

LIME-LACE COOKIES

These crisp, fragile cookies with a lime flavor go particularly well with ices and fruit desserts.

2 tablespoons unsalted butter, softened	Grated rind of 1 lime
1/2 cup sugar	3/4 cup rolled oats (not quick-cooking or instant)
1 egg	
1/2 teaspoon vanilla extract	1/2 teaspoon baking powder
	1 tablespoon flour

Cream the butter with the sugar. Beat in the egg, vanilla extract, and lime rind. Combine the oats, baking powder, and flour and stir into the batter. Chill the batter thoroughly for at least 1 hour in the refrigerator.

Preheat the oven to 375°. Butter and lightly flour a large cookie sheet.

Drop the chilled batter by half-teaspoonfuls, at least 2 inches apart, on the baking sheet. Bake for about 7 minutes or until dry and very lightly browned. Cool on the baking sheet for half a minute, but remove with an inverted nonflexible spatula while the cookies are still slightly warm. If the cookies become too cool and stick, return them to the oven for a minute to soften. Cool on a wire rack.

YIELD: APPROXIMATELY 2 DOZEN COOKIES

MOCHA HAZELNUT CRESCENTS

A coffee-and-hazelnut-flavored cookie dipped in chocolate.

¼ pound unsalted butter,
*   softened*
⅓ cup confectioners' sugar
1 teaspoon instant coffee
*   powder*

4 teaspoons crème de cacao
1 cup flour
½ cup fine-chopped hazelnuts

FOR THE CHOCOLATE COATING

4 ounces German's sweet
*   baking chocolate*

½ tablespoon unsalted butter

Cream the butter and beat in the sugar gradually. Dissolve the coffee powder in the crème de cacao. (If you use freeze-dried granules, it will be necessary to heat the mixture slightly to dissolve them. Then stir off the heat to return to room temperature.) Add the coffee mixture to the butter and fold in the flour and chopped nuts. Chill for 1 hour or until the dough is firm.

Preheat the oven to 350°.

Break off small pieces of chilled dough and roll between the palms of your hands into small logs; then shape into crescents. Place about 1 inch apart on ungreased cookie sheets and bake for 10 minutes or just until dry in the center. Cool on a wire rack.

TO MAKE THE CHOCOLATE COATING

Break up the chocolate and put it in the top of a double boiler with the butter. Stir over hot, not boiling, water until melted. Continue stirring for a minute off the heat. Dip one end of each crescent in the chocolate and dry on a wire rack.

YIELD: 3 TO 3½ DOZEN COOKIES

ORANGE-PECAN WAFERS

2 egg whites
½ cup light brown sugar
6 tablespoons unsalted butter, melted
Grated rind of 1 temple orange

¼ cup flour
¼ teaspoon cinnamon
½ cup fine-chopped pecans*

* Chop the nuts by hand. A food processor or blender will grind all or part of them to powder and the cookies will fail to spread properly when baked.

Preheat the oven to 425°. Grease and lightly flour a large cookie sheet.

Whisk together the egg whites and sugar until combined. Stir in the melted butter and the grated orange rind. Sift the flour and cinnamon into the batter, add the chopped pecans, and stir to combine.

Drop by teaspoonfuls, 2 inches apart, on the prepared baking sheet and bake for 7 minutes or until browned around the edges. Remove with a spatula while the cookies are still warm. If any should stick, return them to the oven for a minute to soften.

YIELD: APPROXIMATELY 2½ DOZEN

Appendix: Sample Menus

T H E menus that follow are intended to give you some ideas and suggestions for planning cold meals. They are, of course, flexible; substitutions can be made to conform to personal preference and the availability of certain foods.

Many cooks who often serve elegant cold lunches find it more difficult to put together the components of a cold formal dinner. But it is much easier than you might think because summer dining should be light and, therefore, simplicity is a guiding principle. If you are serving an elaborate main dish, you do not need much in the way of side dishes. A cold sauce for the entrée, if appropriate; a salad or vegetable vinaigrette; and perhaps a thin, crisp bread are all that is necessary, particularly if you are beginning the meal with soup and ending with dessert. For example, when I serve a fillet of beef in aspic, all that accompanies it is a green sauce, sliced tomatoes and avocados on a bed of watercress, and toasted Syrian bread. Never serve a hot vegetable or side dish with a cold entrée.

The other guidelines for cold cuisine are those you would follow in planning any meal. Avoid duplication in flavor or texture. For instance, don't serve too many creamy, rich items and don't have more than one dish made with gelatin. As in matters of color and design, your choices in food should be governed by your own sense of balance and harmony. For example, I might follow a fish meal with something light and lemony, but never with a chocolate or coffee dessert, although I cannot say exactly why.

My final reason for including sample menus is simply to call attention to some of my favorite recipes in the book in the hope that you will try them and enjoy them.

Picnic and Patio Meals

---

*Senegalese Soup
*Cuban Bread
  Spinach, Lettuce, and Tomato Salad
  Brie
  Fresh Fruit

---

*Herb-Roasted Chicken with Ratatouille
*Lemon-Pepper Toasted Syrian Bread
  Peaches and Green Grapes

---

*Picnic Pâté
*Al Fresco Salad
  Jarlsberg Cheese
  Fresh Fruit

* Indicates recipes included in this book.

*Summerhouse Salad
*Gougère or *Cheese Twists
*Apple-Praline Mousse

---

*Summer Garden Soup
*Wappingham Pie
*Deviled Eggs
 Tomato and Basil Salad
*Peach Ice Cream or *Frozen Peach
    Mousse with Amaretti

---

*Terrine of Sole and Crabmeat with
    *Sorrel Sauce or *Green Mayonnaise
*Cucumbers Vinaigrette
*Tomato Tart
 Fruit Salad
*Lime-Lace Cookies

---

*Country Pie
 Tomato, Arugola, and Basil Salad
 Cheddar and Jarlsberg Cheese
 Fresh Fruit or *Blueberry Ice Cream
*Crisp Granola Cookies

*Insalata Romana
*Cuban Bread
  Brie and Jarlsberg Cheese
  Fresh Fruit
*Florentines

---

*Gazpacho Blanco
*Chicken and Fennel Pâté
  Sliced Tomatoes with Dill
*Stuffed Belgian Endive
*Oatmeal Bread
  Green Grapes and Pears

---

*Curried Coconut-Crabmeat Soup
*Georgian Cheese-Filled Bread
  Green Salad with Tomatoes
*Pear Mousse

---

*Fresh Parsley Soup
*Calamari Salad
*Cuban Bread
  Sliced Tomatoes with Basil
*Biscuit Tortoni or *Pear-Honey Sorbet

Lunches and Suppers

*Iced Honeydew-Pear Soup
*Cold Curried Shrimp
*Lemon-Pepper Toasted Syrian Bread
*Tangerine Ice

---

*Tomato and Orange Soup
*Molly's Cold Curried Chicken
 Green Salad
*Coconut Ice Cream or *Peach Ice Cream

---

*Russian Gazpacho
*Russian Chicken in Aspic with *Sour
    Cream-Horseradish Sauce
*Deviled Eggs
 Tomato Salad
*Lemon Ice

* Indicates recipes included in this book.

*Clear Borscht
*Palm Court Salad
*Caviar Mushrooms
*Mocha Ice Cream
*Mocha Hazelnut Crescents

---

*Tomato-Fennel Soup
*Salmon Mousse
Green Salad
*Lemon Sherbet

---

*Lemon-Mint Soup
*Gingered Shrimp with Lime and Coconut Rice
*Sesame Toasted Syrian Bread
Sliced Tomatoes
*Green Grape Dessert or *Frozen
Honey and Almond Cream

---

*Spiced Peach Soup
*Chicken Salad Madras
*Melba Toast or *Toasted Syrian Bread
*Honeydew Ice

*Lobster Bisque
*Melba Toast
*Mussel, Rice, and Roast
   Pepper Salad
*Watermelon-Cassis Ice
*Lemon-Coconut Wafers

---

*Iced Pear-Celery Soup
*Aegean Salad
*Cuban Bread
*Lemon-Kiwi Mousse

---

*Artichoke Mousse
*Melba Toast
  Spinach, Lettuce, and Tomato Salad
  Oranges and Strawberries with Cointreau
*Orange-Pecan Wafers

---

*Cold Roast Chicken with Lime
   and Tarragon
*Biscuits
  Tomato and Basil Salad
  Sliced Peaches and Raspberries
   with Peach Brandy

*Tomato-Fennel Soup
*Crabmeat Mousse with *Avocado Sauce
     or *Green Mayonnaise
  Asparagus Vinaigrette
*Biscuits
*Lemon Sherbet

---

*Gazpacho
*Mediterranean Pepper Salad
*Whole Wheat Cuban Bread
 Sliced Peaches and Strawberries
*Crisp Granola Cookies

---

 *Chicken in Leek and Gorgonzola Aspic
 *Biscuits or *Cuban Bread
   Tomato, Bermuda Onion, and Dill Salad
   Fresh Fruit

---

*Tomato and Orange Soup
*Lobster Salad
*Deviled Eggs or Hard-Boiled Egg Quarters
*Melba Toast
*Peach Ice Cream

*Gorgonzola Vichyssoise
*Spinach Salad
*Stuffed Cherry Tomatoes
*Cuban Bread
*Lime and Honey Ice Cream

---

*Chicken Salad Othello
*Tomato Aspic
*Lemon-Pepper Toasted Syrian Bread
*Blueberry and Green Grape Tart

Dinner Parties

---

*Curried Coconut-Crabmeat Soup

*Poached Salmon in Aspic with *Green
Mayonnaise or *Salsa Verde

Asparagus Vinaigrette or Tomato and
Avocado Salad

*Toasted Syrian Bread

*Frozen Lime Soufflé

*Lime-Lace Cookies

---

*Shrimp Bisque or *Cream of Mushroom Soup

*Cold Fillet of Beef with Caper-Mustard Sauce

Sliced Tomatoes and Avocados on a Bed of Watercress

*Lemon-Pepper Toasted Syrian Bread

*Frozen Chocolate Mousse with Nut Crunch

*Indicates recipes included in this book.

*Asparagus Soup
*Sliced Veal with Funghi Trifolati in Aspic
    with *Salsa Verde or *Provençal Sauce
Tomato, Arugola, and Belgian Endive Salad
*Zabaglione with Sliced Strawberries
    or *Pear-Amaretti Trifle

---

*Cream of Fennel Soup
*Summer Pork with Apple, Mint, and Ginger Conserve
Julienne Carrots Vinaigrette or Sliced Beets Vinaigrette
*Lemon-Pepper Toasted Syrian Bread
Green Salad
*Frozen Peach Mousse with Amaretti

---

*Cream of Almond Soup
*Lake Trout with Herb Stuffing
    Asparagus or Broccoli Vinaigrette
*Sesame Toasted Syrian Bread
*Pear-Honey Sorbet

---

*Madrilène with Avocado and Caviar
*Veal Roulade with Prosciutto and Salsa Verde
    Green Beans Vinaigrette or Leeks Vinaigrette
*Parmesan Toasted Syrian Bread
*Honey-Hazelnut Blancmange
*Chocolate Hazelnut Cookies

*Cream of Sorrel Soup
*Chicken Breasts Stuffed with Pâté in
    Tarragon-Wine Aspic
*Toasted Syrian Bread
  Spinach, Belgian Endive, and Tomato Salad
*Raspberry Bavarian or *Bombe Favorite

———————————————————

*Clear Borscht
*Beef Salad
*Deviled Eggs
  Tomatoes with Basil
*Cuban Bread
*Frozen Cappuccino
*Florentines

———————————————————

*Iced Tomato Soup
*Sole in Fennel Aspic
  Green Salad
*Cuban Bread
*Lemon Sherbet
*Lime-Lace Cookies

*Cucumber-Mint Soup
*Lemon Duck in Aspic with *Mousseline Sauce
 Asparagus Vinaigrette
 Sliced Peaches and Raspberries with
    Peach Brandy or *Frozen Orange Soufflé

*Iced Pear-Celery Soup
*Vitello Carciofi
 Spinach, Lettuce, and Tomato Salad
*Melba Toast
*Raspberry Tart

Index

For many years Helen Hecht lived in New York City, where she pursued a career in book publishing, and then in Rochester, New York. She now resides in Washington, D.C., with the poet Anthony Hecht and their son Evan. Her food articles have appeared in Vogue *and* Cuisine *magazines. Her earlier cookbooks include* Gifts in Good Taste *(coauthored),* Cuisine for All Seasons, *and* Simple Pleasures, *which was a winner of an* IACP/Seagram Cookbook Award for 1986.